ISAAC
ASIMOV

Also by Michael White

C.S. Lewis: A Life (Carroll and Graf, 2004)

A History of the 21st Century (with Gentry Lee, 2003)

The Pope and the Heretic (Time Warner, 2002)

Tolkien: A Biography (Time Warner, 2001)

Rivals (Secker and Warburg, 2000)

Thompson Twin: An '80s Memoir (Time Warner, 2000)

Leonardo: The First Scientist (Time Warner, 2000)

Super Science (Simon and Schuster, 1998)

Isaac Newton: The Last Sorcerer (4th Estate, 1997)

Life Out There (Simon and Schuster, 1997)

Alien Life Forms (Puffin, 1998)

Mind and Matter (Puffin, 1998)

The Science of the X-Files (Random House, 1996)

Asimov: The Unauthorised Biography (Orion, 1994)

Breakthrough (with Kevin Davies, Macmillan, 1994)

Darwin: A Life in Science (with John Gribbin, Simon and Schuster, 1994)

Einstein: A Life in Science (with John Gribbin, Simon and Schuster, 1993)

Stephen Hawking: A Life in Science (with John Gribbin, Penguin, 1992)

Newton (Exley, 1991)

Galileo (Exley, 1991)

John Lennon (Exley, 1992)

Mozart (Exley, 1992)

ISAAC ASIMOV

A LIFE OF THE GRAND MASTER OF SCIENCE FICTION

MICHAEL WHITE

CARROLL & GRAF PUBLISHERS
NEW YORK

Isaac Asimov
A Life of the Grand Master of Science Fiction

Carroll & Graf Publishers
An Imprint of Avalon Publishing Group Inc.
245 West 17th Street
11th Floor
New York, NY 10011

AVALON
publishing group incorporated

Library of Congress Cataloging-in-Publication Data is available.

ISBN: 0-7867-1518-9

Printed in the United States of America
Interior design by Maria Elias
Distributed by Publishers Group West

CONTENTS

ACKNOWLEDGMENTS

While trying to avoid the horrid cliché, there really are a number of people who have been invaluable to me in writing this book and to whom I would like to extend my gratitude.

First and foremost, I would like to thank Isaac's wife Janet, who has been noble enough to talk to me despite the fact that she, too, has been writing a book about her husband.

I would also like to extend my warmest gratitude to Larry Ashmead, Jennifer Brehl, Janet Hill, Truman (Mac) Talley, and Elizabeth Bolton at the Mugar Library, Boston. Many thanks also to Brian Aldiss, Jack Cohen, Ian Stewart, Maggie McDonald, Nick Austin, Fred Pohl, Rachel Klayman, Chris Holifield, Charon Wood, and Deborah Beale. Thanks also to my wife Lisa, who for months put up with piles of Asimov paperbacks on the dining room table, tucked down the back of sofas, in teetering columns on the stairs, falling out of cupboards, on the bedside table, and in soggy heaps beside the bath. And last but not least, I would like to thank the staff of Oxfam, Oxford, whose tireless assistance helped me track down as many as possible of the absurd number of books I had to read and leave around the house while researching this biography. Thanks, thanks, and thanks again.

PREFACE

I first encountered Isaac Asimov's writing when I was thirteen. There was this odd boy in my class who used to spend the breaks devising codes from logarithm tables and reading dog-eared Asimov paperbacks, priced twenty-five pence.

One day I noticed him reading a book called *Foundation and Empire*. I asked him what it was about and he told me (rather impatiently, I thought) that it was part of a trilogy written by Isaac Asimov. The name sounded exotic and I liked the idea of a book about empires. I asked more questions, and in rather weary tones laced with annoying condescension, he told me that there were these two Foundations created by a scientist called Hari Seldon. The First Foundation was made up of physical scientists who could build nuclear reactors the size of walnuts and travel through hyperspace. The Second Foundation was composed of mathematicians who could read minds.

Now, I thought I was pretty clued up about science; after all, I had beaten this smart bugger in the last physics test with a mark of eighty-seven percent to his miserly seventy-two. I knew that it was pretty difficult to build a nuclear reactor the size of a walnut. Thus, unable to control the sarcasm in my voice, I said: "And I suppose these Foundationers are immortal, too, are they?" To which my classmate devastatingly replied: "Don't be ridiculous. This is science fiction, not a fairy story."

I decided there and then that if I was to maintain my undisputed reputation as the brightest kid in 3A, I would have to find out as much as possible about this science fiction lark as quickly as I could.

It was obvious, even to an adolescent English schoolboy with a very bad haircut and flared gray school trousers, that my lead into this new world was none other than the author of *Foundation and Empire*, Isaac Asimov.

I bought *Foundation* and read it in two days. I then badgered my parents for cash so remorselessly that they had to give in, and I rushed out and bought the second and third parts of the trilogy. By now there was no stopping me. I spent almost my entire weekly allowance of thirty

pence on an Asimov paperback each and every Saturday, reading slowly
so that I would not finish the book by Thursday, leaving me Asimov-less
for a full two days.

Each Saturday, I stood in my local bookshop gripped by a paroxysm of
indecision as to which novel I should read next; should it be *The Currents
of Space* or *The Caves of Steel*? And if you've ever been gripped by a
paroxysm of indecision, you'll know just how painful it can be.

Then, alas, a mere few months into my adventure, I came to my last
Asimov book; there were no more worlds to discover, no new territories
to explore. I felt the way Hillary and Tensing must have done when they
reached the peak of Everest, the disappointment Talking Heads must
have experienced after they had written "Once In a Lifetime"—where
did I go from here?

Of course, I soon calmed down and found that there were other
writers aside from Asimov. I read Clarke and Heinlein, took a detour into
Tolkien and C. S. Lewis, discovered the New Wave, something that really
was new then, and backtracked to H. G. Wells and Jules Verne. But my
first and greatest science fiction love remained Asimov.

Despite the fact that after *The Gods Themselves* there was nothing new
from Asimov throughout my teens, I kept encountering his work. At university I read his popular science books and collections of essays and even
used his textbooks, classics like *Understanding Physics*. For recreation I
foraged around in Hermann Hesse, John Fowles, Dostoyevsky and
Henry Miller, subconsciously waiting for the day when I could pick up
the story of the Foundations where it had been left dangling.

Finally, new Asimovs began to appear, and I was delighted by some,
disappointed by others. But what was really important was that the whole
world of Asimov's peerless imagination was once more in business.

When I visited New York at the end of March 1992, I put the idea of
writing a book about my childhood hero to my editor, Rachel Klayman.
She took me to see her boss, Arnold Dolin, who told me Asimov was
very ill and might not live more than a year or two.

I returned to England on April 5 and awoke the next morning to the
news that Isaac Asimov had died.

Having never met the man and knowing none of his family or friends, my first reaction to his death was a purely selfish one—"God, that means there will be no more Foundation books." But naturally, as I learned as much as I could about Isaac Asimov the man, as well as the creator of those wonderful novels, I have grown to see his passing in far broader terms. And when I met his gracious wife Janet and his close friends in New York and elsewhere, I quickly buried my selfishness beneath an avalanche of sadness that the literary world had lost one of its most colorful, entertaining, and ingenious characters, the like of whom passes this way all too rarely.

In this biography I have tried to bare the truth about his life and to view his work objectively and in the context in which it was written. In places I am candid about his personality and his actions because I believe that Asimov's faults were as much a part of him as were his great strengths.

Isaac Asimov wrote so much, not least of which was on the subject of Isaac Asimov, that it would be all too easy to sit back and accept his none-too-objective account of his own life and work. I am convinced that his story needs to be told from an outside viewpoint. I hope I have succeeded in doing this. I like to think that he would have approved.

Michael White

ISAAC
ASIMOV

1

ÉMIGRÉ

When Isaac Asimov died on April 6, 1992, not only did the world lose the third most prolific writer of all time, but one of the founding fathers of modern science fiction, America's leading science popularizer, orator, incorrigible flirt, writing addict, and lovable personality. Who else, while lying on the operating table, drugged and half-conscious, would stare up at the surgeon and spontaneously compose comic verses:

> Doctor, doctor, in your green coat,
> Doctor, doctor, cut my throat.
> And when you've finished, doctor, then,
> Won't you sew it up again.[1]

The search for the real Isaac Asimov begins in a large, temperature-controlled storeroom in the Mugar Library of Boston University, now home to almost his entire works and correspondence. The special collection numbers almost one thousand boxes, all neatly organized into folders lettered A–Z, each painstakingly cataloged.

Having deposited coats, bags, all save a pencil and paper, a reader may, under the watchful eye of a video camera in the corner, don white reading gloves and plow through this vast collection at Asimov's former academic

---

[1] *In Joy Still Felt* by Isaac Asimov. Doubleday, New York, 1980 (p. 596).

home. The collection comprises an estimated fifty thousand fan letters, bills, postcards, cellulose memorabilia, and, most treasured of all, original drafts of some of Asimov's most famous works, including *I, Robot*, *The Stars Like Dust*, and *Pebble in the Sky*.

To many, Asimov's prodigious output was his own failing. As a counterbalance to his millions of fans around the world, there are those who claim that Asimov was a hack, a smart-ass who simply wrote too many books. To others he was an underestimated genius, an arcane giant, who had the remarkable knack of being able to successfully turn his hand to almost anything.

During his lifetime Asimov wrote over four hundred and sixty books as well as thousands of articles and reviews. So huge was his output that a single publishing house could not deal with his production, and throughout his career he worked simultaneously with several major publishers. Yet it is often forgotten that although Asimov is best known as a science fiction writer, the larger part of his literary output was in the field of popular science, and during one fourteen-year period he wrote almost no science fiction at all.

When asked about his productivity, Asimov always claimed that he simply *had* to write, that it was a compulsion, and that he experienced severe withdrawal symptoms if he was forced away from his typewriter for any lengthy period.

There is no doubt that Asimov was an obsessive character, but, luckily, he found a use for this obsession and it brought him great success. Thanks entirely to his writing, Asimov died a very famous and very wealthy man. He did not play the stock market, dabble with property speculation, or even accept financially attractive deals from Hollywood. Toward the end of his career he is reputed to have been paid advances of a hundred thousand dollars per book, a clear indication of his status within the science fiction and popular science industry, which he had helped to revitalize over forty years earlier.

Asimov lived to write. He traveled little and refused to set foot on a plane. Flying, he believed, was "unfair." With an automobile there was a chance of surviving a crash, but when an airliner went down, you were dead. Yet, ironically, the man who refused to fly gave us fiction that dealt with starship battles in intergalactic space, travelers journeying into the distant future and voyaging through hyperspace and far-flung nebulae.

Despite his almost monastic approach to work, Asimov was certainly no monk. He was a very popular man and enjoyed a number of lifelong friendships with members of both sexes. He was a successful father, maintained a close relationship with his own parents until their deaths, and carved out a second career for himself as a highly successful after-dinner speaker.

He was married twice, his first marriage ending in divorce. Asimov was always more of a ladies' man than his first wife would have liked, but his friends testify to the fact that, once married to his second wife, Janet Jeppson, he never strayed from the straight and narrow. In Janet he had met the great love of his life.

Asimov knew he was good at what he did; he was anything but shy about his own abilities. There were those who thought him a bighead or conceited, but he preferred to call his blunt approach "Asimovian immodesty."

Buried among the manuscripts, newspaper articles, and fan letters in the Mugar Library, in BOX 316 of the archive there is a perfect example of Asimov's confidence in his own fame and success. Inside an obscure mid-'70s magazine called *Bleer*, there is an article about Asimov and his work. Over the top of the first page, with his bold, neat handwriting, Asimov had scrawled: *Note: God knows where the authors got some of the stuff in this essay. Biographers! Please ignore!*[1]

Isaac Asimov was uncertain of his date of birth and from a very early age adopted January 2, 1920, to mark the occasion. The reason for his vagueness is that he was born in a tiny village called Petrovichi, some 250 miles southwest of Moscow. No official records were kept of births, deaths, and marriages.

Isaac's parents were Russian Jews. His arrival in the world was a traumatic event for his mother Anna Rachel. Five years before Isaac's birth, his father, Judah, who was a grain merchant and respected member of the community, had persuaded a doctor to take up residence in Petrovichi; after the revolution, the doctor decided to move away, leaving the village

---

[1] *Bleer* No. 1, BOX 316 Asimov Archive, Mugar Library, Boston University.

without professional medical services. Isaac seemed distinctly reluctant to enter the world, and his mother had to endure three days and two nights of labor with only an inexperienced midwife to help.

Fortunately, Anna Rachel was young and strong. She was twenty-four when Isaac was born, a small woman, four feet, ten inches in stockinged feet, with typical Slavic rather than Jewish features. She had blue eyes and, when she was young, fair hair; very different in appearance from Judah, who was a year younger, almost a foot taller, and had brown eyes and dark brown hair. It was Anna Rachel's coloring that Isaac and his brother and sister inherited, although Isaac himself was the only one of the three to have Slavic high cheekbones. He also grew to match his father's height of five feet, nine inches.

As well as having very different looks, Anna Rachel and Judah were very different in character. Isaac's mother was a fiery, quick-tempered woman who was high-spirited as a teenager, flirtatious and adventurous. Judah was altogether more staid and conservative, a plodder but bright and inclined toward contemplation. He liked to tell moralistic stories to his young son when the boy was old enough to understand, and was definitely the parent who kept the family going throughout the many difficulties that lay ahead of them. Isaac believed wholeheartedly that his father was a virgin when he met Anna Rachel and that she was the only woman with whom he ever had a relationship. Although he could never confirm his ideas, he was convinced that this was not the case with his mother.

Isaac was a tiny baby, weighing four and a half pounds at birth, and his parents had little hope that Isaac would survive his first year. In fact it was not until he was two that he developed his first serious illness, when he nearly died of pneumonia.

According to Asimov family legend, Isaac was the only child survivor of a pneumonia epidemic in the area. Seventeen infants contracted the disease and sixteen died within a few weeks. The doctor who had been called in to treat the epidemic had given up on Isaac. The baby's health deteriorated and Anna Rachel's mother was said to have told her daughter that she should accept the fact that Isaac would die, and that he was only a baby; there would be others.

Outraged by her mother's comment, Anna Rachel discarded the

ineffectual remedies the doctor had given her and held the baby against her breasts until he made a recovery. She never forgave her mother for her callous comment, and Isaac always remembered how, in later years, his mother expressed only contempt for his grandmother.

It was soon after Isaac's recovery that Judah and Anna Rachel had a second child, a girl they named Manya, who was born on June 17, 1922. When she was old enough to decide upon such things, Manya changed her name to Marcia. At almost the same time as Marcia's birth, a letter arrived from the United States that set in motion a series of events that were to radically change the lives of the Asimovs.

Anna Rachel's brother, Joseph Berman, had been living in Brooklyn, New York, for a number of years and wrote to the rabbi of Petrovichi to enquire as to the whereabouts of his sister. The letter was passed on and a correspondence began. It soon became clear that Joseph was keen to open the door for other members of his family who might want to leave Russia.

After a great deal of discussion it was decided that the family would indeed accept Joseph's offer to help them make the move. It would be a journey into the unknown for them, but they had heard stories of how others had created comfortable lives for themselves in a land of plenty. Despite the barriers of language and culture, it seemed that the invitation offered hope against the bleak backdrop of their lives in post-revolution Russia. Joseph would be there to help them settle, and they were still young and ambitious. However, before they could hope to leave the country they would have to secure the permission of the Russian government.

The newly formed Bolshevik state did not make it easy for people to leave Russia. The mere desire to set up home in a foreign country was seen as something of an insult, and the process of obtaining permission was usually one fraught with bureaucratic difficulties. The authorities were slow-acting and beleaguered by red tape. Fortunately for the Asimovs, Judah had a friend who was highly placed in the civil service and assisted the family by writing a letter stating that they wished to join relatives already resident in the United States. This went some way to mollifying the authorities.

Even so, the task of obtaining the necessary papers was still not easy. It took Judah over a week of traveling from Petrovichi to a town called

Gomel and then on to Moscow, where he had to visit one minor official after another. Each transaction cost money, and, of course, once the news was out that the Asimovs were planning to emigrate, even family friends would not lend them rubles for fear that Judah would be thrown into jail for the insolence of attempting to leave his country.

Somehow, Anna Rachel managed to find the necessary cash with which to bribe an endless stream of officials. This was then wired to Judah in Moscow, where, in the depths of a Russian winter, he had been sleeping for a week on friends' floors in subzero temperatures and living on black bread and herring.

After spending all their savings, aside from that required for the journey to America, on December 13, 1922, the Asimov family finally secured passports and permission to leave Russia.

Judah returned to Petrovichi just long enough to organize the sale of everything they could not take with them. He and Anna Rachel then packed their possessions and, on Christmas Eve 1922, the family began their long journey.

The trip took almost six weeks, and together they overcame one diffi-culty after another. Within days of leaving Petrovichi and arriving in Smolensk, fifty miles away, Marcia fell seriously ill. A doctor was even-tually found, and she was treated with a course of drugs. She made a slow recovery, and it was a week before they could leave the town and begin the next stage of the journey to Moscow, where a visa was obtained to board ship in the Latvian capital of Riga.

On January 11, 1923, the Asimovs left Russian soil, and Isaac never returned.

The plan was to sail from Latvia to France and then on to America. The day the Asimovs arrived in Latvia, the French occupied the Ruhr and closed its borders. The family had to divert to Liverpool, where they could board ship for the transatlantic crossing. When they arrived in England they discovered that their papers had gone ahead of them to Cherbourg, their original stop-off point in France.

Thanks to the Hebrew Immigrant Aid Society in Liverpool, which had learned of the rerouting, the papers were obtained from the French authorities, a new sailing was organized, and the family boarded the *Baltic*, bound for New York.

On February 3, 1923, the four members of the Asimov family joined the huge list of European immigrants who disembarked at Ellis Island and went through the formalities of taking up residence in America. The family was separated and interviewed. Isaac contracted measles, and the whole affair proved to be a tiring, arduous obstacle course of red tape following an uncomfortable journey in the cheapest accommodation aboard the *Baltic*.

In many respects, the Asimovs were lucky; 1923 was the last year in which the U.S. government allowed relatively unrestricted acceptance of foreign immigrants. It is quite likely that if they had arrived the following year they might well have been turned back.

With the bureaucratic details settled, four days after arriving at Ellis Island, the family was reunited. Joseph Berman met them and took them to Brooklyn, where they were to establish their new home and where Judah and Anna Rachel would spend the rest of their lives.

Brooklyn in the 1920s was a sprawling mass of tenements and industrial units. When the Asimovs arrived they added four more to a population approaching the one million mark. Immigrants naturally gravitated to this borough, primarily because friends and relatives had already established homes and businesses there. Brooklyn had a strong sense of community, particularly among the large Jewish population. For those who were qualified to take clerical jobs, Manhattan was just across the Brooklyn Bridge, and the six thousand plus industrial plants lining the Brooklyn shoreline could, before the Depression, boast a working population of over two hundred thousand.

Into this human beehive came the Asimov family: father, mother, and two children, with a few dollars in their pockets and no fixed abode, save for the transitory hospitality of the Bermans. Behind them was the pre-industrial, rural simplicity of their homeland. They had to leave behind their native language and customs; ahead lay a new and confusing world, blared out in English. At first it felt like a totally alien, incomprehensible way of life.

Adapting to the new environment was much easier for Isaac than for his parents, and Marcia never knew anything different. Indeed, Isaac claimed that he could remember almost nothing of his life before coming to America, and he was quick to pick up English and to adopt American customs. Although, as a young man, he played up his exotic place of birth for the benefit of the opposite sex, it is difficult to imagine anyone more at home in Brooklyn once he had settled in.

The Asimovs' first apartment was in a slum district, on a street called Van Sicklen Avenue. It had no electricity or central heating; lighting was provided by gas jets and heating by an old cast-iron stove. Judah Asimov worked in a succession of low-paid jobs in local sweatshops and factories. For a short time he tried his hand at door-to-door selling, but this was unsuccessful; he was simply not the type to charm his way into people's homes and off-load encyclopedias or toiletries.

The first two years in America were an unhappy time for Isaac's parents. They resented the help of the Bermans because, back home, Judah was seen as having had a far better education than his brother-in-law, yet here in this strange environment, it was the Bermans who possessed the more practical education and could provide help and advice. The proud Asimovs had to swallow hard in order to accept anything from them.

The name for newly arrived immigrants was "greenhorn," and to be branded as such was a tremendous insult to those who had come from respected families and an environment where they were high in the social order. In crossing the Atlantic, the Asimovs had descended from the highest point to the very lowest, and they were reminded of this each and every day.

Isaac, too, was a little greenhorn. It was not until an irate neighbor complained to his parents that he was made to realize he could not urinate in the street. It was only through learning the language and thereby the customs and secret codes of everyday life that Isaac was able to initiate himself into the new society, for his parents could not help him.

Isaac taught himself to read by pestering the older boys of his neighborhood and constantly asking how words were pronounced and spelled. He had to put up with their teasing and bullying, but his determination paid off. When, at the age of five, he went to his parents to demonstrate his ability, they were astonished. His father had only just reached the same level of understanding the language as his son.

Isaac's first school was a kindergarten unromantically named P.S. 182, and while he settled into a routine there, the family moved out of the dreadful apartment on Van Sicklen Avenue and rented a place a block away, on Miller Avenue. This was an altogether more comfortable home and enjoyed the benefits of electricity and gas central heating. But this was only to be a transitory stage in Isaac's early life. In the spring of 1926, Judah and Anna Rachel Asimov accepted that they could never hope to achieve a respectable standard of living while Judah had to chase one job after another in seedy factories and warehouses. Instead, it was decided that they should invest the little money they had managed to save into opening a candy store. With that decision, Isaac's childhood was transformed overnight.

The first candy store was at 751 Sutter Avenue, around the corner from the family apartment on Miller Avenue. As well as sweets, the Asimovs sold newspapers, soda, cigarettes, cards, stamps and a thousand and one other small household items. It was a convenience store, a place where a customer could buy one cigarette, change money or merely stand and chat with friends as long as they bought sodas.

The store was hard work. It opened at 6:00 A.M. and closed at 1:00 A.M.; and duties did not end with mere sales. There was stock to keep track of, accounts to balance, and trips to the bank. Newspapers had to be unloaded and sorted, the soda machines kept topped up, and business decisions thought through.

Judah knew the ropes when it came to running his own little business. He had come from a line of grain merchants and he was his own master. He no longer had to walk the streets in a vain attempt at selling other people's goods or to sweat out his days in a small industrial plant under the eye of a foreman. For Isaac, the shop spelled an end to an uncluttered childhood of playing in the streets and a simple school routine. Instead, he became as attached to the store as his parents were, and, being the eldest child, his spare time was not to be his again until he left home over sixteen years later.

Despite the rigors of duties at the store, Asimov always recalled with fondness his childhood spent helping his father. Working in the store and keeping up with schoolwork were facts of life, and he claimed never to truly resent the fact that he could only rarely play with others on his block.

What Isaac lost in time with his friends he gained in other ways.

Working in his father's store taught him many lessons that remained with him into old age. As an adult, Asimov was a stickler for punctuality, a result of his father's strict attitude toward timekeeping. He learned how to deal with numbers, bookkeeping, and basic economics long before he was shown these things at school. It is also fair to say that if his father had not owned a candy store, then Asimov might not have become a science fiction writer at all; he might never have encountered a seminal influence—pulp books and magazines.

The pulps were cheaply produced paperback adventure books, full of stories of wise-guy detectives and shady underworld dealings. Judah Asimov did not approve of them and considered them to be gutter-reading for bums. Yet they sold well, and that is why he had them in his store. When he forbade his son to read them, Isaac countered by claiming that he had seen his father doing so. Judah ended the argument by pointing out that they were essential to his learning of English. Isaac was forbidden to read them, and that was that.

Of course it was not. Despite his father's objection, Isaac managed to taste forbidden fruit. In so doing he adopted another lifelong habit. Because he had to read the magazines and return them to the rack in the shop without a mark on them, he developed a technique for reading them without even creasing the spines. Throughout his life, Asimov always read newspapers in the same ultracareful fashion, and claimed that no one could tell that a paper he had read from cover to cover had even been touched.

Whatever the virtues of the pulps, they introduced Isaac to reading. From that time on he was rarely seen without his nose in a book, and he developed a thirst for knowledge that was to lead him not only to academic success but into the writing profession.

Meanwhile, Isaac was receiving a mixed reception at school. On the one hand, his teachers quickly realized that they had a super-bright pupil in their class, but it was soon emerging that this intelligent and versatile child was also a pain in the neck. While displaying impressive feats of memory and achieving high marks, Isaac was also an incorrigible chatterbox and was forever in trouble with his teachers.

These faults aside, Isaac's parents and his teachers were aware of his talents, and it was decided that he should be moved up a year. Because he was already a young member of his year, this meant that for his entire school career he was almost two years younger than his schoolmates. The advantage of this was that he finished school and college younger than his contemporaries, but the downside was that he found it difficult to make close friends.

Asimov was extremely proud of his scholastic achievements. Despite the fact that he was far younger than the others, he was invariably top of his class throughout his school years. It became almost a point of honor that he would beat all opposition when he arrived at a new school or was placed in a higher class. However, he did have his weak areas. Contrary to the famous image of Asimov the total polymath, he admitted to a blind spot when it came to economics. Surprisingly, he also found that mathematics proved easy for him up to a certain stage and then the doors of comprehension closed firmly shut—a fact that caused him considerable problems with elements of his undergraduate college work.

By 1928, Judah Asimov decided that it was time for the family business to move to better premises, and so they made their third move since arriving in Brooklyn, this time to Essex Street, over half a mile eastward.

The new store was a vast improvement on the premises on Sutter Avenue. It was in a smarter area of Brooklyn and, most important to the eight-year-old Asimov, it boasted a slot machine. Isaac seemed to have an almost instinctive feeling that the machine was not to be messed with. He knew that there was no way a gambler would come out on top, but he was instantly hooked on the mechanics of the contraption. He would watch others wasting nickel after nickel, and when it broke down, as sometimes happened, he would make sure that he had a good look at the machine's internal workings just so long as his father was not on hand to demand that he keep out of the repairman's way.

Asimov always claimed that he had an early fascination for mechanical devices. His interest was, even at this early age, centered on how the individual parts of a machine worked together to make it function as a whole. Strangely, he never showed the slightest interest in becoming an engineer or a mechanic; his fascination was all theory and no practice.

The move to Essex Street coincided with an event that was to make a sudden increase in Isaac's responsibilities in the store. His mother had become pregnant. Up to that point, Isaac's main jobs had been collecting the pennies from passersby who bought newspapers on the stand outside the store and running errands straight after school. Now, with his mother less able to help manage the store, it fell on Isaac's shoulders to assist behind the counter, deliver newspapers, and pass on phone messages to regular customers (an important service during an era when very few people in Brooklyn had telephones of their own).

Isaac had had little spare time in which to meet other children; now he had almost no free time at all. When he was away from school, homework, and the responsibilities of helping his father in the store, he found ways of losing himself in the dramatic adventures of pulp heroes, books from the neighborhood library, and the occasional silent movie at the local cinema.

Looking at Isaac Asimov's early life in Brooklyn, tied to his family duties at the candy store, with only his sister, Marcia, near his own age, and cut off from normal life both in and out of school, it is surprising that he grew into such a gregarious and friendly teenager and adult.

A slow starter socially, he made up for lost time by overplaying the extrovert, flirtatious, and sometimes risqué elements of his personality. What this rather unusual family background and strict, disciplined upbringing, this instilling of responsibility and reinforcement of a sense of duty, inevitably did was to make Asimov into a driven, obsessive, self-confessed workaholic who, throughout most of his life, found separation from his typewriter almost physically painful.

At school, as though to compensate for the formalities of working in the store, Isaac developed into a real loudmouth. Not only was he becoming infamous among the staff for his chattering, but among his contemporaries he was gaining the reputation of being an eccentric, uncouth oddball who never kept his mouth shut for a second. It made him popular within the limits of the school, but he could never extend his friendships outside the school gates.

Asimov remembered very few of his colleagues from any period of his school days, but they always remembered him. As an adult he would occasionally encounter a character from his past whom he had totally forgotten, but they always recalled tales of his rowdiness and run-ins with teachers.

This split character remained with Asimov for the rest of his life.

Whenever he visited publishers, agents, and others connected with his work, everyone would know he was in the building. Secretaries could hear him several rooms along the corridor and he was forever fooling around, making jokes, and telling ribald stories to the office staff before settling down to serious business. It was almost as though, because he rarely left his study, he had extra energy and impetus to play around when he took time out to make a business call.

Asimov's liking for solitude and his deep attachment to the inside of his study came from early childhood. He was always attracted to quiet, dark places. He particularly liked the kitchen of one of the family apartments because it had no windows and was always snug and warm. He envied the newspaper sellers in subway stations because they worked from little huts where they could sit and read all day. The paradigm was established early on.

Once bitten by the reading bug, Isaac was completely hooked. He joined the local library and made regular trips there, first escorted by his mother and then alone. He was allowed two books each trip, one of which had to be nonfiction. In this way he was introduced to the Greek myths, Dickens, Dumas, Louisa May Alcott, and others, as well as texts about the Roman Empire, world geography, science, and much more. Asimov always claimed that he had a near-perfect memory, and attributed the ease with which he could turn his writing skills to any subject to his early self-education at the local Brooklyn libraries.

He had a voracious and totally indiscriminate appetite for learning and sated it with one book after another, often started, to the annoyance of his parents, while walking along the road from the library to the store. A consequence of this magpie approach to reading was that very little twentieth-century fiction filtered through to him. The libraries of Asimov's youth had not caught up with contemporary fiction and gave him instead a staple diet of mainly nineteenth-century literature with a smattering of ancient texts thrown in for good measure.

When it came to his choice of reading matter, Isaac faced continuous parental censorship. It was not until several years after the magazine's first appearance in 1926 that Asimov came across his first copy of *Amazing Stories,* a groundbreaking and extremely popular publication that, along with *Astounding,* is viewed by enthusiasts as the granddaddy of SF magazines. Despite the fact that Judah Asimov sold the magazine in his store, for Isaac, glimpses inside the brightly colored covers of *Amazing* were entirely clandestine. It was not until the arrival of *Science Wonder Stories*, set up by the great science fiction publisher Hugo Gernsbeck, that Isaac managed to coerce his father into allowing him to read science fiction magazines at all.

The key to the whole problem was that Judah could see no value in such nonsense as the stories in *Amazing* and thought that his son should be spending his time on more worthwhile pursuits. Isaac managed to circumvent this by pointing out that *Science Wonder Stories* was in fact highly educational. After all, he declared, it contained the all-important word *science* in the title. Judah could not argue against this and conceded. Once Isaac had won that battle, it was a mere technicality convincing his father that *Amazing* was very similar. With the flood of new magazines appearing almost on a monthly basis in the late twenties and early thirties, Isaac had found his true inspiration. He managed to read every edition of every magazine that came into the shop. Some of the thrill of illegality had gone with parental agreement, but the excitement of the stories and the awakening realization of a whole new universe of possibilities were satisfactions enough.

The Asimovs' decision to enter into business was a very wise move and came at just the right time. Three years after opening the candy store and within months of Isaac's brother Stanley's birth in July 1929, the Depression struck.

By owning their own small business, the Asimovs were cushioned. Times were hard for them as for everyone, but even in a Depression people need food. Where large companies went to the wall, small stores for the most part survived. Those in what they considered secure jobs suddenly found themselves without work. The Asimovs did not miss a single meal throughout the Depression, and although they had to work sixteen hours a day to merely survive, they succeeded.

Isaac began junior high school in 1930. His local school was East New York Junior High School 149, a short walk from the Asimov's old apartment on Van Sicklen Avenue, but a school bus trip from the candy store. It was a rough school, but Isaac settled in quickly. Within a short time he had created the same image for himself as that he had left behind at primary school: a very bright but disruptive member of the class, considered by his contemporaries to be eccentric and loud.

Soon after graduating to junior high, Isaac was inspired to make his first literary efforts. He had seen a book called *The Darewell Chums at College*, which was a saga following the antics of a group of college friends. He decided that he would write his own version of the book, calling it *The Greenville Chums at College*.

After eight chapters written in an exercise book over a period of a few days, Isaac gave up. He had quickly learned an important lesson. He could not properly write about something of which he knew nothing. After all, he was a junior high schoolboy from Brooklyn writing about college kids living in a small country town.

After graduating from junior high school in the summer of 1932, the next move was high school. Isaac's parents were very clear about where they wanted him to go. The local coeducational school, Jefferson High, would not be suitable. The best school within the catchment area was the Boys High School of Brooklyn, which took only the most academically successful boys living in the district. Isaac's grades were good enough and he qualified, along with two others from the East New York Junior High School 149. He started at the end of the summer vacation, aged twelve and a half; most of his classmates were fifteen.

Six months into high school, in 1933, the family moved again, this time to a larger candy store in a wealthier part of Brooklyn called Ridgewood. The family were to stay in this, their third store, for over three years.

It was during this period that the family had its first radio in the apartment. Before this it had been locked away in the store. Now the whole family could tune in, and the children were allowed to listen to it on their own. Suddenly Isaac's perspectives were enormously expanded.

Outside, in the wider world beyond the tiny confines of the gray streets and brick tenements of Brooklyn, great powers were moving toward the precipice of the Second World War. Up to 1933, Isaac's sole window on the world had been his school education and the local library; now he could hear firsthand talk of German expansionism and the growing conflict taking place on the other side of the Atlantic.

Reaching his teens, Isaac began to feel the first stirrings of political awareness. Although never an active spokesman on national political issues, Asimov always did have a clear and vocal sense of right and wrong. He was a liberal in a broad sense; no pulpit-beating socialist or radical, but a man with a clear, educated perception of the world, an innate sense of humanitarianism and a well-defined idea of how the world would work best—even if he knew that humankind would find it incredibly difficult to fit that ideal.

Ridgewood helped to harden Isaac's adolescent political feelings. While the countries of Europe were aflame with anti-Semitism, the Asimovs' own neighbors, largely Catholic and with a strong German element, helped in subtle ways to make him realize for the first time that he was different. At school there were mildly anti-Semitic teachers who took a particular dislike to this loudmouthed smart-ass, and there were potential customers in the neighborhood who shunned the candy store for no apparent reason. It was his first awareness of being Jewish and it made him feel uncomfortable, more of an outsider.

Ironically, the family had little interest in religion, and Isaac had only rarely entered a synagogue. Unusually, even for non-Orthodox Jews, Isaac did not even go through the religious initiation of bar mitzvah when he was thirteen.

At school, despite his discipline problems, his studies were progressing well. He was still coming top of the class in most subjects, but even so, when he did not achieve marks in the upper nineties, whatever the subject, he would have to face his father's inquisition. If he slipped in the class ratings, there would be a serious investigation awaiting him.

Isaac's father was typical of the majority of hardworking immigrants who perceived a golden future in the New World, not so much for themselves as for their children. Judah was also wise enough to realize that the key to success in the modern world was education. He was severe in his belief. Being the first son, Isaac suffered the full force of his father's feelings. It was because he believed that Isaac should devote every spare minute doing schoolwork that he viewed with contempt his son's seemingly wayward interest in pulp magazines and science fiction. Later on, Stanley had things much easier.

Over his school efforts, Isaac had more than his father's harsh attitude to face. In 1934, his English teacher, Mr. Newfield, organized a creative writing course at school. Isaac, who was never one to miss an opportunity to display his talents, jumped at the chance of writing some fiction in the guise of schoolwork. It almost nipped in the bud his entire literary career.

The first set piece on the course was a descriptive essay. Without giving it much thought, Isaac quickly decided to write about a beautiful spring day. This was his first mistake. Casting aside everything he had learned from starting and dropping *The Greenville Chums at College*, instead of writing about a spring morning in Brooklyn, he chose to write a description of an ideal spring morning in the country.

The day came when the essays were due to be presented, and the teacher asked if anyone would like to stand up and read their efforts. Isaac then made his second mistake. His hand shot up and he was invited to come to the front of the class to read his work.

Rich with the wordiness of the nineteenth-century novelists whose works he had been reading for several years, Isaac's essay began with tender descriptions of birdsong and opening petals. It was naive and childish, the work of a totally inexperienced fourteen-year-old in a class of fifteen- and sixteen-year-old "men of the world." They began to laugh, and the teacher stood up to stop Isaac in midsentence.

"This is shit!" the teacher apparently declared aloud, and Isaac turned a shade of redder than the blushingest rose in spring.

Fortunately for the world of literature, the intolerant Mr. Newfield's remarks hurt, but caused no lasting damage. By this time Isaac was too deeply engrossed in science fiction, too enamored by the thrill of learning, and too excited by the sheer pleasure of writing to be put off by this early setback. Within a few months, he had written and had had accepted a humorous piece for the school magazine entitled "Little Brothers." His name was in print for the first time. It was an inspiration to the schoolboy, who could already begin to see the huge satisfaction to be gained from writing fiction.

Within a few years of his humiliation at the hands of Mr. Newfield, Isaac had begun to take writing seriously. Before graduating from college, and still only eighteen years old, he had sold his first story.

2

ASIMOV'S SCIENCE FICTION HERITAGE

I t is generally agreed that science fiction originated with a story written as entertainment for a group of English aristocrats holed up in bad weather in the Alps during the summer of 1816.

Mary Shelley and her husband, the poet Percy Bysshe Shelley, had gone on a walking trip with a group of friends, including Lord Byron. Bored and penned in by a sudden storm, they began to relate ghost stories from memory. After a while, one of the party decided that it would be fun if they each attempted to write an original horror story. Mary's effort was called *Frankenstein*.

Many critics claim that *Frankenstein* is not authentic science fiction, that it is actually a horror story. However, they forget to place the tale in the era in which it was written. As part of educated European society, Mary Shelley had been excited by the newly publicized discoveries of Volta and others concerning electricity. No one at the time understood this strange phenomenon or realized its potential, but Mary Shelley used it as the basis for her famous plot, a technique that lies at the very heart of science fiction. During the next hundred years science fiction changed enormously, but at the heart of the genre remained the extrapolation of accepted scientific ideas.

Science fiction did not find its feet as an independent literary form until late in the nineteenth century, when it was propelled into the spotlight by a great burst of activity in the real world of scientific discovery.

The turn of the century in Europe and America marked a time of tremendous change in the way people perceived the world. In the arts and the sciences human perception was altering in many different ways. Within the space of fifty years, from the 1870s to the 1920s, painting had gone from Realism to German Expressionism via Post-Impressionism. Music had thrown off the mantle of Romantic influences—Chopin, Mendelssohn, and others—and had metamorphosed into the atonal experiments of Schoenberg and the imagery of Mahler and Shostakovich. Simultaneously, science had made the irreversible leap from Newtonian physics to quantum theory and relativity. The world was ready for science fiction.

Pioneers of the genre in this new age of discovery included the American writers Edgar Allan Poe, Edward Bellamy, and Edgar Rice Burroughs, and the Frenchman Jules Verne.

With such books as *Thuvia, Maid of Mars* (1920), *The Men of Mars* (1922), and *Pirates of Venus* (1932), it was Burroughs who instigated the interplanetary myths that acted as a springboard for the empire and galactic adventure dreamed up by the likes of E. E. "Doc" Smith, which in turn led to the creations of Asimov, Heinlein, Van Vogt, and Arthur C. Clarke. It is Burroughs, more than any other writer of his generation, who can be seen as the progenitor of the space operas of the Golden Age.

If Burroughs gave science fiction its swashbuckling adventure, it was the English writer H. G. Wells who gave it a thoughtful, contemplative side. By the time Burroughs hit the scene, Wells had given science fiction genuine respectability and at the same time reached a far wider public than any writer before him.

Wells's great contribution to science fiction was that he managed to keep the science accurate and plausible and yet remain a storyteller extraordinaire—a crucial skill that Asimov later realized was at the very heart of great science fiction writing.

In all, Wells wrote nine science fiction novels. Most important of these were *The Time Machine* (1895), *The Island of Dr. Moreau* (1896), *The Invisible Man* (1897), and *The War of the Worlds* (1889), all of which young Isaac read as a boy working in his father's candy store. By the early 1930s, when Asimov borrowed his quota of two books from the local library, Wells was considered a respectable member of the literary establishment and, although not quite required reading, Isaac would have found little difficulty in getting Wells's work past his father's censorship.

The first two decades of the century were a boom time for science popularization. Engineering and technological developments in the early part of the century produced a wave of interest in science on both sides of the Atlantic. The Wright brothers had built their first aircraft, Edison had become a household name for his inventions, and the world was changing fast. Popular literature had to reflect those changes and expand upon them. For working-class kids in the drab backstreets of Brooklyn, pulp magazines provided an escape into a world populated by aliens where they were starship commanders.

The pulps, or dime magazines, began life as collections of westerns and other terrestrial adventure stories. They only embraced the still unchristened genre of science fiction through the determination of one man— Hugo Gernsbeck.

Controversy surrounds Gernsbeck's contribution to science fiction. Although he has been lionized by his many fans in the field as "the father of science fiction," Gernsbeck is seen by others as a destructive influence. At least one respected science fiction writer and critic, Brian Aldiss, perceives Gernsbeck as not only dragging science fiction into the immature pastures of space opera but also hindering the development of the European line of the genre, which, thanks to the lead of such literary figures as Wells, could have blossomed earlier.

In 1911, Gernsbeck was editor of a magazine called *Modern Electrics,* a typical nonfiction pulp publication of the time. Whatever Gernsbeck's faults, he had daring, and he decided to begin serializing a self-penned fictional piece in the magazine. He gave it the catchy title *Ralph 124C41+: A Romance of the Year 2660.*

The story was well received and Gernsbeck continued to insert his fictional pieces into *Modern Electrics* until the magazine folded a few years later. Meanwhile, other publications that dealt mainly with adventure stories began to publish tales previously outside their remit. Edgar Rice Burroughs had his first Martian stories published in *All-Story* during 1913, and magazines specializing in horror and fantasy sprang up featuring stories by well-known horror writers such as H. P.

Lovecraft and Edgar Allan Poe. Despite this proliferation, a decade passed before Gernsbeck was able to expand upon the idea of fiction in science magazines.

By 1923, Gernsbeck was the editor of a new magazine called *Science and Invention* and secure enough to take the bold step of devoting an entire issue to fiction. He called it the "scientifiction issue." It was another great success and prompted him to try to persuade his publishers to launch a new magazine catering entirely to readers interested in a form of fiction he defined as "the Jules Verne, H. G. Wells, and Edgar Allan Poe type of story—a charming romance intermingled with scientific fact and prophetic vision."[1]

The new magazine was called *Amazing Stories* and was perhaps the single most important pulp science fiction magazine of the 1920s. The first issue kept true to Gernsbeck's definition of science fiction (a name attributed to Gernsbeck after much messing around with his original, rather unfortunate cognomen "scientifiction"). The magazine included over thirty items by Wells, nine by Verne, and five short pieces by Poe, as well as a smattering of Gernsbeck's own work. But before long Gernsbeck realized that he had to develop a new crop of writers and to shift the emphasis of the writing in the magazine away from the pseudointellectual to a machine-age "gosh-wow" style.

In the real world outside the pages of *Amazing*, technology and society were changing rapidly. In order to stay ahead of the game, science fiction authors could not dare to write about the near future or to merge sociology and science in their speculations. By the mid-twenties scientists had launched the first rocket and were publicly suggesting that space travel was feasible. In 1926 a surgeon in London had carried out the first operation involving open heart surgery, and the BBC was broadcasting to an estimated ten million worldwide. Achievements that had been seen as ridiculous fantasy a decade earlier were now science fact. In Asimov's childhood, the forward charge of technology was already gaining momentum, and the writers and editors of science fiction made the move further into the distant future.

---

[1] *Science Fiction* by Robert Scholes and Eric S. Rabkin. Oxford University Press, New York, 1977 (p. 37).

While Asimov was growing up in Brooklyn and smuggling copies of *Amazing Stories* into a back room to read in secret, Gernsbeck's baby was going from strength to strength. In the space of a year he created, almost single-handedly, an establishment of young writers with fresh ideas going way beyond the old school of Wells, Verne, and others. Gernsbeck's concoction of science wonder and pangalactic adventure was a perfect formula for the times.

After a temporary blip caused by the stock market crash of 1929, Gernsbeck established other magazines to cater for the expanding market created by *Amazing Stories*. There was *Wonder Stores and Science Wonder Stories,* and a rival publication appeared in 1930 called *Astounding*. In the years that followed, the lines of commercial warfare were established by *Amazing* and *Astounding,* which remained great rivals for a generation of writers and readers, yet most readers managed to scrape together the money to buy both publications.

After establishing the pulp market for science fiction, perhaps Gernsbeck's second greatest contribution to the form was his discovery of E. E. "Doc" Smith, who was to have a profound influence on the generation of writers succeeding him, including Asimov.

Smith's most important work is undoubtedly the Lensman series, first serialized in *Amazing* between 1934 and 1947 and later published as a set of novels. The Lensman stories are the first to be given an intergalactic setting. They are vast in scope and truly mind-boggling in the way Smith deals with interstellar distances and galaxy-wide civilizations, wars, and high adventure. The original "space opera" books, they have since spawned a plethora of imitations.

Today, Smith's work is seen as incredibly naive. His characters are wooden and the plots juvenile. Nonetheless, the Lensman stories have a definite charm about them; it is easy to forget that they were written in the 1930s, when a flight across the Atlantic was on the borders of the possible.

Smith undoubtedly sacrificed characterization and sensitivity for adventure and thrills, but swashbuckling adventure and the creation of almost psychedelic settings were what he was interested in and very good at, and the readers of *Amazing,* including the teenage Asimov, lapped it up.

Smith's influence on Asimov's work is obvious. Although the Foundation series is infinitely more subtle and accomplished than the Lensman series, through Smith's adventures, Asimov discovered that a story could be built around a monumental theme, and an author could handle unimaginable distances, time periods, and incredibly far-fetched ideas without diving too far into fantasy. What Asimov managed was to amalgamate Smith's intergalactic vision with the greater scientific and literary maturity of the times in which he wrote.

During the same period in which Gernsbeck was publishing E. E. Smith, a writer appeared on the scene who was to have the greatest of all influences on Asimov's career and the development of science fiction in general. This was John W. Campbell. Ironically, it was not Campbell's writing that would have such an influence on Asimov and others in the field but his peerless skills as an editor. In Brian Aldiss's view and in the opinion of many modern commentators, it is Campbell who really propelled science fiction into the modern era.

Campbell first appeared in *Amazing* as a writer in January 1930 with a story called "When the Atoms Failed" and quickly rose in importance as a potential rival to E. E. Smith. At the same time, he began to appear in the rival *Astounding* under the pseudonym Don A. Stuart, trying out a new form of science fiction story, an altogether more downbeat, emotional tale, low on adventure but more searching and challenging than the one-dimensional thrills and spills of Smith.

Many readers, including the teenage Asimov, initially found Stuart's writing hard to cope with. Asimov claimed that it was many years before he could accept many of Campbell's stories in the guise of Stuart and that they were largely beyond him as a teenager.

Despite his success as a science fiction writer, before long Campbell wanted to try his hand at life on the other side of the editor's desk, and in the spring of 1938, the twenty-seven-year-old took over the helm of *Astounding*.

Astounding had previously been edited by F. Orlin Tremaine and had already run to fifty issues before Campbell's appointment. Tremaine had been a good editor but more inclined toward Gernsbeck's vision of science fiction. With Campbell's succession, *Astounding,* and with it the whole genre, soon came of age.

Much has been written about Campbell's time at the magazine, and many saw him as the man who created the careers of the greats of the genre. Campbell's first decade at the magazine is regarded by many science fiction fans as the Golden Age.

Campbell was certainly the most important coordinator of early science fiction publishing. Under his editorship he succeeded in nurturing many of the important names of a generation of science fiction writers. Asimov was always deeply indebted to Campbell for the help and encouragement he gave, and saw him as the single most important influence in his early career.

Campbell was a tough editor who was utterly determined to drag out the best from his writers. He was a master coaxer with an instinctive feel for how best to treat an author and how to surf their egos and shifting temperaments. He knew when to be forceful and when to cajole. As Aldiss says in his survey of science fiction, *Trillion Year Spree*:

> It must have been a painful experience to write for the pulps
> in the thirties. One had to conform to get the formula right
> or get out. There was no sort of cultural tradition to appeal to.
> Low rates of pay engendered much hack-work.[1]

Campbell was almost solely responsible for sweeping away this attitude and entered the genre with a perspective based on logic and maturity. He wanted to develop a central core of great science fiction writers and to lead magazine writing away from the naive worlds of "Doc" Smith and give it a believable, coherent framework.

Asimov was not the only one to benefit from Campbell's wisdom. Robert Heinlein, A. E. Van Vogt, Theodore Sturgeon, and Harry Harrison, to name but four other first-class science fiction writers, were all first exposed to the public through Campbell. Each was allowed to mature and develop under his guidance, and each cut his teeth writing for his magazines before moving on to become internationally famous science fiction novelists.

The relationship between Asimov and Campbell was not always a

[1] *Trillion Year Spree* by Brian Aldiss with David Wingrove. Paladin, London, 1988 (p. 261).

smooth one. As Asimov found his feet and independence from the pulps,
he and Campbell had many falling-outs. They disagreed on many issues,
including politics, but remained friends until Campbell's death in 1971.

Campbell was interested in the sort of science fiction story that had
some substance as well as thrills. He was not a particularly great fan of E.
E. "Doc" Smith's swashbuckling high adventure but he loved big, universal themes. He was a man deeply homocentric concerning the place of
our species in the great scheme of things and believed that Homo sapiens
was the most important life form on Earth. In his stories and those of his
writers, he liked his aliens to be either human and cooperative or else
dominated by human beings. This was an aspect of Campbell's character
that Asimov found hard to accept. Yet, in order to get work from
Astounding, Asimov soon learned to incorporate such ideas into his early
efforts.

In the spring of 1938, when Campbell took up his position at
Astounding, Asimov was in his third year at junior college and had already
had a letter published in *Astounding* (during the editorship of Campbell's
predecessor, Tremaine). But it was several months before the name of
Isaac Asimov became known to Campbell and the two men actually met.

At the time, Asimov was more concerned with saving his floundering
college career than nurturing dreams of becoming a famous writer. When
Asimov and Campbell did eventually meet, the encounter provided
exactly the catalyst Asimov needed and was instrumental in launching his
career as a science fiction writer.

3

COLLEGE AND CAMPBELL

I n the spring of 1935 Isaac Asimov was a spotty, untidy youth who was a poor conversationalist and quite uninspiring to most adults who met him. During the course of the next seven years he was to totally transform himself, metamorphosing from an awkward adolescent into a confident, outspoken adult and establishing himself as an important figure in the world of science fiction story writing.

By his fifteenth birthday Isaac was fully grown and stood five feet, nine inches in stockinged feet; his voice was breaking and he was about to change schools yet again. This time he was moving from high school to college.

Isaac's parents had decided that he would attend medical school and eventually qualify as a doctor. Being a doctor was considered the pinnacle of success by Jewish immigrants of the era. Isaac himself had little choice in the matter, and in any case had no other ideas of his own.

The first step on the road to entering the medical profession was to graduate from college. If he later failed to make medical school, then at least a college education would hold him in good stead for some other career.

Medical schools were notoriously difficult to get into, particularly for the children of Jewish immigrants, and attending a good college was important. The obvious choice was the nearby City College, but this was largely Jewish in enrollment and, according to all reports, certain death for those wishing to go on to medical school. A better bet was Seth Low

College. Although entry was more difficult, graduation from here would give him a head start.

Seth Low was affiliated with Columbia College, part of Columbia University, the elite undergraduate school. It was really a catchment college for those considered, for one reason or another, not quite appropriate for Columbia College itself. It catered primarily for the brightest children of immigrant families, not just Jews, but Italians and other ethnic groups.

Isaac did not do very well at the college interview. Not really knowing how to conduct himself, he came across as a rather introverted and uncharismatic adolescent, and left feeling that he was almost certainly destined for the down-market City College and therefore complete failure in his embryonic medical career.

Thinking that he had not qualified, Isaac spent the end of his last term at school and his entire graduation under a black cloud of impending doom, dreading the fact that he would have to break the news to his parents.

Much to his amazement, a couple of weeks after the interview, he received surprising news. He had been accepted into Seth Low. His parents realized that the college was not as good as Columbia itself, but were equally well aware of the ethnic factors involved in college selection. They accepted this second-rate placing as unavoidable, but Isaac would, for his entire time at the college, feel like a third-rate student.

It was during his last term at school that Isaac acquired his first type-writer, a secondhand Underwood No. 5, which his father bought for the princely sum of ten dollars.

Isaac found learning to use the machine difficult. Never one for easy-to-learn courses or manuals, he plunged in and started to type using one finger. When his father realized what he was doing, he insisted that Isaac learn to type properly, a demand for which Asimov was always grateful. A young girl named Mazie, who lived across the street from the store, was taking a commercial typing course. Lessons were arranged and Isaac never looked back.

As an adult, he recalled that it was not so much Mazie's instruction that interested him but that for the first time in his life, he would be alone with a pretty girl.

He was a fast learner and was soon outstripping Mazie in typing speed; before long, he was accurately typing at the rate of ninety words per minute.

Once he could use the machine, Isaac almost immediately began to write fiction. He had very little recollection of these early efforts and no trace of them remains on paper. The only memory of his early fiction was an effort that dealt with magicians and elves. As far as he could remember, the story had a Tolkienesque feel, before *The Hobbit* or *The Lord of the Rings* first appeared in print.

College started in September 1935. The campus, in the Borough Hill district of Brooklyn, was about five miles from the candy store. He had to take a short subway journey to the college, which cost five cents each way.

Isaac knew no one at the college. Most of his classmates had gone to City College, and he remained pretty much a loner during his student days. He had one good friend at Seth Low. Sidney Cohen was an academic and determined student who shared many of Isaac's scientific interests, but their friendship faded into the background after college ended.

Isaac did not enjoy his first years at college. He discovered that he was poor at languages and art and found that he was not a very good practical scientist. Dissection proved to be especially difficult. Isaac had always loved cats and felt terrible having to kill even a stray. So, when he was required to catch an alley cat, kill it, preserve it, and dissect it for biology class, he forced himself to do it, but only just. As soon as he could, he dropped zoology as a major.

Isaac's second or sophomore year at college brought a number of changes. Seth Low, as a separate institution, closed down, and the students were made "university undergraduates." Much to Isaac's annoyance and fueling his increased awareness of ethnic discrimination, Seth Low undergraduates were not brought into the larger body of the colleges of Columbia, but segregated by their new title, which meant that they were still second-class citizens even though they did the same work and, on some occasions, attended the same lectures as the bona fide Columbia students.

The new arrangement also involved a much longer journey to college, which took up to an hour each way on the subway. This served to further alienate Asimov from his peers and to make any form of relationship outside college almost impossible.

The Asimovs moved again at the end of 1936, to their fourth candy store and the one Isaac remembered best. It was on Windsor Place, near Prospect Park, a place where he passed through his adolescence increasingly lost in a fictional world.

The new apartment, this time not above the store but across the street, was the best place Isaac had ever lived in. The Asimovs' candy store had been doing well for a number of years and a strong financial base allowed them to move to a more spacious home in a smarter district. For the first time Isaac had his own room, and with it came permission to keep his science fiction magazines in the closet. There had not been room for such things in Ridgewood, and what are now considered valuable collector's items—copies of *Amazing* and *Astounding* from the early thirties—were simply thrown away.

Isaac had fond memories of this family home. The Asimovs lived there for sixteen years, their longest stay in any one place. Isaac lived with his parents on Windsor Place for six of them and was greatly saddened when, twenty-five years later, he returned to the old neighborhood and found the shop and apartment derelict and boarded up.

Windsor Place was where Asimov began writing in earnest. He could remember the exact day he began his first serious and coherent fictional piece on the typewriter; it was May 29, 1937. Up until then he had been learning to type and writing reports and juvenile journalism for the school magazine, along with occasional unstructured, ill-conceived fictional efforts.

His first story was called "Cosmic Corkscrew" and centered on a time traveler. Even in this first effort, Asimov began with current scientific concepts and extrapolated on them, weaving the story around a plausible extension of an idea at the fringes of science.

Meanwhile, in the spring and early summer of 1937, as he messed around with this first story Asimov realized that he really needed to earn some money to help pay his way through his sophomore year. The previous summer he had worked as a laborer for fifteen dollars per week, and this had helped with the cost of books and transport to college, but his savings were running out. To alleviate the financial burden on his parents he worked as an assistant in the college psychology department.

Asimov's job was to number crunch for the head of psychology,

Professor Gregory Razran. The job involved working in a team preparing a table of statistics for the professor, but Asimov soon realized that he was no team player. He was forever going off and preparing his own tables and doing his own research outside the professor's remit. When he did actually work with the others in his department, he ended up arguing over all manner of minor points and making it very clear that he thought he was right and the others were wrong. He soon reached the conclusion that he could not work on the team into which he was placed, and spent most of his time on his own. The professor only kept him on because, despite his inability to cooperate with others, Asimov did actually deliver useful results.

He always did find it difficult to work with others involved in the same job. According to publishers, he was a dream to work with in preparing a book, but that was because he wrote them and they published them. Publishers respected his contribution, and he theirs. They were not doing the same job or working too closely on a particular project. This is undoubtedly one of the reasons why, with the exception of a brief spell with Fred Pohl, Asimov never had a literary agent.

Asimov celebrated New Year 1938 by starting a diary. The date also almost exactly coincided with his eighteenth birthday. Despite periods where his enthusiasm waned, he faithfully maintained the habit of writing his diary his entire life.

These diaries were, by his own admission, incredibly dull efforts. They were simply reportage and lent precious little insight into his deeper feelings or motivations. From the outset, he intended his diary to be merely factual, for later use to settle arguments and disputes rather than for providing insights into any erotic fantasies, dreams, or deeper thoughts on life.

At school, Asimov had shown himself to be a talented but disruptive pupil; he did not change when he started college. He continued to get good grades, but almost immediately turned a number of lecturers against him. Before the completion of his first year, he was almost kicked out of at least two courses because he so antagonized the lecturers with his constant wisecracks. Asimov's lecturers quite naturally did not take kindly to this flippant student sitting at the back of the lecture hall undermining their authority by making smart remarks. It is clear that if he had not been such a talented student he might well have found himself out on his ear.

One particular incident remained in Asimov's memory into old age and almost spelled the end of his college career. In his junior year, he had decided to take an English literature course given by a flamboyant and eloquent teacher called Professor Lyon.

Lyon was fanatical about the theater and would frequently enthuse to the class about the latest production he had seen. He was also incredibly strict, and nobody ever crossed him or argued over any point he made. In one particular lecture, Lyon decided to tell the class about the latest Shakespeare play he had seen performed in the city and was describing the event in great detail and with almost comical enthusiasm.

It so happened that Asimov had only recently heard of burlesque—a risqué theater of the time. Big news of that year was that the puritanical mayor of New York, Fiorello LaGuardia, had closed down all the burlesque theaters in the city.

As Lyon paced around the classroom describing the splendor of the performance, he declared that he felt sorry for the class because never in their lives would they see the spectacle, never would they experience the incomparable beauty of the performance . . . at which point, Asimov, bored by Lyon's over-the-top delivery, suddenly remarked aloud, "No we won't, not as long as LaGuardia keeps those places closed."

As soon as he had said it, Asimov regretted it. The lecture hall fell silent and then, as one, the entire class burst into uncontrollable hysterics. A po-faced Lyon tried to placate them but they were too far gone. Asimov was saved by the bell, and a few moments later Lyon left and the class filed out after him, still smiling and joking about Asimov's comment. Asimov and Sidney Cohen remained in the lecture hall discussing what Asimov was going to do for a job after being expelled from college.

Fortunately for Asimov, Lyon did not seem to mind Asimov's comment and took it in the spirit in which it was meant. The following week Lyon entered the lecture hall, gave his errant student a wink and a knowing nod, and the incident was forgotten, except that Lyon gave Asimov high marks and special praise at the end of the course.

Asimov's talent for quick, off-the-cuff comments combined with a naturally analytical bent were turned to good effect in another area of his life. As Asimov was coping with the college establishment and developing his academic life, he started writing to science fiction magazines and reviewing the stories in each issue as well as grading them according to what he considered were the essential ingredients of a story. This sparked off a response that was to prove far more significant than he had imagined.

The initial thrill of seeing his name in print in *Astounding* led him to delve deeper into the science fiction world. When, on May 10, 1938, *Astounding* did not appear as scheduled, Asimov grew concerned. Several days passed and the magazine had still not appeared. He decided to take some positive action and set off for the offices of the publishers, Street and Smith.

Directed by a receptionist to the fifth floor, he was shown into the offices of a Mr. Clifford, who explained that the publication date had been changed to May 20. Asimov went home contented and waited for his copy to arrive, which it did the next day.

In retrospect, Asimov realized that this seemingly insignificant incident was actually an important turning point in his life and set him on the road to writing his own science fiction stories. His heroes were the writers of the stories he read in each issue of *Astounding* and *Amazing Stories*. When one issue had not appeared on schedule, he discovered just how much he had built his life around the magazines. If they were to go, the only way to compensate for the loss would be to write his own fiction.

The visit to Street and Smith had also made Asimov realize that the writers featured in the magazines were by no means untouchable. He had simply walked into the publisher's offices, the very place where the stories arrived and were selected for the magazine. Why shouldn't he also step into that world as a writer? It was at this point that he remembered "Cosmic Corkscrew," which had been sitting incomplete in his desk drawer at home. Within minutes of returning on the subway from Street and Smith, he had picked up his first serious dog-eared literary effort and decided there and then that he would rework it and submit it to *Astounding*.

Asimov kept "Cosmic Corkscrew" and all his ideas about writing fiction very much to himself. After he was satisfied with the story, he had to decide how best to submit it to *Astounding*. He decided to talk to his father about it, and was surprised when Judah gave him what turned out to be the best advice he had ever received—"Go to Campbell with the manuscript personally," his father said.

Asimov and Campbell first met on June 21, 1938. On that first occasion Asimov was an eighteen-year-old college kid and Campbell a highly successful and experienced magazine editor ten years his senior.

Campbell took Asimov's first story and promised to read it and to get back to him with comments within a few days. What was almost as important to the young college kid sitting on the other side of Campbell's desk was the mere fact that the great editor had agreed to see him in the first place.

Of course, Campbell rejected "Cosmic Corkscrew," and, as promised, sent the manuscript back to Asimov within two days. He was unemotional in his criticisms and took the story apart in almost every aspect; he criticized the beginning, the characterization, the thin plot, and the ending. Yet, despite what appeared to be a complete rejection, Campbell added a hint of encouragement at the conclusion of his letter and planted a seed in Asimov's mind that all was not lost, that he should persevere and try again. Campbell had the great and rare knack of doing this— firmly pointing out the weaknesses of a story, totally destroying it if need be, but still leaving a crumb of hope for the writer; an essential skill in any editor.

Asimov immediately set to work on a new story. He had learned a lot from this first rejection and he had established a relationship with Campbell. He believed he now had the measure of the style and essential ingredients for an *Astounding* story and set to work on a new, six-thousand-word story entitled "Stowaway."

"Stowaway" tells the story of a voyage to one of Jupiter's moons, Callisto, which turns out to be inhabited by a colony of strange animals that respond to magnetic fields.

Meanwhile, Asimov continued to have his letters of criticism published each month in *Astounding*, and even received letters back from established writers who contributed regularly to the magazine. Some were puzzled by his comments; others wrote to thank him for his opinions. Without realizing it, Asimov was networking. It was through these letters that he had first managed to get into Campbell's office that June afternoon, and it was also through them that he was beginning to make contact with the great backdrop of writers and readers who made the science fiction revolution happen and kept *Amazing* and *Astounding* in business.

"Stowaway" took Asimov eighteen days to complete. He submitted it to Campbell on July 18 and received the rejection on July 22. This time Campbell rejected it on far more specific grounds. The plot was a good one and the idea quite strong, but the dialogue was unnatural and lacked the professional touch needed for a successful story.

Thus things continued. It was over six months before Campbell accepted an Asimov story for *Astounding*. The successful yarn, called "Ad Astra" and about a trip to the Moon, was accepted on January 31, 1939. It took Asimov seven visits to Campbell and a total of nine rejected stories before his work was accepted.

Early 1939 turned out to be a very fruitful and successful period for Asimov's writing. By the time Campbell introduced him to *Astounding*'s readership, Asimov had already had a story accepted. His very first published piece had been rejected by Campbell. "Marooned Off Vesta," now one of Asimov's most famous stories, was taken by *Amazing* on October 21, 1938, and appeared in the January 1939 issue.

In February 1939 Asimov made a third sale to one of the smaller magazines, *Science Fiction*, a sister magazine to *Wonder Stories*. This time it was a story called "Ring Around the Sun." By now he was well and truly in business.

In accepting "Ad Astra," Campbell had not been influenced by Asimov's success with *Amazing*. He took the story on its own merits. But "Marooned Off Vesta" had been very well received by *Amazing*'s readers, and Asimov received a number of cards and notes telling him that it had been the best story in the January issue.

Quite naturally, Asimov got a great buzz from these, his first sales. The writing business at this stage in his career was certainly not very lucrative, but he did receive between a half and one cent per word, which meant that "Ad Astra," at 6,900 words, earned him sixty-nine dollars. The word rate depended on the magazine. The big magazines quite naturally paid more because they had larger circulations. *Science Fiction* paid only the lower rate.

Asimov was beginning to attract attention among the fans and readers of the popular science fiction magazines. The stories were also coming thick and fast. Fred Pohl, one of Asimov's friends and a fellow science fiction writer, offered to act as Asimov's agent and to help him rework rejected stories. At first Asimov was not keen on the idea. Knowing himself to be a very difficult person to work with, he nonetheless gave it a try later in the year. The partnership lasted no more than a couple of months during 1939, and was only marginally successful. Pohl helped his friend to place a couple of stories with minor magazines.

Pohl was far more helpful as a critic than as an agent, and Asimov always remembered the assistance and encouragement he gave him at sticky moments in his career, times when Asimov, still relatively new to the business and more than a little naive, had bitten off more than he could chew in promising to deliver a story for which he had only the vaguest plot.

Through this brief liaison, Pohl and Asimov became very close friends, but both agreed that their relationship was far better on a personal level than as a formal business partnership.

With these early successes under his belt, Asimov was up and running as a writer for the pulp magazines, and, except for a brief period during 1942 when domestic responsibilities and the intrusion of the war brought things to a temporary standstill, there was rarely a month during which he did not appear in one science fiction magazine or another. What is often forgotten is that during this enormously productive period, Asimov was still at college, struggling with his degree and trying to juggle responsibilities at home, as well as cultivating his writing ambitions.

The new craze of science fiction clubs sprang up all over America during the late thirties and early forties and most particularly in New York, where the major magazines were published. It was through his writing and membership in a succession of science fiction clubs that Asimov finally made a number of personal friends.

The first club Asimov joined had given itself the rather bland name of the Greater New York Science Fiction Club. It consisted of a group of adolescent pulp science fiction fans who lived in the five boroughs and held regular meetings in Queens.

At these meetings members would discuss stories that had appeared in the various magazines, and from time to time they would read each other their own efforts, compose letters to the pulps concerning some minor detail of a story, and, most crucially, bitch about other clubs. This ferment of teenage enthusiasm was incredibly stimulating to someone as isolated as Asimov had been. It was an adventure traveling across New York in the early evening after finishing his college work and his duties at the candy store. Being away from home for an evening, even at the age of eighteen, was a relative rarity and added spice to the proceedings.

The science fiction clubs of the day never lasted very long. At some stage or another, internal politics, usually aggravated over some minor disagreement about science fiction, erupted into internecine conflict. After this the club would fragment, realign, and form new, equally short-lived clubs of like-minded souls.

Considering his difficulty with team efforts and working with others, it is surprising that Asimov always tended to act as arbiter between the warring factions, and after a breakup he always tried to keep his hand in with both camps simultaneously. Asimov did not take seriously the petty squabbles between the different factions within the clubs and cared very little for gaining any form of "leadership" or merit within the close-knit little community of science fiction fans. He was more interested in reading and writing science fiction than attempting to be a big fish in a small pond.

Membership of the science fiction clubs of Asimov's youth was almost exclusively male. With few exceptions, during the thirties and forties, science fiction was really an all-male preserve. This has changed a great deal in recent times, perhaps largely due to the influence of Hollywood.

Thanks to the science fiction clubs he joined, Asimov made many male friends. Some of them became lifelong buddies, including Sam Moskowitz, Fred Pohl, L. Sprague de Camp, and others.

The most important club of the period was called the Futurians. At one time or another it included within its membership such future luminaries as Fred Pohl, James Blish, Damon Knight, Robert Heinlein, and, of course, Isaac Asimov. This was an important phase in Asimov's development as a science fiction writer because it enabled him to discuss his ideas with others of similar mind and to explore what was possible in the fiction field and what was not. Science fiction, especially during this era, was written by fans for fans, and an essential ingredient in the development of any author is an understanding of the field they are working in. The cross-pollination of ideas that came as a result of meetings of the Futurians provided the basis of Asimov's early work as well as the launch pad for Heinlein, Pohl, and others.

Because Isaac spent so much of his time discussing spaceships and time travel in science fiction clubs, his teen years were almost totally devoid of female company. He did not have a date with a girl until he was almost twenty years old.

Isaac's first girlfriend was a fellow chemistry student at college called Irene. Although their relationship did not last long and never developed into anything serious, their occasional dates during the winter of 1939 and early 1940 gave Asimov his first real experience with girls of his own age.

Despite having some success as a short story writer and accruing several hundred dollars in his own bank account, Isaac did not believe in splashing out. He appears to have been totally clueless when it came to the art of seduction and acting the part of the gallant gentleman. He was a little miserly with his early dates and always took girlfriends to cheap restaurants. He hated the thought of forking out money for theater tickets or expensive meals.

One particular incident almost ended his relationship with Irene soon after it had begun. In May 1940 Isaac took her to the World's Fair. Deciding that their relationship, after more than six months, needed a boost to take it from the purely platonic to the mildly carnal, Isaac thought that a trip on the roller coaster at the fair would help. The theory was that at the top of a particularly formidable peak in the ride, Irene would be so terrified that she would throw herself into his arms and he could steal a kiss.

Things did not go exactly to plan. Isaac had not realized that *he* was terrified of heights. The roller coaster hit the first peak and he panicked, grabbed hold of Irene, and screamed. By the time the cart had arrived back at base he was a gibbering wreck and had to endure Irene's sarcasm and scorn for the rest of the evening.

The relationship with Irene did not last much longer and Isaac returned to his circle of male friends, college work, helping his father in the candy store, and, more importantly, his science fiction writing. Then, a few months later, he met a young lady called Gertrude.

Their first meeting in early 1942 was thanks to a friend of Isaac's called Joe Goldberger. Isaac had met Joe at the Brooklyn Authors Club, to which Asimov had graduated after a spell with the Futurians.

Joe's girlfriend, Lee, wanted one of her friends to meet Joe and assess his suitability as a "serious" prospect. Obviously it would be best if a four-some could be arranged, so Joe approached Isaac.

It took several weeks to find a time and place for the date but eventually the four of them met up in New York. Joe had described Isaac as a Russian chemist with a mustache.

Isaac had indeed grown a mustache over a year earlier, but by early 1942 he had shaved it off. He could not speak a word of Russian, and was at that stage still struggling with his college chemistry course. Nonetheless, the first date went well.

From his own recollections, Isaac was apparently more concerned about the cost of the event than whether or not he was going to get on with his date, Gertrude.

Isaac was still a very naive young man. He had little dress sense, showed no interest in fashion, and did not have the first clue how to manipulate a social situation to his advantage. He was a rather young twenty-two-year-old academic, an odd mix of introvert and loudmouth. His family were working-class immigrants with little money. He had an air of absent-mindedness about him; the "nutty professor type," uncool and a little gauche. He had a broad Brooklyn accent (which stayed with him his entire life) and was, by his own admission, sometimes embarrassingly unsophisticated. That aside, something worked with Gertrude, because, after that first date in February 1942, others followed, at first with Joe and Lee and then just the two of them, traveling into Manhattan to see a movie or to go for a cheap meal.

Isaac, even in his clumsy youth, was a very lovable character. In his teens and early twenties he was quite clearly at a loss as to how to behave with women and often proved socially inept with his superiors. He frequently ran into trouble at college. But he was affectionate and open, honest and reliable—women always appreciated these qualities in him.

He was also quite evidently extremely clever and was clearly not shy in demonstrating his intelligence.

Around the time of this first serious date, Isaac began to change. He never did acquire great social sophistication, and always had a rather childish, simplistic sense of humor, but suddenly he began to gain a new self-confidence.

It was at this juncture that he suddenly realized the potential of flirting. Many who met him in later life would find it hard to imagine a shy and introverted Asimov who felt uncomfortable in the presence of women. But in his early twenties he went through a very definite change in his social manner, and from that time on, he behaved totally differently with the opposite sex. Almost overnight he changed from a young boy who was tongue-tied and jumpy with women to a man who never let pass an opportunity to make an impression on any female he encountered.

The most likely explanation for this is that by early 1942 Isaac had emotionally and intellectually broken away from his family. Coupled with this, he had settled down at college and was now enjoying some academic success. In Gertrude he had met a girl with whom he felt comfortable and had managed to impress quite easily. But, most of all, he had written a number of successful stories. He had proven to himself and the science fiction community that he could write well and commercially. Seeing his name in print obviously did wonders for his ego. Asimov always was a sucker for flattery, and a little success obviously went a long way in allowing suppressed aspects of his personality to emerge just at the point where he was ready to break free from a protracted childhood. At last he was beginning to throw off the mantle of the eccentric, otherworldly boy obsessed with science fiction. Suddenly he found that he could communicate with that hitherto unknown quantity—girls. With a newfound sexual awareness, Isaac's wise-guy quips were broadened into a mildly lascivious manner with women. From this point on, Isaac was still a wise guy but he had also become a flirt.

Ironically, Gertrude was really the catalyst for Isaac's transformation. His settled academic life and early promise as a writer provided the backup; Gertrude pushed him into adulthood.

She had a pretty face and a mass of dark hair; she was a little over five feet, two inches, with a full figure. Isaac thought she was extremely beautiful and pictured her as the spitting image of Olivia de Havilland.

Gertrude had lived in Canada for most of her life; her family had moved to New York when she was nineteen. Born in 1917, she was almost three years older than Isaac. She had led a far more varied life than he and had had a number of boyfriends.

Isaac was a virgin when he met Gertrude and had experienced little in the way of sex, but he and Gertrude seemed to click almost immediately. It is clear, however, that in the early stages of their relationship Isaac did all the running and Gertrude behaved with far greater reserve. Nonetheless, the romance blossomed and she was invited to meet Isaac's parents. The invitation was returned and they settled into serious courtship.

The three years at college had been a constant struggle for Asimov. This era in his life was marked by three matters of great importance to him. Firstly, his work as a science fiction short-story writer was going from strength to strength. He had received a large number of rejections, but he kept coming back for more and eventually stories were sold. Campbell was a continual source of inspiration, as were his friends and fellow science fiction fans and young writers. By the time he met Gertrude, he had sold over a dozen stories and in 1941 alone had earned over a thousand dollars from his efforts—not a fortune even then, but it went a long way to paying for his college tuition.

The second major concern for Asimov was the war. He felt involved in the conflict from the start. Despite the fact that he had absolutely no religious leanings, he did feel himself to be part of a global Jewish community. He believed that Hitler's actions against European Jews were actions against him. He felt frustrated and impotent.

By 1941, the war had stagnated into a stalemate, with the Germans simultaneously fighting on two fronts. The Russian winter and the Soviet army had stopped Hitler in his tracks to the east; and on the western front, in the Far East and in Africa, the two great armies of Britain and Germany had come to an impasse.

Then, on Sunday, December 7, 1941, the Japanese bombed Pearl Harbor and the United States was in the war. Asimov was incredibly excited by the conflict. He realized that the war was a crazy exercise, millions of people were losing their lives and homes, and great nations were exhausting themselves; but he also realized that Hitler had to be stopped at all costs. He believed that America was on the side of good, and never doubted for a moment that the Allies would win. It was simply a question of time.

The third aspect of his youth, and its heaviest burden, was his academic life. Having met the required academic standard, in September 1939 Asimov entered graduate school. He was at Columbia but still not a first-class member of the college. At the root of this was once again ethnic segregation. He had also made things more difficult for himself by antagonizing several influential professors at Columbia, who decided to make it harder for him to carry on there.

Professor Urey, a Nobel laureate and head of the Columbia chemistry department, did not like Asimov. The two had had a number of petty run-ins, and Urey had made it clear that he had little time for Isaac. Asimov had not done well in Urey's courses and had barely reached the expected standard in several others. Urey believed him to be a bigheaded and lazy student who would never make anything of himself. Asimov could never mention the fact that he was trying to complete his college work as best he could while helping to run the family store, traveling for hours each day on the subway, and finding his own fees from writing science fiction.

In 1939, Urey tried to get rid of Asimov at the college selection meeting to choose graduate students, but he was outvoted. However, much to Isaac's annoyance, Urey did succeed in forcing through a motion that Asimov only be given probationary graduate status. This ranking was to last one year. If at the end of that time he had not made the required grades, he would be out. If he did make the grades, he would be given the status of full studentship.

Throughout 1939, as the war developed and reached crisis point in Europe, Asimov temporarily decreased his commitment to writing and pulled out all the stops at college. He studied late into the night and rose early to work at the store. He read throughout the subway journey to and from college and cut himself off from his contemporaries. At the end of 1940 his grades were excellent and he was rewarded with full studentship at Columbia.

The next hurdle Asimov had to face was the problem of medical school. For some time he had not only given up hope of being accepted, but had decidedly turned against the idea. Unfortunately, his parents had set their hearts on their son becoming a doctor. They saw no real, long-term worth in acquiring a Ph.D., only a medical doctorate. Asimov, of course, saw things differently.

By this time he had discovered a love for pure science, and chemistry in particular. He struggled at college, not because of any lack of academic skill or lack of interest, but because of the other pressures in his life. He also disliked the system of education at Columbia. Before the end of his first year at Seth Low, he had realized that he was far brighter than most of the professors who taught him. Many of them were incredibly boring individuals who knew little outside their specialist areas. Asimov could find little respect for such people.

As it happened, he was saved from any painful arguments or decisions over medical school—they all rejected him out of hand. Asimov breathed a sigh of relief and set about trying to plan what he was going to do instead.

Naturally Judah Asimov was upset by what he saw as his son's academic failure. It took a great effort to convince his father otherwise—that it was a blessing in disguise and that there was life after medical school rejection.

He decided to remain at Columbia and to take a master's degree in chemistry, which would put him in line for research toward a Ph.D. placement. Between passing his exams in 1940 and acquiring his master's degree from Columbia just before meeting Gertrude in early 1942, Asimov had a much easier time. He still had to work hard at college, the master's exams were by no means easy, but he could concentrate on passing those when the time came. He knew that as long as he attended lectures, kept clear notes, and maintained an interest in chemistry through his own reading, he would be fine.

It was during this period that he was able to return to science fiction writing with fresh interest and enthusiasm. Renewing his links with Campbell and his friends in local science fiction clubs, Asimov made huge progress during this time. The period 1940 to 1942 saw in print the original robot stories, the classic short story "Nightfall," and the early parts of what became *The Foundation Trilogy*.

Asimov's decision to relax a little at college and to concentrate on his writing paid off. Compared to his graduate exams of 1940, the master's qualifiers were straightforward. On February 12, 1942, he discovered that he had passed with flying colors and straightaway began to apply for a Ph.D. course at Columbia.

With a master's degree under his belt, upwards of a thousand dollars in the bank, and more than a dozen published stories to his name, the early part of 1942 was a good time for Asimov. Despite the fighting in Europe and the uncertainties about his future, he felt optimistic. And, with great daring and perhaps a degree of overenthusiasm, he decided in April 1942 to propose to Gertrude.

They had known each other only a few months, and Gertrude must have been completely taken aback by the suggestion, but Isaac was very serious about it. His proposal was certainly a further sign of his newly acquired self-confidence.

Gertrude rejected him and tried for a short time to end their relationship. She even told Isaac she did not love him. But, despite her matter-of-factness, he was persistent. He left the matter for a while, but less than a month later, and after persuading Gertrude to continue with their relationship on a less serious footing, he tried again. After a long walk beside the Hudson River and hours of discussion, he finally persuaded Gertrude to accept his offer of marriage.

At an astonishing pace Asimov's world had changed dramatically. From being close to college expulsion, he had managed to pull the academic irons from the fire and achieve entry to a Ph.D. program. He had achieved recognition in the world of science fiction from both the fans and his peers, and he had got the girl he wanted. Ahead lay many hurdles, but in the spring of 1942, Asimov was on the crest of a personal and professional wave.

In terms of his work, the early 1940s are seen as Asimov's most fruitful time as a short-story writer and an era in which he began to establish himself as one of the great American science fiction writers, one of Campbell's chosen few, and a leading light in the Golden Age of science fiction.

4

ROBOTS

t is an astonishing fact that Asimov wrote the majority of *The Foundation Trilogy,* a dozen or more robot stories, and the science fiction classic "Nightfall" before reaching his mid-twenties. And this was not simply a case of the author sparkling when young and then burning out. Although Asimov will probably be best remembered for *Foundation* and the creation of his robot stories, he used these early successes to launch a phenomenal career.

Asimov's first professional story was "Marooned Off Vesta," which appeared in the January 1939 issue of *Amazing Stories.* It is a simple tale of survival through the application of science and established Asimov's trademark of accurately fictionalizing science in his stories. A recurring theme in Asimov's work is that of solving problems through scientific understanding. In the case of "Marooned Off Vesta," this technique is about all there is to the story. It is a single-idea tale with no subplot, scant attention to characterization, and no twists. It is actually little more than a literary conundrum, famous because it was Asimov's first professional story. With the exception of his early robot stories, it was really not until his thirty-second story, "Nightfall," that Asimov began to establish himself as a short-story writer of merit. "Nightfall," like so many of Asimov's earliest efforts, began life through a visit to Campbell.

The visit took place on March 17, 1941. Campbell, reading a story called "Nature" by Ralph Waldo Emerson, had been particularly struck by a few lines in the first chapter:

> If the stars should appear one night in a thousand years,
> how would men believe and adore and preserve for many
> generations the remembrance of the city of God . . .

Campbell handed Asimov the book and asked him to read the quote. When he had finished, Campbell asked, "What do you think would happen?" When Asimov gave him a blank look, Campbell smiled and stated matter-of-factly, "I think if people only saw stars one night in a thousand years, they would go mad. I want you to write a story about that."

The rest, so they say, is history. Asimov delivered the manuscript to Campbell on April 9.

In later years, Asimov very clearly remembered writing "Nightfall." At the time he did not imagine that he was writing one of the most famous science fiction stories of all time, the story that has many times been voted the best ever written. To Asimov, it was merely story number thirty-two.

He is also rather sensitive about "Nightfall" because some people have made too much of Campbell's contribution to the story. Asimov rightly believed that it was one thing to be asked to write a story about a certain subject, quite another to actually go home and face the first blank page, type out the title, and get started.

Asimov himself later saw the creation of "Nightfall" as a major turning point in his career. Although by 1941 he had become a regular contributor to the magazines of the time and was viewed by Campbell as perhaps his most promising protégé, "Nightfall" really did project Asimov into the limelight of the science fiction world. Before its publication, bigger names in the genre included many of Campbell's other writers—Heinlein, Van Vogt, and de Camp—but after "Nightfall," Asimov was seen as the brightest young star in the science fiction firmament.

Year after year "Nightfall" has been cited as the single best science fiction story ever written, a declaration reinforced over thirty years later by no less a fraternity than the Science Fiction Writers of America. Yet it was never one of Asimov's favorites. (These are "The Last Question," "The Bicentennial Man," and "The Ugly Little Boy," in that order.)

So what is it about "Nightfall" that hit a chord with so many readers and has enabled it to remain so highly regarded for over half a century?

The story is set in the city of Saro on the planet Lagash and centers upon a small cast of characters, which include a journalist, Theremon 762; the head of the Saro Observatory, Aton 77; and the psychiatrist Sheerin 501.

Lagash has six suns. Every 2,049 years, all six suns, bar one, set simultaneously and the last one, Beta, is eclipsed by a giant moon. This event plunges the planet into total darkness for over half a Lagashian day. Legend has it that when this occurs, the population of the planet goes mad, because, being inhabitants of a planet with six suns, they have never known anything but intensely bright light, day and night.

A religious cult has grown up on Lagash based on the superstitions of "the nightfall." This group, simply known as "The Cult," preach the Book of Revelations, which claims that when the suns set, the cult's followers see things called "stars."

The action takes place in the observatory of Saro University. Everyone is twitchy. They are scientists, but the influence of "The Cult" runs deep. The women and children of the scientists and government officials have taken the precaution of keeping away from centers of population. But, because the civilization has never known anything other than bright light, they have never developed any form of light technology. Consequently, they cannot lock themselves away in a well-lit bunker and wait until the suns rise again. The best they can manage is flares and burning brands.

At the observatory, the psychologist, Sheerin 501, and the skeptical but quite ignorant journalist, Theremon 762, sent there to report the event, conduct private darkness experiments to see what the phenomenon is like. Two of the observatory astronomers are missing and turn up later in the story announcing that they have tried their own experiments in a darkened room and felt severely claustrophobic. Naturally, none of the characters yet realizes the true problem facing them.

There are two neatly crafted subplots to "Nightfall." The first involves "The Tunnel of Mystery," which relates how a fairground attraction at the Jongler Centennial Exposition—it features a totally black tunnel—two years earlier caused hundreds of customers to go mad and killed three before it was shut down.

The second subplot involves the presence at the observatory of a cultist called Latimer 25, who sneaks in on a mission to destroy what he and his leaders perceive to be sacrilegious experiments.

The story reaches a climax as the total eclipse of the last remaining sun plunges the planet into total darkness, and, for the first time in over two hundred years, the inhabitants see stars. But they do not simply see a lame spattering of stars through a polluted haze, as we do on Earth. Lagash is situated in the heart of a giant star cluster. As darkness falls, the heavens blaze with the light of thousands of nearby stars.

The beauty of "Nightfall," and what I suspect is at the root of Asimov's success with it, is that he is dealing here with a deep-rooted archetype, a universal theme. It is not simply darkness that turns the inhabitants of Lagash mad, for that is very short-lived; it is the sudden realization that there are other stars out there, possibly other civilizations. It is the realization—absolutely horrible to any creatures so sheltered from the concept—that the universe is not the size of their own little stellar system, but that it is infinite.

"Nightfall" moves at a perfect pace. Asimov succeeds in creating an empathy between the reader and these strange aliens, the Lagashians, so totally different from you and me. At the same time, the story moves with the speed of a thriller.

Asimov also manages to interweave historical depth into the plot. We learn about the development of Lagashian science—how they had only recently worked out the law of gravitation, yet are more advanced than twentieth-century Earth scientists in many other ways. And, of course, this would be so. On a planet with six suns, the gravitational effects experienced on Lagash would be far more difficult to calculate than Newton found it to be with just one sun to take into account.

"Nightfall" is a terribly bleak story, full of subconscious nightmare qualities. We know something the characters playing out their parts do not, and we realize long before the end that they are not going to like what they see. As the inhabitants start to go berserk and set fire to whatever they can find, anything to blot out the ghastly stars, the last lines send a chill down the spine:

> On the horizon outside the window, in the direction of Saro City, a crimson glow began growing, strengthening in brightness, that was not the glow of a sun.
>   The long night had come.[1]

---

[1] "Nightfall" by Isaac Asimov. *Astounding,* September 1941.

And with this, all hope dies. In this story, Asimov succeeded in bringing out something deeper, more personal, more human in his characters than in almost anything else he wrote.

The most common criticism leveled against Asimov is his seeming inability to express true human emotions, to cut beneath the outer veneer of humanity. He is always far more interested in machines, technology, scientific correctness, intrigue, and clever plotting than anything emotional or even truly philosophical, with the exception of this short story.

The literary critic and author of a critique of Asimov's work, Dr. Joseph F. Patrouch Jr., has claimed that "Nightfall" "creaks a little,"[1] but I disagree. Many of Asimov's stories do; his exposition is often pained, his characters wooden, and many other facets of what is required in a great story are sacrificed at the altar of plot, but not so in "Nightfall." We can even forgive Asimov (with a forgiveness not exclusively reserved for "Nightfall") for such terrible English as ". . . demanded Latimer frozenly,"[2] and "It was very horrible to go mad and know that you were going mad—to know that in a little minute you would . . ."[3] For me, it is Asimov's best short story and I fully expect it to be receiving the accolade of "best science fiction story" in another fifty years.

Campbell was also pleased with "Nightfall." After a few minor alterations he accepted the story for *Astounding* in his usual way: he did not send Asimov an acceptance letter but instead simply dispatched a check.

The check arrived on April 24. It was for 150 dollars. Asimov stared at it in disbelief. At the rate of a cent per word, the 12,000 words of "Nightfall" should have netted him 120 dollars. Campbell had inadvertently overpaid him. Being scrupulously honest, Asimov straightaway called Campbell and pointed out the error. To Asimov's delight, Campbell had not made a mistake. He had held the story in such high regard that he had paid him at the higher rate of 1.25 cents per word. Furthermore, "Nightfall" made the front cover of *Astounding*, something Asimov had been dreaming of achieving for over three years.

---

[1] "Science Fiction Classics Revisited: Isaac Asimov's *I, Robot,*" lecture by Dr. Joseph Patrouch Jr., 1972.
[2] "Nightfall."
[3] Ibid.

One minor disappointment for Asimov concerning "Nightfall" was also thanks to Campbell. Without consulting Asimov, he included a paragraph of his own in the final draft—an emendation that caused Asimov three problems.

Firstly, he did not agree with Campbell's policy of editorial change without consultation. To be fair to Campbell, he did this rarely and with far greater discretion than many other editors. Secondly, the paragraph made a mention of Earth, which, as Asimov quite rightly pointed out, was inconsistent with the rest of the story. The inhabitants of Lagash obviously did not know of the existence of Earth, and Asimov had carefully not mentioned it in the story. What particularly rattled Asimov was the fact that many readers and critics later cited this paragraph as evidence that, against frequent comments to the contrary, Asimov could write poetically.

Asimov rightly points out that the paragraph is not his own and that by its mention of Earth it stands out as a serious literary flaw. Campbell's inserted paragraph appears in the tale just after the stars appear and reads:

> Not Earth's feeble thirty-six hundred stars visible to the eye; Lagash was in the center of a giant cluster. Thirty thousand mighty suns shone down in a soul-searing splendor that was more frighteningly cold in its awful indifference than the bitter wind that shivered across the cold, horribly bleak world.[1]

Definitely not Asimov, and perhaps part of the reason why he never rated it in his top five, but probably why Campbell liked it so much.

Before starting "Nightfall," Asimov had already written three robot stories. In chronological order these were "Robbie," "Reason," and "Liar!" The first of these, "Robbie," was published in the September 1940 issue of *Super Science Stories,* at that time under the editorship of Asimov's friend Fred Pohl, who paid him the princely sum of thirty-five dollars for the story.

---

[1] "Nightfall."

"Robbie" (which actually appeared in Pohl's magazine under the title "Strange Playfellow," a title Asimov later changed back to "Robbie"), was certainly not the first story ever written dealing with a friendly robot. Asimov is quite candid about the fact that, in writing it, he was enormously influenced by a story by Eando Binder called "I, Robot," which had appeared in the January 1939 issue of *Amazing*.

On May 10, 1939, Asimov began to write his own sympathetic robot story and thereby initiated a series that was later to become one of the central pillars of his fiction-writing career.

"Robbie," set on Earth in 1998, tells the story of the eponymous robot employed as nursemaid to a little girl called Gloria Weston. Robbie is the most unsophisticated of Asimov's robot creations; he cannot speak and has very limited capabilities, but Asimov does manage to imbue him with a lovable character that immediately endears him to the reader.

Unfortunately, "Robbie" exposes Asimov's immaturity as a writer. He had just turned nineteen when he began the story. He had almost no experience of women and even less of family life outside his own. Compared with stories he was writing a mere two years later, "Robbie" belongs to his juvenilia. The characters are wooden and most of the time they behave in a rather extreme and overemotional fashion. Gloria Weston comes across as a horribly spoiled child and the henpecked Mr. Weston and the domineering Mrs. Weston are rather absurd stereotypes.

The plot of "Robbie" revolves around the fact that Mrs. Weston, fearing that her daughter has become overdependent on her mechanical nursemaid, sends him back to the manufacturers. Gloria is of course devastated, and the rest of the story is concerned with Mr. Weston's attempts to resolve the problem by pleasing both his pushy, slightly obnoxious daughter and very pushy, very obnoxious wife.

The ending, in which Weston manages to get Robbie back for his daughter and simultaneously escapes the wrath of his dragon wife, is rather fairy-tale and some way short of believable. The overall effect is that of a lightweight, lighthearted, gentle story that almost succeeds as a fairy tale.

Asimov submitted "Robbie" to Campbell on May 23, 1939, and it was rejected within days. The story languished in Asimov's desk drawer for almost a year until Fred Pohl, as editor of *Super Science Stories,* shocked

Asimov by inviting him out to lunch and announcing that he wanted to use the story for his magazine.

After Campbell's rejection of "Robbie" back in May 1939, Asimov had not tried to write another robot story. Instead, he had concentrated on other projects, including his first novelette, "Half-Breed"—which appeared in the December 1939 issue of *Astounding*—"Stowaway" and "Homo Sol," which showed up in what Asimov considered to be one of the very best issues of any science fiction magazine of the Golden Age, the September 1940 *Astounding*.

Asimov's robot stories did not really get under way until his second, "Reason," which began life strangely, and was once again greatly influenced by Campbell.

In both his own stories and in those written by his authors, Campbell was keen on the principle that "humans are best" and he greatly respected their aggressiveness. He would not accept a story in which an alien race ended up dominating humans or tales in which humanity was cast in a bad light or played second fiddle. However, his philosophy did not end there.

Campbell made no bones about the fact that his racial prejudice ran deeper than the pangalactic racism he expressed in his stories. He viewed American and European humans as superior to other races, strenuously argued this corner with Asimov, and even went so far as to insert paragraphs expressing these views in Asimov's (and other writers') stories. These insertions were invariably against the wishes of his writers. For all his greatness as an editor, after a couple of years knowing Campbell, Asimov began to realize that he could also be a severe pain in the neck.

Asimov found Campbell's attitudes particularly unacceptable because he had himself been at the receiving end of mildly anti-Semitic behavior. He found it extremely difficult to find any respect for humanity embroiled as it was in a bloody war stretching across a substantial part of the planet. To solve the problem and escape Campbell's unwanted influence, Asimov turned to robots.

On October 23, 1940, Asimov presented the idea to Campbell of a story based on a robot that refused to believe it was made by humans and had to be put right on the subject. As Asimov had expected, Campbell went for it and the idea was up and running.

The result was "Reason," the first of Asimov's robot stories to involve the soon-to-be-regular characters Michael Donovan and Gregory Powell. Donovan and Powell are a couple of troubleshooters hired by the global robot manufacturers U.S. Robots to sort out robot problems whenever and wherever they crop up.

"Reason" is set on Solar Station 5, where an energy converter concentrates solar energy and beams it back to Earth. During a suitability trial, a robot, QT-1 (Cutie), left in charge of a team of robots maintaining the station, decides that it was not created by what it sees as inferior humans but that the energy converter is its God.

Donovan and Powell are sent to the station to sort out the problem. During the course of the story they become quite emotional, declaring "Sizzling Saturn, we've got a lunatic robot on our hands."[1] And in exasperation at the course of events they utter such wonderful lines as ". . . but this takes the iridium asteroid!"[2]

Despite their best efforts to convince Cutie that it is sadly misguided, the robot refuses to listen. This would not be such a serious problem if it were not for the fact that during their visit to the station, a solar storm threatens to knock the energy beam out of line—with disastrous consequences for Earth. Cutie believes Earth to be an optical illusion rather than the place of its manufacture.

Eventually they realize that they do not need to convince Cutie of the fact that it is man-made in order for it to keep the beam on course; the laws of robotics ensure that, whatever it believes, Cutie must comply with its programming.

"Reason" is a clever story and a subtle attack on religious fundamentalism. At one point, when our intrepid troubleshooters draw the robot's attention to the ship's library and the documented history of humanity, Cutie declares that the books were put there by "the Master"—the energy converter.

Campbell loved the story because, as well as spinning a good yarn, Asimov had the human characters winning out in the end. It was submitted to him on November 18, 1940, and was immediately accepted.

---

[1] "Reason" by Isaac Asimov. *Astounding,* April 1941.
[2] Ibid.

Between this, Asimov's second robot story, and "Liar!," his third, a great many changes were to occur in Asimov's entire concept of the robot story.

Most readers are familiar with Asimov's robot tales because of the collection *I, Robot*, which was first published by Gnome Press in 1950. The volume contains nine stories written between 1939 and 1950. These are "Robbie," "Runaround," "Reason," "Catch That Rabbit," "Liar!," "Little Lost Robot," "Escape!," "Evidence," and "The Inevitable Conflict."

The book was typed up by Gertrude to allow Isaac time to cope with his responsibilities at college and to work on fresh projects. It originally had the working title *Mind and Iron*.

At a late stage in the editing of the manuscript, Martin Greenberg, who was publishing the collection, suggested the title *I, Robot*. Asimov liked the idea but protested that Eando Binder's story of the same name in the January 1939 issue of *Amazing* precluded its use. "Fuck Eando Binder!"[1] was Greenberg's response.

Over the years we have seen *Robots and Empire, The Robots of Dawn, The Complete Robot*, and others, but none, with the exception of *The Rest of the Robots* (a direct descendant of *I, Robot* and published by Doubleday in 1964) can match *I, Robot*.

I, Robot was produced soon after "The Inevitable Conflict" had appeared in magazine form and was merged into a series after *Pebble in the Sky* had established Asimov's reputation as an author.

For those familiar with *I, Robot* rather than the original stories published over a ten-year period, it may come as a surprise that Asimov's famous Three Laws of Robotics were not actually formalized until he began to write "Liar!"

The creation of the three laws came about, not surprisingly, through a conversation with Campbell that took place in his office on December 23, 1940.

Asimov had gone there to discuss the idea of a story plotted around a robot that had, by some accident on the production line, become endowed with the ability to read minds. Campbell liked the idea but stopped Asimov in midflow of his plot description to say, "Asimov, you do realize that any robot built would have to obey three rules. Firstly, they

---

[1] *In Memory Yet Green* by Isaac Asimov. Doubleday, New York, 1979 (p. 591).

could not harm humans, second, they have to follow orders without harming humans, and lastly, they would have to protect themselves against harm.'

These inspired words got Asimov thinking about the feasibility of "Three Laws of Robotics." They appeared in his fourth robot story, "Runaround," which he started nearly a year later, on October 4, 1941. In the story the laws are phrased as:

The Three Laws of Robotics

1. A robot may not injure a human being or, through inaction, allow a human being to come to harm.
2. A robot must obey the orders given it by human beings except where such orders would conflict with the First Law.
3. A robot must protect its own existence as long as such protection does not conflict with the First or Second Laws.[1]

At first sight the three laws look incredibly pretentious. After all, we are talking science fiction here, and by using expressions like "through inaction," they ape Newton's three laws of mechanics rather too neatly. However, Asimov was a scientist (albeit a student scientist at the time of creating the laws) and he strongly believed in the application of science to science fiction—why not then imitate established scientific laws?

In terms of fiction, the three laws became cast in stone. All science fiction writers after Asimov used the laws as a matter of course. With these three laws, Asimov liberated the entire subject of robots in fiction, making obsolete the paranoia of *Frankenstein* and the absurd hulks of the pre-Campbell era. To function properly, Asimov's robots had to be so strictly programmed that they would self-destruct before breaking the three laws: any plot that involved robots turning on their creators left the accepted limits of science fiction and became fantasy.

Asimov was flattered that he had established a set of pseudoscientific

[1] First stated in "Runaround" by Isaac Asimov. *Astounding,* March 1942.

laws. Despite the fact that in the early 1940s the science of robotics was a purely fictional thing, he somehow knew that one day they would provide the foundation for a set of real laws.

As with the creation of "Nightfall," many have said that it was Campbell and not Asimov who really created the three laws. After all, even if he did not formalize them in the way Asimov later did, it was Campbell who suggested three laws and set them out. However, as Campbell was always quick to point out, he had actually gleaned the three laws from Asimov's first two stories, "Robbie" and "Reason," and indeed there is a version of the first law in "Robbie," when Mr. Weston declares: "You *know* that it is impossible for a robot to harm a human being; that long before enough could go wrong to alter the First Law, a robot would be completely inoperable."[1]

Along with the formalizing of his laws of robotics, Asimov created a few more institutions. He was the first to use the word "robotics" and was surprised when he found that there was no such word in the dictionary (it is there now). Following the established tradition of "mechanics," "ballistics," and others, Asimov simply used "robotics" in the same fashion.

Asimov needed to build a consistent framework for his robot stories. He described their brains as being made from platinum-iridium sponge and working on the principle of positronic pathways. The positron, or positive electron, was one of several new particles postulated at the time Asimov was writing the early robot stories. He had no real idea how the robot brain would actually work, but "positronic brain" sounded good.

The collection of stories is held together by the contrivance of a journalist investigating the history of robots in the year 2057. U.S. Robots, we are told, was established in 1982, when one Lawrence Robertson set up a company called U.S. Robots and Mechanical Men, Inc.; a company that "became the strangest industrial giant in man's history."[2]

Most importantly, by the time Asimov had completed his third robot story, "Liar!," he had introduced the three central characters who later appeared in the majority of his robot short stories. Alongside the

---

[1] "Robbie" by Isaac Asimov. First appeared as "Strange Playfellow" in *Super Science Stories,* September 1940.
[2] Introduction to *I, Robot* by Isaac Asimov. First published by Gnome Press, 1950.

troubleshooting robot engineers Donovan and Powell, who appear in "Reason," came robopsychologist Susan Calvin.

In the introduction to "Satisfaction Guaranteed," Asimov claimed that as time went on he fell in love with his creation, robopsychologist extraordinaire Susan Calvin. He described her as "a forbidding creature to be sure—much more like the popular conception of a robot than were any of my positronic creations—but I loved her anyway."[1]

Susan Calvin was based on a woman with whom Asimov did, at the time, have close academic contact—his graduate adviser at Columbia, Professor Mary Caldwell. Professor Caldwell's character was nothing like Susan Calvin but she was definitely on Asimov's mind when he was writing "Liar!" and in the first draft of the story he actually called his character Susan Caldwell.

A few days before the story was due to go to press, Asimov got cold feet over the idea of using the name of one of his professors. He went to Campbell's office to ask him if he could change it. Campbell was off sick. Becoming more certain that he must change the name, he asked Campbell's secretary, Katherine Tarrant, if this could be done.

"I suppose you want me to go through the entire manuscript changing the name, do you?" she declared with a smile. To Asimov's polite "please," she said, "Well, what do I change it to?"

Trying to think of a name that would require as little alteration as possible he came up with "Calvin," and this it remained.

In his entire body of work, Susan Calvin is Asimov's strongest female creation. She is intelligent, resourceful, high-powered, and often outwits the male characters with whom she interacts. She is also, to all outward appearances, cold, entirely asexual, and androgenous—in fact, a clichéd dried-up prune of a woman, which perhaps again demonstrates Asimov's naivete about women at that time. Nonetheless, in her first appearance at least, Calvin does have depth and is strangely charming.

"Liar!," which is considered by some critics to be Asimov's best robot story, is unusual for him in that plot plays second fiddle to the human problems of the characters involved. It is really a story about human

[1] Introduction to "Satisfaction Guaranteed" by Isaac Asimov. From *The Rest of the Robots,* first published by Doubleday, New York, 1964.

emotions—vanity, in particular. It makes a refreshing change from many of Asimov's robot stories, which end up as little more than clever and highly entertaining intellectual exercises, often based on solving a technical conundrum.

"Liar!" revolves around a robot called Herbie, which, through a fault during manufacture, can read minds. This talent obviously conflicts with the three laws because Herbie must tell his masters what they want to hear. During an investigation into the fault, the research team works itself up into a froth of misunderstanding, all caused by Herbie's innocent interference triggering their own weaknesses. Susan Calvin's particular weakness is her secret interest in a male member of the team, Milton Ashe, who, Herbie convinces her, is equally interested in her.

Asimov uses the clever device of writing seven separate scenes involving only five central characters. Each scene gives the reader an omniscient insight into the action, and Asimov moves us in and out of these scenes with great skill. We really feel for Calvin as, against her better judgment, she is taken in by Herbie's suggestions, starts to pay unaccustomed attention to her appearance, and even begins to subtly flirt with Ashe.

When Calvin finally realizes that the robot has been lying all along, her feelings boil over and she directs a lifetime of frustration and inhibition toward destroying poor Herbie. This she does by making him blow a fuse over a paradox in the First Law.

Calvin's destruction of Herbie is powerfully written and very disquieting, especially for those who perceive Asimov's robots as mechanical men rather than machines. Calvin does not simply "kill" Herbie, she drives him "insane."

Although in this first appearance Asimov gives us Calvin's most brutal side, the reader can still admire her strength. Within the same story, Asimov makes her alternately vulnerable and savage; but in the end she does what she has to do, and in her very viciousness we gain an insight into her emotional makeup, her self-image and sexual frustration. In no other robot story does Calvin display such a range of human emotion, and she is often portrayed as pure intellect, sometimes disparagingly described by other characters as being a robot herself.

Asimov made Susan Calvin the most important human character in many of his robot stories, and by constructing the book around her long career, it is Susan Calvin's presence that holds *I, Robot* together.

After his initial success with his stories of the forties and early fifties, Asimov went on to write four full-length robot novels—*The Caves of Steel* (1954), *The Naked Sun* (1957), *The Robots of Dawn* (1983), and *Robots and Empire* (1985)—all of which featured a human character, the plain-clothes policeman Elijah Baley, and the robot R. Daneel Olivaw. All four books received great commercial success and critical acclaim, with one reviewer describing *The Naked Sun* as "Asimov's finest novel."

The characterizations of Baley and the robot are strong, and they work well together. Here Asimov produced a paradigm for human "buddy stories" of the *Starsky and Hutch* variety. As well as this, the settings are well drawn. In *The Caves of Steel*, Earthmen live in vast covered cities hundreds of miles across, each one home to hundreds of millions of inhabitants. Earth is ostracized by the rest of the inhabited worlds because the Spacers, the descendants of human colonists who long ago cut ties with the home planet, see Earth people as unclean and inferior.

In *The Naked Sun*, Baley is whisked off to one of the Spacers' planets, Solaria, inhabited by a tiny populace of introverted, isolated Spacers: a world diametrically opposed to Baley's home world, Earth.

In three of the four novels, Baley is called upon to solve a crime—which, with the help of R. Daneel, he succeeds in doing. There is a neat interplay between Baley and Daneel because Earthmen have been brought up to fear and despise robots. In true Hollywood fashion, Baley learns to overcome his distaste and the two become friends.

Yet, notwithstanding the fact that Asimov viewed *The Caves of Steel* as the first perfect fusion of the detective novel and science fiction, some critics remain skeptical of all four of his robot novels.

The "big idea" in Asimov's first three robot/mystery novels is the combination of detective novel and robot story. They fail, it is argued, because, as much as Asimov tries to surprise us, the plots are quite transparent, the characters other than the two stars are weak, and the books lack the pace needed for a truly gripping crime story.

There may be some truth in these suggestions. In the first two robot novels at least, the secondary characters—Commissioner Enderby, the Spacer, Dr. Fastolfe, Gladia, Klorissa, and others—are all sketchy, and the whodunit aspect is perhaps not in the same league as an Agatha Christie mystery. But then, Asimov is blending genres, and for the majority of readers he succeeded in this.

For Asimov, his return to writing robot novels in the eighties served a particular purpose beyond a desire to resurrect some of his favorite characters from where he had left them in the fifties. But I will return to this subject in a later chapter.

Of all the robot stories Asimov wrote during his career, his favorite, and indeed his favorite story of any genre he delved into, was "The Last Question."

This story was written by invitation—from Bob Lownes, the editor of *Science Fiction Quarterly*, in June 1956. It was actually the second story involving a computer called Multivac. (The first, called "Franchise," was written four years earlier, during the 1952 election.)

Asimov wrote "The Last Question" in two sittings without a sentence hesitation. On the first of June he received the letter from Lownes requesting the story, sent the manuscript off on the fourth, and received payment on the eleventh.

Asimov viewed "The Last Question" as "the science fiction story to end all science fiction stories."[1] In *Opus 100*, Asimov's hundredth book, he recounts how "The Last Question" became the story for which he received the greatest quantity of mail. Many readers of "The Last Question" could not remember the title or even if it was an Asimov story at all, but they could remember the tale itself. Asimov believed the reason for this lay in the fear conjured by the story. He supposed that the story left readers with an uncomfortable feeling, a kind of existential terror, which held it in their memories despite their best efforts at eradicating the facts behind it.

"The Last Question" even became the subject of a sermon at the Unitarian church at Bedford, Massachusetts, soon after the first appearance of the story in *Science Fiction Quarterly*. Asimov somehow discovered that

---

[1] *In Joy Still Felt* by Isaac Asimov. Doubleday, New York, 1980 (p. 59).

one of his stories was to be included in a sermon, and decided to attend. He sat quietly and unobtrusively in the back row, listening attentively. He never related what he thought of the sermon.

An entrepreneurial science fiction fan also adapted "The Last Question" for a planetarium spectacular that involved a word-for-word narration of the story, accompanied by a light and slide show. Asimov saw the first performance in Rochester on April 16, 1972. He was stunned by it, and only then realized the full power of the story and the unintentionally clever technique (in the written version) of making each of the six sections of the story shorter and more melodramatic than the last. This creates an almost palpable sense of unease and angst, strikingly unusual for Asimov.

This story fits neatly into the "heavy science" side of Asimov's work. If we imagine for a moment Asimov's fictional work stretching from, at one end of the spectrum, the more human-based, emotional story, epitomized by "Liar!" or "The Mule" of *The Foundation Trilogy*, and at the other, the purely scientific, analytical story, then "The Last Question" resides at this extreme end of the scale.

In 4,700 words, Asimov manages to span ten trillion years of human life. He does this by describing six scenes taken from human history in which the same question is asked of the greatest computer of the age. The question is: "How can entropy be reversed?"

Different generations of Multivac become increasingly sophisticated as the story progresses. Beginning with the first computer, built to establish stellar energy for the Earth in 2061, it evolves through a Planetary Multivac to a Galactic AC, and eventually culminates in the giddy heights of the Cosmic AC.

The final question arises as humanity fears extinction. In the opening scene, two engineers ask the question of the gigantic first Multivac, which has switched the planet onto solar energy. Ostensibly they do this in order to solve an argument about how long the human race might exist, but they are terrified when they realize that even the Multivac cannot give them an answer.

This same naive, fearful question is then asked time and again through eons of human evolution. Humankind becomes hyper-space-traveling sophisticates, galactic colonizers, and eventually pure energy, and as the suns die, they finally merge with the Cosmic AC, but still the question is the same: "Can entropy be reversed?" The answer always comes back unaltered: "There is insufficient data for a meaningful answer."

It is not until the last drop of energy has dissipated and the Cosmic AC has fallen into a timeless period of contemplation that it eventually finds the answer. The Cosmic AC has, of course, become God, and the answer to the final question is: "Let there be light . . . And there was light."

"The Last Question" is science fiction exposition at the very limit of the genre. It can barely be thought of as fiction in the conventional sense, but, as Asimov made very clear, he wanted to take the robot or the computer to its ultimate extreme and felt he could not do this in a formal setting. Ideas of this type can, he believed, be best expressed in the form of fiction because the narrative captivates the reader and makes the point of the story wholly more palatable.

Which leads us to the question: What, if anything, is Asimov's message in his fiction? Does he consciously or subconsciously attempt to communicate his philosophies in his writing, and if so, what are they?

Are robots a metaphor for racial minorities, and is Asimov either consciously or subconsciously expressing his abhorrence of racism when he has humans turning against robots, as he does in so many of his stories?

Asimov deliberately used allegory only rarely in his science fiction. The best example is his failed attempt to lampoon McCarthyism in "The Martian Way." In his own writings about his work he makes no reference to approaching his robot stories with allegory in mind. The closest Asimov came to modeling his robot culture on ethnic minorities was creating them in order to circumvent John Campbell's homocentricity.

The question of Asimov's subconscious modeling of robots along ethnic lines is, of course, open to question. Asimov was certainly a liberal thinker and strongly democratic. He hated racism and had experienced it peripherally. There is no question that Asimov's heroes are always democratic and righteous. He always imbues his good guys with a powerful sense of justice. Because of this, it has been suggested that his robots were subconsciously modeled on suppressed (or repressed) humanity.

What is irrefutable is that Asimov viewed his robot stories as his greatest literary achievement. He has said himself that, although his

Foundation books were slightly more rewarding financially, he personally always preferred his robot stories.

The theme of Asimov's robots has been taken up by others. There are several collections of science fiction novels now available that have been written by other authors but based on Asimov's creation. A recently produced CD ROM called *The Ultimate Robot* chronicles everything you ever wanted to know about robots, fictional and factual.

With the exception of the later robot stories discussed in this chapter, Asimov's early literary efforts were the work of a naive young man. Yet, in places, they show remarkable maturity and self-possession. In the years spanning those early efforts and his acceptance as a globally important writer, Asimov's life changed beyond recognition, and this naturally manifested itself in his fiction, the evolution of which is best exemplified by his greatest work, *The Foundation Trilogy*. But before we take a look at this masterpiece, we must consider the personal changes in Asimov's life and how they played a role in developing his skills as a writer.

5

MARRIAGE AND WAR

n February 1942, soon after meeting Gertrude, and with the ink still wet on his master's degree certificate, Asimov began a Ph.D. at Columbia under the supervision of Professor Charles Dawson.

They immediately hit it off; Asimov straightaway appreciated Dawson's acute intellect. Asimov was assigned a room, which he shared with another research student, and began work. However, the course at Columbia was not to last long.

In March Asimov met the famous science fiction writer Robert Heinlein, who was visiting John Campbell at his home in New Jersey, and Campbell decided that it was high time the two writers should meet.

Asimov almost never made it to Campbell's house because for him, even at the age of twenty-two, a trip to New Jersey from New York was a major undertaking and he nearly lost his way several times. After arriving late and making his introductions, Asimov was offered an alcoholic drink. He unwisely accepted it, and after a second, rapidly became drunk. In spite of all this, by the end of the evening Heinlein had offered Asimov a job as chemist at the Philadelphia Navy Yard, where he worked.

For some time Asimov could not decide what to do. The job would provide him with his first salary, initially set at 2,600 dollars a year; but by this stage in his academic career he had found a degree of independence and enjoyed working with Dawson. Nonetheless, the offer of a real salary was hard to resist, especially as he also liked Heinlein's company.

Eventually, after discussing the situation with his parents, Gertrude, and Dawson, he came to the conclusion that, should he pass the interview for the post, he would accept it and return to his Ph.D. after the war. Meanwhile, wedding plans were progressing fast and the date had been set for July.

Asimov visited Philadelphia twice before he was offered the job. Then, after taking up the post, he had to live there on his own during the week and travel back to New York at weekends to visit Gertrude and his family.

Asimov never got on well with Gertrude's mother, whom he found to be a domineering dragon of a woman. According to Asimov, she never appreciated her son-in-law's talents and always considered him to be unworthy of her daughter. For his part, Asimov developed a loathing for Mary Blugerman and lost all control of his sharp tongue when she was around.

Gertrude's mother had a morbid fascination with cancer and was forever talking about it. Asimov relentlessly teased her about this, claiming that she was jealous of anyone she knew who had contracted the disease. On the other hand, Gertrude's father, Henry, was a quiet, passive man, beloved by everyone in the family. He was totally dominated by his wife, and kept himself very much to himself. Asimov liked him but never got to know him very well.

He later declared many times that he believed his mother-in-law's hold over Gertrude played a major role in the destruction of their marriage, that Gertrude was too submissive toward her mother and always put her wishes before his.

Despite the animosity between Asimov and Mrs. Blugerman, on July 26, Isaac and Gertrude were married in a simple service at the Blugermans' home in Brooklyn. It was an intimate affair; the guest list included both sets of parents as well as Gertrude's brother, John, and Asimov's siblings, Marcia and Stanley.

Neither family was religiously inclined, and the rabbi who conducted the service was found in the Yellow Pages. The rabbi insisted that an independent witness be present before the service could begin. Gertrude's father was therefore obliged to drag in the first person he could find to act as a witness. Things became almost farcical when the rabbi then declared that the witness was unsuitably dressed and had to wear a hat. Mr. Blugerman scrambled around in his closet, found a hat to lend to the stranger, and the service finally got under way.

Afterward the families traveled to Coney Island for a celebratory dinner at the Half Moon Hotel. The newlyweds departed early to spend their wedding night at the Dixie Hotel, a downmarket hotel in midtown Manhattan, and the guests were left to enjoy what apparently turned into a drunken and hilarious evening.

As the couple drove away from the reception, Mrs. Blugerman yelled out, "Gertrude, if you're unhappy, just remember, you come straight back to me."

Asimov freely admitted that their wedding night was something of a disaster. Both of them were virgins when they married and neither of them had the first idea what to expect. They had both led very sheltered lives and had had absolutely no sex education or any form of parental guidance on the subject. Among Asimov's friends and colleagues it was well known that Gertrude was never very interested in sex. One of his favorite jokes was: Question: What is Jewish foreplay? Answer: An hour and a half of begging.[1] Asimov claimed this joke always reminded him of Gertrude.

At the time of their marriage, their unsuccessful sexual relationship did not seem to bother Asimov too much. He was absolutely besotted with Gertrude and found her incredibly beautiful. In the early days he felt humbled by his wife's good looks, especially as he knew that she had not married him for his appearance. Later, their almost nonexistent sex life led to discontentment, marital problems, and eventually divorce.

The couple spent their honeymoon in the Catskills, at Allaben Acres, a rather cheap holiday resort frequented by working-class New Yorkers. It seems that neither Gertrude nor Asimov thought much of the place, but like any newly wedded couple, the surroundings were less important to them than the fact that they were in each other's company.

The honeymoon lasted a week, and by August 2 they were back in New York. It was decided that Gertrude would join Isaac in Philadelphia, and they straightaway began to search for their first apartment.

The job at the Navy Yard represented a totally different environment from any Asimov had previously experienced. He was part of a team of chemists working on war materials such as explosives, materials used in

---

[1] *Asmov Laughs Again* by Isaac Asimov. HarperCollins, New York, 1992.

camouflage paints, foodstuffs, and field drugs. Each chemist had his own project, so Asimov did not have to work in a team, which pleased him, but he did have to share the lab with a small group.

Asimov had a plethora of stories about the Navy Yard and created the distinct impression that it was not really such a bad time in his life. The Yard, situated in the marshlands near Philadelphia, was an ugly place, and the weather was often atrocious. But Asimov enjoyed Heinlein's company, and although the two men did not work together, they often met up for lunch and sometimes socialized in the evenings.

Asimov's particular gripe with the Yard was the cafeteria food. In his opinion, the meals served there were so bad that he considered it his duty to stir up some support and make an official complaint about it to his superiors. Heinlein, who had particular responsibility for the cafeteria and was also several ranks senior, became quite offended by Asimov's complaints and in response instigated a new rule that anyone complaining about the food had to pay a fine according to the degree of insult. As a consequence, after losing several dollars, Asimov decided that he would bring sandwiches to work rather than run the risk of losing more money. The whole affair was lighthearted and a source of great amusement for the two men when they met up at science fiction conventions many years later.

From their shared experiences in the Navy Yard and their common foundation as science fiction writers, both coming from the John Campbell and *Astounding* stable, Asimov and Heinlein became close friends, a relationship that proved to be lifelong. It is gratifying to know that despite a healthy degree of rivalry, the three greatest science fiction writers of the era, Asimov, Heinlein, and Arthur C. Clarke, were all good friends.

Asimov did not meet Clarke until after the war. Clarke was working on the development of radar in Britain during the time Asimov was at the Navy Yard, and it was not until the early 1950s, through highly acclaimed books like *Childhood's End*, that Clarke joined the top rank of science fiction writers. By the 1960s Asimov and Clarke had become both friends and rivals, and in 1972 they drew up the Clarke–Asimov treaty, which stated that Clarke was the best science fiction writer in the world and Asimov was the best science writer in the world. Their egos knew no bounds.

Whenever Clarke was visiting America, such as the period during 1969 when he worked for CBS covering the Apollo moon landings, he would often call up Asimov, and they would go out to dinner or meet up at parties. When in later years Clarke was inundated with mail from cranks suggesting crazy scientific schemes, he would often reply to them with the comment: "This may be of interest to Dr. Asimov, whose address is . . ."

Asimov's favorite story from the days at the Navy Yard involved a rather pretentious secretary who worked in the complex. One day she arrived at work wearing a very showy bracelet that her boyfriend had given her the previous evening. It was gold with large jewels encrusted around the entire circumference. The only problem with it, she complained, was that it had become a little dirty during the morning. Overhearing her, Asimov suggested that there were chemicals in the lab that could clean up the bracelet for her. The secretary suddenly brightened up and offered Asimov the bracelet.

"No, no," he said quickly. "I don't have time. One of the technicians will clean it for you."

The secretary followed Asimov into the lab and he called over a female technician, who gasped and cooed over the beautiful object the secretary held out to her and immediately set about cleaning the bracelet with the mildest agent available, a dilute solution of alcohol.

Moments later the technician, ashen-faced, approached Asimov.

"Something terrible has happened," she stammered. And with shaking hands, she held out the wreck of a bracelet, now steel-colored, with half the jewels out of their settings and lying at the bottom of the beaker.

Asimov just laughed and said. "I shouldn't worry about it if I were you. But I wouldn't like to be in her boyfriend's shoes this evening."

Asimov's acid tongue was not tamed by age. Instead of targeting teachers and lecturers, he was lightning-quick in putting down anyone who tried to verbally outsmart him.

Another secretary, who happened to be rather hirsute, got on the wrong side of Asimov's insensitivity. Asimov had decided to try to grow another mustache. A couple of days into its development he turned up at the lab in the morning and the secretary said to him: "Isaac! You're not trying to grow a moustache, are you?" To which Asimov snapped back: "And why not? You've managed it."[1] The poor girl burst into tears and would not speak to him for over a week.

On another occasion, a very slim girl risked comment on Asimov's potbelly, a recent development enhanced by the comfort of living with Gertrude and an aversion to physical exercise.

Asimov was filling a beaker with a corrosive chemical and as a precaution he was wearing a rubber apron, which accentuated the curve of his stomach. Picking up a length of glass tubing, the girl said: "I've a good mind to puncture your stomach and let out the air so that you look more like a man." To which Asimov instantly snapped back: "And, if you do, I suggest you use some of it to pump up your chest so that you look more like a woman."[2]

This time Asimov almost received an injury for his rudeness. The offended woman picked up a chair and went for him. Dropping what he was doing, he made a dash for the door and only returned when he was convinced that her temper had cooled.

During the first years of the war, the Asimovs enjoyed a rather cozy home life. In the early days they were happy in each other's company and shared a number of interests, tastes, and aspirations. Gertrude was a good cook and a dedicated wife. Yet, from what Asimov himself has said and written about his personal life, it is clear that, of the two of them, Gertrude was the more mature. Asimov seems to have created a mother figure out of his wife, and increasingly he relied on her for material comfort and emotional support, which at times appeared almost childlike. He could hardly bear to be away from her, and went through emotionally fraught periods whenever Gertrude had to go away for a few days.

Shortly after they were married, Gertrude discovered that despite having an American husband she still had only temporary-resident status in America. She had to return to Canada for a couple of weeks to acquire relevant documentation and then reenter the States in order to gain permanent-resident status. Fearing that his wife would be refused reentry into America, Asimov was filled with anxiety the whole time she was

---

[1] *In Memory Yet Green* by Isaac Asimov, Doubleday, New York, 1979 (p. 386).
[2] Ibid. (p. 374).

away. He could not concentrate at work and spent his evenings moping around the apartment, counting the days until Gertrude's return.

Asimov had a great and lasting affection for the early days of his marriage to Gertrude and in particular the weekends they shared during his spell at the Philadelphia Navy Yard.

Living in what was only their second home as a couple, a place called Wingate Hall, they would make a special event of Saturday evenings. After dinner, Asimov went to the local store to buy the early editions of the Sunday papers, and the two of them would curl up to read. They would turn to the comics first and then to the news of the day, dominated by war news. Asimov particularly enjoyed this routine in the depths of winter, when he would trek through the snow and be welcomed home by the warmth of the apartment, a cup of hot cocoa, and a Cole Porter song on the radio.

The two of them would sometimes spend weekends in New York, taking the train straight after work. On the Sunday they would occasionally go for walks along the entire length of the boardwalk on Coney Island. Sometimes they would be joined by Gertrude's brother John, who was about to be inducted into the army, and they would talk about their respective plans for the future, relaxing in the warm glow of a New York summer evening.

By the spring of 1944 the war in Europe was clearly going the Allies' way, but the draft was still a threat to those, like Asimov, who had no desire to volunteer. There were soldiers who had been in active service for over eighteen months. They needed relieving, and so a second wave of young men was necessary.

At the start of the war, Asimov had been given a 2B draft rating, which meant he was safe from the call-up. The B referred to his health; he had not been given an A because of his shortsightedness. The 2 signified that he was not on the priority list because of his war work at the Navy Yard. Despite this, Asimov spent most of 1944 and 1945 in a state of anxiety about the draft. As a result, his creativity seemed to freeze up for long periods, and for much of the time he could not bring himself to write at all.

In spite of these attacks of panic and writer's block, he did manage to write what many consider to be one of his strongest stories, what later became the cornerstone of *The Foundation Trilogy*—"The Mule."

When he could work, the old magic was still there, and what he produced was charged with themes that occupied his mind at the time. "The Mule" is full of military imagery, as well as the inclusion of that rare thing in Asimov's literature—a young married couple as two of the lead characters.

During that nerve-racking period, Asimov also had to undergo a series of medicals and appear before a number of boards to determine his suitability for the army. A 1A meant call-up at any time, a classification he dreaded receiving.

He tried everything to avoid it. At an eye test, part of the army medical, the doctor asked Asimov to read the letters on the chart at the end of a room, to which Asimov, in true Groucho Marx fashion, replied: "What chart?"

Although by no means a pacifist, Asimov found the concept of military action rather backward, perceiving it to be the least effective way of settling a dispute. Throughout his fiction we encounter heroes who use violence only as a last resort, and he often wrote in support of passive resistance. Having said that, it was evident to him that the moral issues involved in the Second World War were clearly defined, and he had no doubts about the need to stop Germany. Also, he was no coward. He never actively sought out violence but could be very strong-minded when he felt that he had been treated unjustly. In later years he often displayed righteous indignation when faced with unreasonable behavior. He usually invoked the law to right a wrong, but on one occasion he had to be physically restrained from hitting an arrogant and unrepentant driver who had rammed into his car and endangered his children's lives. Asimov believed in his own edict: "Violence is the last refuge of the incompetent," but, like any man, he could prove himself incompetent, given a suitable cause.

What really disturbed Asimov about the draft was the prospect of having to leave his wife and his family in New York for an unspecified time and being sent to some far-flung part of the globe. In his naivete he was worried about what would happen to Gertrude and did not realize that his wife would be given government support in his absence. Most of all, he hated the thought of being alone.

For eighteen months, from the middle of 1944 to November 1945,

Asimov was engaged in a battle to escape the draft. The age limit was twenty-six, so he had to hang on until January 2, 1946, to be clear.

The war in Europe ended in May 1945, and after the atomic bombing of Japan in August 1945 the fighting stopped in the Far East. Consequently, work at the Navy Yard wound down. Along with a group of other scientists and technicians, Asimov was kept on, but the position had become less formal, allowing him to make frequent trips to New York and occasionally take time off. Using this, Asimov managed to gain time with the Draft Board by insisting that he have his medicals in Philadelphia if he was based in New York and in New York if he was based in Philadelphia. It almost worked.

Asimov very nearly escaped the draft. With little more than two months to go until he was over the age limit, while in New York with Gertrude, he received the dreaded 1A classification and his call-up date of October 26. Even then he managed to extend his freedom until November 1 by pleading that he needed more time to arrange his personal affairs. But he could do no more. His immediate future was sealed and he was enlisted into the army.

Asimov hated every moment in the army and spent his entire time contriving ways of getting back to civilian life and longing for his return to Gertrude. He also missed working in an academic environment with others of like mind. Although the Navy Yard was a military institution, he was working in a laboratory and enjoyed the company of his colleagues. For Asimov, the army proved to be a totally alien environment.

It began in Philadelphia with an induction procedure and yet another physical, and the same evening he was put on a train bound for Ford Meade, an army base near Baltimore, Maryland.

Asimov was chronically lonely, and reading his own account of this morose period of his life one is filled with a mixture of pity and impatience at his immature attitude. He simply would not accept the situation in which he found himself and appears from the outset to have decided he would make the worst of a bad deal. He made very few friends in the army, at least until toward the end of his time, and seems to have gained nothing from the experience. It is clear that his attitude from the moment he received his call-up papers was: "Well if they're forcing me into this against my will, I'm damn well not going to join in any more than I absolutely have to."

On his very first morning at Fort Meade, Asimov managed to get himself on report by being flippant to a corporal. He quickly learned to curb his tongue, realizing that he could not get away with his typical wisecracks in the way he had at school and college.

His first night at Fort Meade was one of the lowest points of his life. So homesick he was actually nauseous, he felt as though he was a million miles from home and that he would never see Gertrude or his family again. His only consolation was that there was now no actual war to fight.

Realizing that first evening that it was a Friday, he decided to visit the camp chapel and joined in a Sabbath service. He had never had any religious inclinations; he had always been a complete rationalist and was fully aware that at the point of greatest vulnerability religion can indoctrinate the most effectively. Mostly he sang, and sang and sang. So loudly did he belt out the hymns that the rabbi walked over and asked if he would like to lead the singing. Petrified at the prospect, he continued to sing from then on in a muted whisper.

A few days after arriving at Fort Meade, the recruits had to undergo a series of psychiatric tests. One of these was an army intelligence test, called the AGCT. Asimov stunned everyone in the barracks by getting the highest score ever recorded by the psychiatrists assigned to the Fort— a rating of 160.

The average AGCT score was a little over 100, and Asimov's 160 immediately branded him as "a genius" to his companions and the authorities. He only learned several months later that his exceptionally high AGCT score had persuaded his superiors that he would be a total waste of time in the army and should be practically ignored by them. He might perform brilliantly in written tests, they had agreed, but he could not tell his left foot from his right.

When Asimov heard about this years later, he was furious, not because he disagreed with his superiors' opinion of him, but because if he had known what they thought of him he could have relaxed a little during his basic training.

After Fort Meade, Asimov and a few other recruits were sent to Camp Lee, in Virginia, about three hundred miles south of New York. This was to be his home for the next four months while undergoing basic training. It was here that he had to face up to a succession of new and, to him, very unpleasant experiences. For the first time in his life he had to shower with other men. Asimov was not at all confident about his own physique and disliked the male body. Friends claim that in later years when Asimov became involved with a succession of women, he was very body-conscious. One intimate revealed that Asimov would never fully undress in the woman's company because he knew he was physically ugly and felt very uncomfortable, especially if the woman was much younger and attractive.

Because of his acute dislike of his own and other men's bodies, Asimov found the daily routine of communal ablutions extremely difficult and never grew accustomed to it. Even more than showering in public, he hated facing the humiliation of defecating in the company of others. He developed the habit of making himself wake up at 3:00 A.M. in order to visit the latrines, but somehow there would always be someone else there, even at that time of the morning.

He hated training almost as much as being so far from home and his loved ones. Asimov always had an aversion to physical exercise. Although, being away from Gertrude's cooking, he was gradually losing weight, he was still out of condition and carrying at least twenty-five pounds of excess fat. He found basic training both physically and psychologically exhausting. As with most aspects of army life, he set his face against it.

Asimov found that in spite of the training and tests, drills and parades, he had plenty of time on his hands. Even then, it took him a while to realize that the camp had a reasonably well-stocked library.

He wrote to Heinlein, a friend from the Navy Yard called Leonard Meisel, John Campbell, Sprague de Camp, to his parents and, each and every day, to Gertrude, who had moved back to her parents' home in New York.

Gertrude wrote to her husband only occasionally. Asimov claims that she was extremely busy working for her father's new company—The Henry Paper Box Company, which Henry Blugerman had established toward the end of the war. The company was going through a series of crises. Mr. Blugerman had fallen ill, John Blugerman was in the army, and the staff were causing further problems by making unreasonable wage claims. Most of the responsibility for keeping what had been from the outset a rather precarious business fell on Gertrude's shoulders. However, from Asimov's own account of the situation, it is clear that Gertrude was not missing her husband in the way he pined for her. Once again she was showing a far cooler, more mature attitude to their relationship and predicament. To be fair to her, she was working all hours to keep her father's company alive. Yet it is apparent that during her early life with Asimov, Gertrude exhibited a more stoic, realistic approach to life. She accepted the situation and tried to make the best of it.

After several weeks at Camp Lee, early in December 1945 Asimov was entitled to his first weekend leave, and naturally he visited New York. He hitched rides to Washington and then caught the train to New York.

The journey took him most of the day and he did not arrive in the city until after midnight. Gertrude had taken time off from Henry's and the couple stayed in a New York hotel for the night. On the Sunday, Asimov had to set off early on the return journey in order to make it back to camp before evening.

Soon after his return to Camp Lee, Asimov stumbled on something in the library that was to change the course of his time in the army. He came across an order that stated that chemists engaged in research were allowed to be released from service. During the following few months he tried everything to make the authorities realize that he was indeed a chemist engaged in research and to try to persuade them that he should be allowed to return to Columbia.

Asimov's efforts at securing an honorable discharge constantly fell on deaf ears. It was generally perceived by his superiors that he was a shirker, someone who could not face up to his responsibilities. To them it was inconceivable and an active insult that this cocky little man with the ridiculously high IQ should not appreciate his time in the great U.S. Army.

The months passed, and during his spare time Asimov began to read his way through the camp library. In spite of the opinions of his superiors, he was oddly confident that his requests would eventually have the desired effect. Because of this, his attitude changed and he now decided to make the most of his time. He quickly discovered that he could use the library typewriter, and his ability to type at the rate of ninety words per minute made him very useful to the camp office. He was soon seconded as the camp typist, which enabled him to gain release from many of the duties he found most objectionable. It also gave him the opportunity to begin writing fiction again.

Buoyed up by the belief that he would soon be home, he found inspiration and wrote the robot story "Evidence," which later appeared in *I, Robot*.

It was during the early spring of 1946, five months after being drafted, that Asimov came close to being unfaithful to Gertrude for the first time. He met a girl at an army dance and took her home. However, when it came to it, he made his excuses and returned to barracks. He was lucky. He realized later that the first morning train back to camp would have made him hours late for roll call and he would have been declared AWOL.

Soon after this incident, Asimov's hopes for an early return to civilian life were dramatically destroyed when he was given a new posting. At first he had no idea where he was going. His imagination ran riot; it could be anywhere—Europe? The Far East? Then the destination was announced. It could hardly have been worse—he was going to Hawaii.

They left on March 3 and arrived on the West Coast, at Camp Stoneman, California, on March 6. The company then boarded the *President Hayes* and set sail for Hawaii on March 9, 1946. It was the first time that Asimov had left the mainland of the United States, and apart from the journey to America at the age of three, it was his first time on board ship.

The first posting was on the island of Oahu, and it proved to be the least painful period in Asimov's army career. The soldiers had little to do there except wonder why they had been sent to Hawaii. Asimov found the inhabitants delightful and the scenery breathtaking. He took tours around the island and did his best to enjoy himself. His greatest regret was that he could not be there with Gertrude on vacation rather than at the insistence of the U.S. Army.

Asimov soon discovered why they were in the region. Because of his scientific training he was a "specialist." He and a small group of other scientists were to be sent to Bikini Atoll to take part in a joint forces project called Operation Crossroads. The object of the project was to explode an atomic bomb and study its effects. It was the first atomic test to be conducted after the bombings of Hiroshima and Nagasaki.

On May 13, he received a letter from Gertrude that informed him that her monthly army payment of fifty dollars had not arrived as expected. When she had inquired about it in New York, she had been told that her husband was to be discharged.

Asimov immediately investigated the matter. After repeating the story to one officer after another, he finally reached the commanding officer of the project. Asimov showed him the letter from Gertrude and explained the situation. Unaware of Asimov's desperate campaign to get out of the army, the officer asked if it was true that he had applied for a discharge. Asimov said yes. The officer thought for a moment, looking the soldier up and down. "Operation Crossroads is too important to allow this," he sighed. "We can't involve anyone who could be called back home at any moment." He picked up a release order from one side of his desk and immediately began to fill in the details.

After all his efforts, his discharge had come about as a result of a bureaucratic mix-up in Washington that had precipitated the cutting off of Gertrude's payment. Asimov could hardly believe his luck. Only days before the ship was due to leave for Bikini Atoll, he received a full, unconditional discharge from the army. Before his colleagues had arrived at the test site, he was on a plane heading in the opposite direction, back to California.

This was the only time Asimov flew in a plane and then only because he had been given a direct order to do so by an officer. By June 5, he had arrived back in New York. His sojourn in the army had lasted seven months, and it was, as he recorded in his diary, 101 days, or 2,418 hours, since he had last seen Gertrude. Meeting her off the train in New York, he believed, was the happiest moment of his life up to that point.

Asimov was free to return to his research position at Columbia and arrived back there in the autumn of 1946. But before he could settle back into his studies, he and Gertrude had to spend the summer hunting for a suitable home in the New York area. At the time Asimov felt particularly concerned about money. He had saved a little from writing and had a grant, but he still felt insecure. He had been awarded funding from the army to help reestablish himself in education, but the amount depended on his length of stay in the army. As he had been a soldier for only a little over half a year, this did not amount to much.

Throughout his life Asimov always did worry too much about money. Even after earning millions of dollars from his writing and living in great comfort, his anxieties about money diminished only slightly.

Asimov's concern stemmed from the austerity of his childhood and his family's concern for the value of things. He had arrived in America a penniless immigrant. The deeply ingrained fear of being forced to return to such humble roots never left him—a fear common to many successful people who come from the poorest backgrounds.

He always resented spending a penny over what he thought to be a justifiable price and only rarely let himself or Gertrude throw caution to the wind and indulge in a little luxury to make life easier. In these, his younger, poorer years, he was only vaguely interested in material luxuries.

During the first six months after his discharge from the army, he and Gertrude moved from one apartment to another. By the time he returned to research at Columbia in late September 1946, they were living on Dean Street in Brooklyn. It was a tiny place, little more than one and a half rooms, and commanded a rent of seventy dollars per month, a sum Asimov believed extortionate.

Back at college, Asimov initially found work difficult. The subject had moved on during his years away from research and he had to read a number of modern books and the latest papers in order to catch up. He enjoyed the challenge and soon found his feet. His gift for rapid learning had not left him.

Once again under the supervision of Professor Dawson, Asimov slipped easily into the comfortable and creative relationship they had enjoyed before the war.

The Asimov who returned to Columbia was a very different person from the rather shy and solitary figure who had first attended lectures there eleven years before. Gone was the awkward and uninspiring clumsy teenager, part wise guy and part introvert. The Asimov who walked through the gates in September 1946 and quickly reestablished himself was a married twenty-six-year-old Ph.D. student who had worked in another city, been in the army, and traveled to Hawaii. Because he had matured he now enjoyed an even better relationship with Professor Dawson and interacted with his fellow research students far more readily than he had as an undergraduate. He no longer needed to rush home on the subway to help in the candy store or to deliver newspapers. Instead he involved himself in college life as much as possible.

Under Dawson's supervision, Asimov's Ph.D. research progressed well. There were times when he backed himself into corners and relied heavily on his supervisor. Dawson was a very attentive and helpful professor who managed to do his own research but at the same time devoted a great deal of energy to the needs of his students. He realized that Asimov was a talented theoretical chemist but that his experimental work was lacking, and assisted him with this whenever he could, nudging him along the correct path, playing on his strengths and getting Asimov to make good his own weaknesses.

During his Ph.D. course Asimov was required to conduct seminars and to give occasional talks. The first time he did this Dawson was in attendance, along with a number of other members of the faculty. Asimov was very nervous, but still performed brilliantly. Dawson realized straightaway that Isaac had a natural gift for explaining things clearly and was able to engender inspiration in his audience, a gift Dawson always thought rare and precious. It was these early lectures that really gave Asimov the idea that he might attempt writing nonfiction as well as continuing with his science fiction stories.

In spite of all the upheavals of moving house and settling back into college, Asimov had not forgotten about science fiction altogether. While writing up his doctoral dissertation, he was working on the first draft of his first serious attempt at a novel—what eventually became *Pebble in the Sky*.

Asimov received his Ph.D. in May 1948. He was so delighted by the fact that he could now be called Dr. Isaac Asimov that he went to a bar with Professor Dawson and a couple of friends from Columbia. To celebrate, he asked for a manhattan. He enjoyed it so much that he ordered a second, third and fourth. . . . It was only while drinking his fifth that the full force of the alcohol hit him. Within seconds he was completely drunk.

Professor Dawson and the others managed to get him home to Gertrude. Although he could remember nothing about the evening, Gertrude's most vivid recollection of the event was getting her husband into bed and then sitting in the kitchen overhearing him giggling to himself in a drunken stupor, occasionally emitting the slurred exclamation, "Dr. Asimov! Dr. Asimov!"

After the elation and the hangover had subsided, Asimov was brought back to the sobering realization that he now had to leave college and find a job. Dawson again came to his assistance. Through the professor's contacts, Asimov was offered the position of postdoctoral research assistant to one of the other Columbia professors, Professor Elderfield.

Despite the offered salary being below average for his age and academic status, Asimov gladly took the post and started work in the late summer of 1948.

The job did not last long. The following January Elderfield discovered that his research grant for the following academic year was to be cut and informed Asimov that he could not afford to keep him after the end of the 1948–49 academic year.

However, Asimov was lucky. He had until the end of June that year to find alternative employment, and early in 1949 he heard of a job from a most unexpected source. A professor of biochemistry at the Boston University School of Medicine, Professor William Boyd, had been corresponding with Asimov for a period of years in connection with Asimov's science fiction stories. He now wrote to him to ask if he would be interested in accepting a post as assistant professor in his department.

Asimov could not decide what to do. On the one hand, the funding for his position at Columbia was about to dry up; on the other, he had only recently reestablished himself in New York and did not want to cut himself off from his friends. Should he wait to see what other opportunities might present themselves, or should he grab the chance of a promotion when it was offered?

After lengthy discussions with Gertrude, his family, and his friend and mentor Professor Dawson, he was persuaded to accept the invitation to an interview.

On February 9, 1949, Asimov caught the train to Boston. Ahead lay the prospect of a new life in a city he had never before visited. If he liked the job being offered, it would give him the opportunity to settle down there with Gertrude and lay the foundations of his academic career.

During the return journey the next day, Asimov knew that the interview had gone well and was already making plans for the future. Gertrude was for the move and, despite his trepidation at leaving the city in which he had spent most of his life, he realized that if he was given the job in Boston he should accept it and set up home there.

6

FOUNDATION

To most critics and fans alike, *The Foundation Trilogy* is Asimov's greatest literary achievement. To many readers coming to Asimov for the first time, it is this science fiction trilogy they read, and it is often their first introduction to science fiction in general. Being weaned on science fiction in novel form, as most readers are today, it comes as a surprise that the trilogy was created as a series of short stories. They were written over a period of seven and a half years between August 1941 and March 1949, and it took a further four years for the complete series to be published in book form.

Once again, the story began life after a visit to John Campbell's office at a time when the majority of Asimov's work was being rejected by *Astounding* and the other pulps. Asimov was traveling on the subway reading a collection of Gilbert and Sullivan operettas. He opened it at *Iolanthe*. The illustrations and their military theme started him thinking in terms of armies, wars, and empires. Before he had arrived at Campbell's office he had the idea of writing about a galactic empire, based on the historical structure, rise, and fall of the Roman Empire.

Walking into Campbell's office, Asimov was bubbling over with enthusiasm for the new project, and within moments Campbell was equally excited by the idea. Campbell immediately realized that they were on to something far bigger than a short story, or even, as Asimov had suggested, a novelette. Campbell envisaged a series of stories, shorts and novelettes, all fitting coherently together to form a history of the decline and fall of an empire, with a second empire rising from its ashes. He told Asimov to go home and write an outline of a "future history." Campbell wanted him to design a scheme charting the historical progress of the galactic empire based on what they had envisaged that sunny afternoon in his office.

Asimov always hated the idea of outlines. He had never written one before, and all his short stories had been written straight from his head. Later in his career he was sometimes forced to present outlines for a number of his novels and factual books, but he always resented and disliked it.

As early as 1941, Asimov saw little point in doing a "future history." He thought the whole idea unoriginal, as he knew that Robert Heinlein had already done it, albeit in a slightly different form from Asimov's. Following orders, he started on the project, but after a while it grew to such a crazy level of complexity that he tore it up and threw it in the trash. He decided instead to get down to writing an actual story.

On August 11, four days before "Nightfall" hit the newsstands in the September 1941 edition of *Astounding,* Asimov sat down and began to write the first story in what became *The Foundation Trilogy.* It was finished by September 8. Campbell accepted it immediately and Asimov received a check from *Astounding* on the seventeenth. At one cent per word, the 12,600 words of the story netted Asimov 126 dollars. It was to be the first 126 dollars of several million paid for the Foundation saga during the following decades.

This first installment, called "The Encyclopedists" in the book form (Part II of *Foundation*), appeared under the title "Foundation" in the May 1942 issue of *Astounding.*

The Foundation Trilogy is massive in scope. With the possible exception of E. E. "Doc" Smith in the early thirties, nothing like it had been attempted before Asimov. Smith's Lensman books had also been conceived in terms of a series of short pieces that appeared in the pulps of the time, but Asimov eclipsed even that.

Asimov fully acknowledges a number of influences in the creation of his fictional empire. Most critics point to Edward Gibbon's *The History of the Decline and Fall of the Roman Empire* as the primary inspiration, but there were other books that gave him just as many ideas. He later joked that he never had to think up a plot for his Foundation books because they had already been written for him.

The first three stories in the series were directly influenced by Gibbon and another vast historical survey, the twenty-four-volume *The Historian's History of the World*. From the fourth story onward, the Gibbon influence began to wane. Fresh inspiration came from a popular series of history books, *A Study of History* by Arnold Toynbee. This greatly influenced him with what later became *Foundation and Empire*, but was discarded by the time he began to write the stories in *Second Foundation*.

The Foundation Trilogy begins on Trantor in the far future. Hari Seldon is a mathematician who has created and refined the science of psychohistory. This is a powerful discipline that provides a precise insight into the future of the human race. It only works if two basic assumptions are met. The first prerequisite is a very large population. In other words, accurate prediction of future trends can only be formulated for numbers in the billions. This means that an entire galaxy may be a subject for psychohistorians but the individual or small groups may not. The second assumption is that the subjects of the analysis—human beings—must be *unaware* of psychohistory. This ensures that their actions are not influenced by knowledge of their future.

In creating this imaginary science, Asimov was greatly influenced by his own academic life. In particular, the rules of psychohistory are loosely based on the laws of an area of chemistry called chemical kinetics. This is a system that tries to predict the behavior of gases, and one of the main premises on which it is based is that a large number of molecules have to be considered in order for there to be any accuracy in the predictions.

Asimov actually makes an allusion to this in his second story, "The Mayors," where he has the character Salvor Hardin saying:

> . . . even Seldon's advanced psychology was limited. It could not handle too many variables. He couldn't work with individuals over any length of time; any more than you could apply the kinetic theory of gases to single molecules. He worked with mobs, populations of whole planets, and only *blind* mobs who do not possess foreknowledge of the results of their own actions.[1]

[1] "The Mayors," *Foundation*. Gnome Press, 1951.

Armed with his deep understanding of psychohistory, Hari Seldon has come to the extremely unpopular conclusion that the empire, now at its peak, will very soon begin to crumble and collapse and that it will be totally devastated within the space of a few hundred years. He further predicts that, following this, humanity will face twenty thousand years of barbarism before a Second Empire can rise from the ashes.

Seldon does have a solution—of sorts. He proposes establishing a community he calls "a Foundation" at each end of the galaxy. Here the sum total of all human knowledge may be accumulated and the seed of a new empire created, which will (in theory) shorten the period of barbarism to a single millennium.

Naturally, Seldon's theories are extremely unpopular with the aristocracy, but he manages to persuade the one man who wields the real power behind the empire, the Chief Commissioner, Linge Chen. Thus, two Foundations are established "at either end of the galaxy."

The first half of the Foundation series concentrated on the First Foundation established on Terminus, a tiny planet at the extreme end of the galaxy, at the periphery of the Galactic Empire.

The first six stories[1] deal almost exclusively with the First Foundation. They center upon the leading characters in its history and the tales of how they overcome one obstacle after another along the path to the creation of a Second Empire.

The first of the stories, "The Encyclopedists," is set on Terminus, and was the first to be written and published in *Astounding*. Set fifty years after the death of Seldon (who died within a year of the establishment of the Foundations), it revolves around a handful of characters. These include Salvor Hardin, who is seen by future generations as a folk hero and legendary patriarch of the Foundation. It is Hardin who realizes that the history of the Foundation has been mapped out by Seldon, and that at intervals they have to face what he calls "Seldon Crises":

---

[1] First five published—the introductory chapter in the novel version "The Psychohistorians" was only written when the stones were collected in book form.

> ... the future isn't nebulous. It's been calculated out by Seldon
> and charted. Each successive crisis in our history is mapped
> and each depends in a measure on the successful conclusion
> of the ones previous.[1]

Before his death Seldon had established a "Time Vault" on Terminus, in which his holographic image appears, usually just after a crisis. He appears whether or not he has an audience and declares how the Foundation has fared in the crisis and how closely it is sticking to the Seldon Plan. The heroes of the Foundation are invariably those who foresee a Seldon Crisis and (in most cases) attempt to steer the Foundation through it.

The first crisis is relatively simple and involves a power struggle with the Foundation's nearest neighbor, Anacreon.

Applying rudimentary power politics and armed with the fact that Anacreon has lost its nuclear capability, Hardin staves off domination from Anacreon by playing off one planet against another. On another level, "The Encyclopedists" is about the way in which the worlds of academia and politics operate by a totally different set of rules. The encyclopedists of the Foundation are rather naive, self-obsessed individuals, ill-suited to positions of power; whereas Hardin is streetwise and manipulative.

Asimov was perhaps the first pulp writer to create a hero who was not a ray-gun-toting superhero, but a middle-aged politician. He succeeded with this by giving his political heroes (of which Hardin is the first) other facets to their character. What makes Hardin so attractive is that he is not a one-dimensional power freak, but often inclined to philosophical musings. He is remembered by future generations as much for his aphorisms as his strategies. Such statements as "Violence is the last refuge of the incompetent" pepper his monologues.

The second foundation story gave Asimov enormous trouble in its conception and writing. He had deliberately forced himself into a sequel by having Salvor Hardin declare, at the end of the first, "Foundation":

---

[1] "The Mayors."

> . . . the solution to this first crisis was obvious. Obvious as
> all hell![1]

After the flush of self-satisfaction at creating the need for a sequel and
getting it past Campbell, Asimov suddenly realized that he had very little
time in which to actually write the thing. The second story would have
to appear in the issue following publication of the first.

Panicked into it, he sat at the typewriter and the story just flowed out.
He managed to write seventeen pages in three days. Puffed up by his own
achievement, he popped in to see Campbell on some other matter—and
the first words the editor said to him were, "Asimov, I want that Foundation story!"

That killed it. He dried up completely, and instead of finishing the
story he just sat and stared at the typewriter. In later years Asimov
recalled this incident as one of the rare times in which he suffered from
writer's block and it almost halted his blossoming career before it had
really got off the ground. He could not face letting Campbell down but
equally he could not get anywhere with his original plot line.

He tried everything: forcing himself to write, revising the original
plot, leaving it to stew for a while; but nothing worked. Finally, in a blind
panic, he talked it over with his closest friend, Fred Pohl, who occasionally acted as his literary adviser and was back in action helping to sell his
friend's stories to the pulps. They walked over Brooklyn Bridge (a journey
they often made because apparently Fred Pohl's first wife, Leslie Perri,
could not stand the sight of Asimov and would not allow him in the
house).

During the walk, Pohl helped him to unravel the threads of the plot
and guided him along the way. Asimov dashed home and polished it off
there and then.

"Bridle and Saddle," as he called the second part, once again has
Salvor Hardin as the hero. This time the story is set some thirty years
later, eighty years after the establishment of the First Foundation on Terminus. Hardin has created a religion extending throughout the Four
Kingdoms where the Foundation is now the power base. Terminus and

---

[1] "The Encyclopedists," *Foundation.* Gnome Press, 1951.

the Foundation are perceived by the increasingly barbaric inhabitants of the region as being at the very hub of this religion. It is the place where ordinary citizens are sent for training and initiation into the Priesthood. Priests control technology provided exclusively by the Foundation and veiled in a mystique of religion, presided over by the omnipotent Galactic Spirit.

Asimov uses this religious power base as a lever for Hardin to extend the influence of the Foundation, to defeat the renewed belligerence of Anacreon and create an embryonic empire in the Periphery.

Some have claimed that herein lies a major flaw with this second story. The plot hinges on the people of the Four Kingdoms accepting, unequivocally, the religion created by the Foundation. This, it has been suggested, simply requires too much of a suspension of disbelief. The Foundation has had only thirty years in which to indoctrinate an entire region of the Periphery. That region falling into such barbaric behavior so quickly and within a generation becoming willing to discard all historical understanding and civilization, along with adopting what is in essence a rather lame religion, is hard to accept.

One can only assume that Asimov based his premise for this story on the time scales operating during the fall of the Roman Empire and the subsequent slide into the Dark Ages. But his flaw lies in the fact that the people of the Galactic Periphery would be descending from a much more advanced position than the Romans. Perhaps Asimov applied the principle that "the bigger they are the harder they fall." Campbell either did not notice or did not care about this flaw in the plot of "Bridle and Saddle" and snapped up the story as soon as he received it in November 1941.

With most of his writers away fighting in the war, between 1941 and 1945 Campbell was desperately short of stories and was paying a higher rate to attract contributions. Consequently, Asimov was paid the largest fee he had so far received. At the new increased rate of one and a half cents per word, payment for "Bridle and Saddle" came to four hundred dollars.

During the time between the creation of the second and third *Foundation* stories, Asimov's writing career was halted because of the war, and it was to be almost two years before he picked up the series again.

"Bridle and Saddle" (called "The Mayors" in *The Foundation Trilogy*) appeared in the June 1942 issue of *Astounding*, but "The Merchant Princes" (or "The Big and the Little," as it was originally called) was not started until October 1943. At over 22,000 words, it turned out to be the longest story Asimov had written up to that point in his career.

"The Merchant Princes" was not finished until January 1944 and appeared in the August 1944 edition of *Astounding*.

It deals with the expansion of the Foundation's influence by use of trade combined with the religion created in "Bridle and Saddle." Our protagonist is Hober Mallow, who, through his bravery and daring, by the end of the tale joins the elite band of Foundation heroes in the Hardin mold.

As the Foundation expands its trade empire, it begins to run into trouble. The biggest hurdle is trying to dominate local powers without resorting to military power.

"The Merchant Princes," set 150 years after the establishment of the Foundation, tells the story of an attempt by a warlord, the Commdor Asper of Korrell, to overpower the Foundation using the final vestiges of the empire's influence.

It is clear to our hero Hober Mallow that a third Seldon Crisis looms. Mirroring the Crisis faced by Salvor Hardin, Mallow has to do battle on two fronts. First, he has to convince the Foundation government of the Korrellian threat, and second, he has to try to overcome a new social problem on Terminus—the establishment of the eponymous Merchant Princes (a group of ultrarich traders who have become too powerful for the good of the Foundation). He succeeds with the first and helps to save the Foundation from military defeat, but fails in the second. Asimov was obviously unperturbed by his earlier problem with leaving an ending open for a sequel and left the Foundation's unresolved social problem dangling in order to create the background for a later story.

The success of the Foundation against Korrell was, of course, predicted by Seldon, and depends not on military superiority but simple economics. The Foundation has cleverly infiltrated the entire economic system of the enemy, indoctrinating their huge population and allowing them to rely on the gadgets produced by the Foundation and sold to them in the years before the war. When these atomic devices begin to break down and cannot be repaired or replaced, economic needs overcome military dreams.

In this story there are close links with Roman history. Ancient Rome engaged in two major "trade wars" in its Imperial phase, firstly with Russia, which resulted in four separate military campaigns; and more significantly with China, when the Emperor Justinian broke the Chinese silk trade monopoly by importing silkworm eggs into Constantinople, which enabled the Romans to produce their own silk. These historical events undoubtedly encouraged Asimov to think about the potential of economic power overcoming military superiority.

Asimov's fourth story, which he called "The Wedge," was taken by Campbell in April 1944 and it appears as the fourth part of the book, where it is given the title "The Traders." At approximately seven thousand words, it is the shortest part of the entire trilogy and is little more than a vignette describing a tiny fragment of Foundation history. A few months later, Asimov finished "Dead Hand," which in the book version became the first section in Volume Two of the trilogy, *Foundation and Empire*. In this book form it was given the title "The General."

Asimov delivered this to Campbell in August 1944, and at twenty-five thousand words it was the longest installment he had so far written and earned him 437.50 dollars from *Astounding*. Both "The Wedge" and "Dead Hand" were written during Asimov's time at the Navy Yard at the height of the war. The fact that matters military were very much at the forefront of Asimov's mind at the time comes across very clearly.

"The General" is one of the most entertaining parts of *The Foundation Trilogy*, high on thrills and beautifully crafted into the overall structure of the whole vast epic. The central character is the general of the title, Bel Riose—the last strong general of the old empire.

As the empire enters its death throes, some two hundred years after Seldon, it has, in the person of Riose, one last stab at imperialism. But who is there in the galaxy for the empire to fight? The empire is falling into savagery and there are no aliens or other inhabited galaxies within reach. It is during this search for an enemy that Riose discovers the Foundation, and he is immediately off in search of blood and honor.

As foretold by Seldon, Riose cannot possibly win. He lives in an era when the empire is ruled by a strong emperor. The mix of strong emperor and a general looking for glory is unstable. The emperor feels threatened when Riose becomes too successful and so disposes of him. Thus Seldon's fourth Crisis is solved and the Foundation survives to fight another day.

By the time Asimov had written "Dead Hand" in August 1944, "The Big and the Little" had appeared in that month's issue of *Astounding*. It made the cover and was announced as "a Foundation story by Isaac Asimov"—the first time Asimov's Foundation stories had been formalized as a series.

Despite the push this gave Asimov toward continuing with the theme, in the autumn of 1944 he was tiring of the whole concept. He had written three Foundation stories in succession, which had occupied his entire creative energies for the major part of a year. He wanted to turn to something new.

Because of this and the upheavals created by the war, the series languished for several months. Then, in January 1945, during a visit to Campbell, the editor declared that he wanted Asimov to write a story that completely broke the Seldon Plan.

At first Asimov was horrified by the idea. After all, the Seldon Plan was the central pillar around which the entire plot revolved. To break it was almost sacrilegious. But Asimov could not convince Campbell that it was a bad idea, and had to go along with it.

"The Mule" shows a far greater maturity in its writing, plot, and characterization than any of the preceding Foundation stories. Many of the characters are quite evidently taken directly from Asimov's own experience. The three key characters are Magnifico, Bayta Darell, and Toran Darell. In terms of physical appearance, Bayta is closely based on Gertrude, and the personality of Toran is modeled on Asimov himself. Toran is portrayed as a young man who is a little vague about what is happening around him, quick-tongued, and a little oversensitive at times. In physical appearance, Toran, athletic and muscular, is the opposite of Asimov.

The most important character in the story and, with the exception of Seldon himself, the central character of the entire trilogy, is Magnifico, the Mule. Physically, the Mule was modeled on Leonard Meisel, Asimov's friend at the Navy Yard. Meisel was a cheerful fellow who on at least one occasion saved Asimov from the pits of depression. Meisel's most distinctive physical characteristic was his huge, pointed nose. He was also a good musician who loved to sing and tell jokes. One of Magnifico's most prominent physical characteristics is a huge proboscis, and in the story, Magnifico not only acts the role of the court jester, but for a large portion of the story he also plays a musical instrument called the Visi-Sonor, a talent that has quite devastating applications.

The other major character is Ebling Mis, who plays a key role within the story, especially in the final scenes. It is unclear who Asimov based this character on, but Mis is possibly a combination of Asimov's college professors and the archetypal wise old man, perhaps rooted in Russian folklore.

It is certainly relevant that Asimov introduced a newly married couple into the story and built the plot around a young woman. It was the first time Asimov had used a strong female character in any of his stories other than those involving Susan Calvin. At the time of writing "The Mule," Asimov was happily married. This undoubtedly had a significant influence on his writing. It is no coincidence that Bayta, modeled on Gertrude, saves the Foundation in the final reel.

"The Mule" is set three hundred years after the establishment of the Foundation and recounts the story of how the Foundation is defeated for the first (and only) time in its history by a mutant with psychic powers who overrides the Seldon Plan. Bayta saves the future of the galaxy by preventing the Mule from discovering the location of the Second Foundation, which, after the fall of Terminus, is the only hope for the salvation of Seldon's new empire.

Written during the war, it is the story most concerned with military matters. There is little doubt that Asimov had Hitler in mind when he was modeling the character of the Mule. However, the personality of the Mule is more complex than this might suggest. He is not a one-dimensional totalitarian dictator, although he is driven and ultraambitious. What is most interesting about the Mule is his vulnerability. Why did he become so power-crazy? By using his power to conquer the galaxy, is he really trying to flee that very power? What are his ultimate goals? Why is he so attracted to Bayta?

All of these questions are dealt with in varying degrees of detail. We learn very few hard facts about the Mule, but Asimov provides us with just enough to enable us to fill in the gaps and to build a picture of a strangely attractive, rather sad man with a power unbalanced by emotional maturity, more telepathic misanthrope than sadistic madman.

"The Mule" constitutes the first part of the *Foundation* story involving the Mule and details his conquest over the First Foundation. It makes up the second half of *Foundation and Empire*.

Asimov wrote the entire story in three and a half months, delivering the manuscript to Campbell in May 1945. It was the most ambitious project he had ever undertaken and ended up at around fifty thousand words, almost the length of a novel. It also earned him the largest check he had ever received for a writing project—875 dollars.

Oddly, Asimov's triumph at completing this marvelous piece of storytelling fell flat, because, he concluded, he had found it too easy. In a rare introspective passage, Asimov wrote in his diary: "Certain success evicts one from the paradise of winning against the odds."[1]

At the time, Asimov was also plagued by fears that he would be drafted at any moment. The only cheering news was that the war in Europe was over and that it would only be a matter of time before the war in Asia would end, too.

By the time "The Mule" appeared in the December 1945 issue of *Astounding*, Asimov had found himself drafted into the army and read the issue on Thanksgiving Day 1945 at Camp Lee. It was not until after he had been discharged and had reestablished himself in civilian life, during the autumn of 1946, that he was once again able to start planning a new Foundation story.

With this, Asimov returned to the strongest character of the series—the Mule—and the story eventually became the first part of *Second Foundation*, where it was given the title "Search by the Mule." It deals with the Mule's obsessive and eventually unsuccessful search for the Second Foundation.

In its published form the story concludes with the Second Foundation defeating the Mule in a psychic battle and influencing him to return to

---

[1] *In Memory Yet Green, The Autobiography of Isaac Asimov 1920–1954.* Doubleday, New York, 1979 (p. 420).

his empire. But this was not how the original ended. Asimov's title for the story was "Now You See It" and he delivered it to Campbell on February 2, 1947. At twenty-five thousand words it was only half the length of "The Mule," but most importantly, Asimov had decided that it was to be the last of the series and finished it off with what he saw as a neat ending.

Campbell was not at all happy about this and insisted on a rewrite that left the ending open for later installments. After working on the Foundation stories on and off for five and a half years Asimov was tiring of the whole Foundation concept. He wanted to concentrate on other ideas, to develop his robot stories, which he had always found more interesting, and to work on a novel. However, as he had precious few contacts in the publishing world, he had to keep in with Campbell. He went away and followed orders, delivering the revised version after a single evening reworking it. This time he left the ending open as it is seen in the novel version of *The Foundation Trilogy* and Campbell was happy enough to immediately mail Asimov a check for five hundred dollars.

Feeling pleased with himself and flush after the austerity of the war years, in a rare impulsive gesture, Asimov took Gertrude out and bought her a mink-dyed opossum coat costing two hundred dollars.

"Now You See It" took a long time to appear in *Astounding*, not showing up until the January 1948 issue of the magazine, nearly a year after its completion. Despite having an impressive body of work behind him, early 1948 was a bad period in Asimov's career. He wrote only a few stories, as he was concentrating on writing and placing his first novel, a task that was proving to be more difficult than he had imagined. Although he loved writing short stories, he realized that it could never be treated as a career and that if he was to have a serious second career as a writer, then he would have to break out of just writing for the pulps. At the same time his academic job was going well and taking up a lot of his energy.

Throughout the first half of 1948, Campbell continued to badger Asimov to get started on another Foundation story, which he had agreed would be the final one in the series. He finally succeeded and a little over eighteen months after delivering "Now You See It," Asimov was persuaded to dive back into the world of the two Foundations and came up with the final installment, which he called "And Now You Don't" to link up with the previous story in the series.

Asimov began to write the final Foundation story in October 1948, but the going was slow. He realized at the very beginning that because the stories all related to those before them, he would have to start this story with some form of résumé. After all, it had been some time since the last installment had appeared in *Astounding* and six and a half years since the first Foundation story. What made it especially difficult was the fact that he was forced into increasingly complex plotting to make the tale fit in with all that had gone before it.

Asimov begins "And Now You Don't" ("Search by the Foundation" in the novelization) by recapping the story of the Foundation through one of the principal characters, a teenage girl called Arcadia Darell, writing a history essay as a school project. We soon realize that Arcadia is actually the granddaughter of the great Bayta Darell, who identified Magnifico as the Mule and saved the Second Foundation some sixty years earlier.

The pace of the story rapidly picks up with the uncovering of a First Foundation conspiracy that involves a group of intellectuals led by Arcadia's father, Dr. Toran Darell (Bayta's son). The conspirators believe that the Second Foundation is a serious threat to the future of the First Foundation and set out to destroy it.

The plotting of "Search by the Foundation" is the most complex of all Asimov's Foundation stories and deals, on the one hand, with a simple tale of Arcadia becoming enmeshed in the conspiracy and, on the other, the labyrinthine plans of the Second Foundation. By the end of the story, the First Foundation pulls through once again. They win a physical war and are also led to believe they have destroyed the Second Foundation.

Naturally, the notion that Seldon would set up the two Foundations simply so that one could destroy the other at some crisis point in the future would be quite ridiculous. Asimov had conceived from the beginning the idea that, in Seldon's Plan, the two Foundations would develop in quite separate ways, one pushing back the limits of technological progress, the other, the Second Foundation, developing an understanding of mental powers.

The final purpose, at some point in the future, would be for the two

Foundations to unite and create a new Empire, one quite different and infinitely more powerful than the purely technological First Empire.

The entire plot of this final story is secretly directed by the Second Foundation. The Second Foundation completely manipulates the characters and guides events to save the Seldon Plan and push the First Foundation along the correct path.

When Asimov delivered the final installment of the Foundation epic at the end of March 1949, he knew, as did Campbell, that that really was it. There would be no more Foundation stories and the epic had been tied up—at least for the time being.

Asimov received a new record check of a thousand dollars for "And Now You Don't" which brought his total earnings for the entire collection of eight stories to thirty-six hundred dollars.

The stories themselves may have ended, but the delivery of "And Now You Don't" (which was published in three parts starting with the November 1949 issue of *Astounding*) was not to be the end of the overall story.

After several false starts trying to get the entire Foundation series accepted for publication in book form, Fred Pohl managed to convince a colleague in the publishing world called Martin Greenberg to accept the stories for novelization.

Greenberg had set up a publishing company called Gnome Press. By 1951, they had already published the collection *I, Robot* and the New York publisher Doubleday had published Asimov's first novel, *Pebble in the Sky*.

Having had both Doubleday and Little, Brown reject the idea of publishing *Foundation*, Asimov was obviously delighted that Gnome Press wanted to take it.

On February 28, 1951, Asimov received his first advance of a hundred dollars for the first book of what became *The Foundation Trilogy*. After Fred Pohl had taken his 10 percent share, Asimov actually received the stately sum of ninety dollars.

Greenberg suggested that the books be divided into three volumes, but the way they naturally separated left the first volume, at sixty thousand words, a little short. He also felt that the series began too abruptly and suggested that Asimov write an introductory chapter. This he did, and thus was created the first part of the trilogy, "The Psychohistorians," the opening section of the book and the last part to be written. This introduced Hari Seldon in person and set the stage for the future history of the embryonic Second Empire.

Asimov delivered the finished version of *Foundation* to Greenberg in May 1951, and over the next two and a half years revised versions of the other two sections were delivered and published. The final part, *Second Foundation*, appeared in 1953.

It is difficult to overestimate Asimov's achievement with *The Foundation Trilogy*. These three books are generally regarded as being the best example of "mature" science fiction from the 1940s and '50s. However, as we shall see in a later chapter, Asimov's achievement did not register with a wider audience beyond the limited arena provided by the pulps until the 1960s, when the trilogy sold worldwide and in the millions. It was these books that really established space opera in the minds of teenagers throughout the Western world who had never even seen a pulp magazine.

For science fiction writers already established in the field and old enough to have been pulp buyers themselves, the Foundation stories in *Astounding* also provided a platform for their own writing. Such blockbusters as the series of Dune books written by Frank Herbert and first published in 1965 have a definite Foundation stamp on them (and even include the device of a futuristic encyclopedia to scene-set). James Blish's *Cities in Flight*, which first appeared in the magazines in 1950, owes a debt to the Foundation stories, not least in showing the way to combine historical perspective and sociology with the adventure of "Doc" Smith.

For many years following the initial publication of *Foundation*, those uninterested in science fiction still viewed the genre as a cheap form of literature that, they imagined, involved bug-eyed monsters and green Martians; they had no appreciation of its complexity. As late as the 1960s, the uninitiated thought that science fiction dealt with nothing beyond the effectiveness of ray guns and the possibilities of flying saucers. Little did skeptics know that, since the Golden Age of the early 1940s, writers such as Asimov had been dealing with complex and sophisticated sociological and psychological matters, interlinking them with science pushed a few stages beyond the reality of the present.

The Foundation Trilogy, perhaps more than any other science fiction work, paved the way for the grander future of science fiction and undoubtedly inspired the creation of *Star Trek* in the mid-1960s. It also helped to create the sudden boom in science fiction in the cinema of the 1970s, best exemplified by the wonderful *Star Wars* films of George Lucas. There is no doubt that *Foundation* acted, at least in part, as the inspiration for *Star Wars.* The pangalactic empire presided over by Trantor is not so very different from the empire of Luke Skywalker et al.

However, *The Foundation Trilogy* is not without its critics. Writer Brian Aldiss remembers with great pleasure the excitement created by the Foundation stories as they appeared in *Astounding* between 1941 and 1949, but never really rated the book versions. "You can't imagine how exciting it was waiting for the next issue of *Astounding* to appear containing the latest Foundation story," he says. "But when you read them collected together in book form you can see their literary flaws. For example, the device of the Mule disguised as Magnifico is used in exactly the same way with Preem Palver in the final story."

For Asimov, the trilogy was, along with his robot stories, work that elevated him into the upper echelons of the science fiction world. As the stories appeared in the pulps he was already achieving celebrity status within the science fiction community, but in book form the stories gave him far greater credibility within the broader publishing world. This led inevitably to a succession of science fiction novels that in the course of time, as they sold in vast numbers around the world, established him globally as arguably the greatest science fiction writer of his age.

7

FAMILY AND INFIDELITY

The Asimovs moved to Boston at the end of July 1949 and stayed there for the next twenty-one years, until 1970, when Isaac and Gertrude separated and Isaac moved back to New York.

At the time of the move they had been married for seven years and had celebrated their wedding anniversary on July 26, just before leaving New York. On many levels they were a happy couple, ambitious and brimming over with high-minded plans. But beneath the public image they were deeply troubled. By the late forties the Asimovs' sexual relationship had degenerated beyond repair.

At this time Asimov was assiduously pursuing two careers simultaneously. He felt neither financially secure nor confident enough to abandon his academic career in favor of full-time writing. It must be remembered that in 1949 *Pebble in the Sky* had not yet been published and Asimov's sole market was in pulp magazines. It would take another nine years of university work and a gradual acceptance by the publishing world before he and Gertrude could comfortably live on his writing income alone.

Asimov was a natural teacher. He had lectured occasionally and successfully while gaining his Ph.D. at Columbia and had enjoyed it. In later years much of his writing was, in a sense, teaching. With his nonfiction books Asimov's talent lay in revealing the wonder of pure knowledge. At first this was solely within the realm of science, but then, as he became more confident as a nonfiction writer, he tackled any subject that took his fancy.

At Boston University he became a first-class lecturer. His position at the university was not an assistant professorship (as had originally been suggested by Bill Boyd) but an instructorship. This was one grade below assistant professor, which meant that he was responsible for a certain amount of teaching as well as pure research.

His first lecture course began in February 1950. The subject was "Simple Lipids." Later Gertrude declared that she had never been so sick of a phrase as "today we take up simple lipids," because Isaac insisted upon walking around their apartment repeating this, his opening line, over and over again.

Despite the fact that Asimov had contracted laryngitis a few days beforehand, the first lecture was a success. He was always popular with the students, who came to him for advice during his first months at the university and enjoyed his laid-back and friendly lecturing style. But Asimov was never that much of a hit with many of the conventional members of the department, who resented Asimov's popularity. They found him eccentric and cocky—by now a familiar reaction. Asimov simply took it in stride.

He was particularly taken with the female students in the course, and on more than one occasion he was accused of fraternizing with them. Jealousies soon arose among a small group of less able male students, who claimed that Asimov treated the pretty female students more favorably. Asimov then quickly realized he had to be careful. With the group of resentful lecturers who had no time for him on the one hand and accusations of favoritism and worse on the other, he was treading a very fine line. These problems soon subsided but others grew during the following eight years, and for Asimov, peaceful times at the university were rare.

With his typical immodesty, Asimov made things worse for himself. Without a further thought, bolstered by his popularity with many of the students, he loudly proclaimed that he was the best lecturer on the faculty.

One story from the early fifties relates how a visitor walking along a corridor heard a loud roar from another floor, followed by cheers and applause. "What the hell is that?" they asked the academic showing them around. "Oh, probably Asimov lecturing," came the chagrined reply.

Asimov did have some friends at the university. Bill Boyd returned to the faculty in 1950 after traveling abroad for nearly a year. He and

Asimov became good friends. Asimov often made friends with the people he worked with in the publishing world, although most of them were based in New York. Campbell, Pohl, and other close associates often visited the Asimovs in Boston, so Asimov's initial fears of isolation away from the heartland of New York City were unfounded.

As much as Asimov was a brilliant teacher, he was a lousy researcher. From the very beginning of his time at Boston University this caused additional conflict with certain members of the faculty. His immediate superior was Dr. Henry Lemon, who was head of the project to which Asimov was assigned. The two men never got along. Lemon was the opposite to Asimov in almost every respect. He was a thorough, meticulous, and dedicated researcher, had little talent dealing with students, and was extremely conservative. He disliked Asimov's loudmouthed, playful manner and often eccentric attitudes. He was of the opinion that an academic should spend as much time as possible on his research. He disapproved of Asimov's writing ambitions and saw them as an embarrassment to the college and beneath the dignity of Boston University. He tried to make life as difficult as he could for Asimov.

Fortunately, Isaac got along well with Professor Walker, the head of the department. Walker was also very different from Asimov, but he had a great deal of respect for him and did not share Lemon's criticisms.

Asimov avoided research as much as possible, and he hated writing research papers. He disliked the required formal style, which left him no room for free expression.

As each year of the 1950s slipped away, Asimov did less and less research and more and more teaching at the university. Despite the fact that he had only been living and working in Boston for a few years, by the early 1950s he could have given up his academic career altogether and devoted his time entirely to writing. His literary earnings for the year 1952 were 8,550 dollars, compared to his college salary of 5,500 dollars. In 1953, they jumped to a fraction under the 10,000 dollar mark. By the end of that year he had nine books in print and was writing as much for the pulps as he had ever done. His writing career looked rosy. But then in December 1950 Gertrude became pregnant with their first child, David.

At first Isaac, with his usual lack of awareness of anything going on around him, failed to read the signs, and appears to have been one of the last to realize that Gertrude was pregnant.

To be fair, there was some reason to be surprised. Isaac and Gertrude did not exactly have what could be called an active sex life and, several years earlier, Asimov had learned that he had a low sperm count. By 1950, they had more or less consigned the idea of having children to the land of maybe and thought little more of it. Nonetheless, when Gertrude told him she was pregnant, Isaac was both shocked and delighted.

Their first thought was that they would have to move out of the small apartment they had been renting since arriving in Boston over a year earlier, and they immediately started looking around for a larger place.

At first things did not go smoothly with the pregnancy. Toward the end of January 1951, when Gertrude was around two months pregnant, she began to experience terrible pain and in a fit of panic Isaac rushed her to the Massachusetts General Hospital in the new car they had purchased six months earlier. Fearing a miscarriage, the doctors kept Gertrude in the hospital for two days. Isaac's distress was so apparent that after a couple of days of his pacing and interfering, and after Gertrude was given the all clear, the joke went around the ward that "Gertrude had not had a miscarriage, but Isaac had had five."

David was born on August 20, 1951. By then the Asimovs had found an apartment on Lowell Street, in Waltham. It boasted a telephone with a dialing mechanism so that they no longer had to fuss around with getting an operator to make a call for them. The only problem was that it turned out to be a party line. Upon moving into the apartment they also invested in a refrigerator costing an astronomical 270 dollars.

The summers in Boston are often incredibly hot and humid, while the winters are savagely cold. Asimov enjoyed cold weather and only felt it when the temperature really plummeted. At the same time, he hated hot weather. He was never interested in sunbathing and he loathed the humidity of the Boston summer. All the apartments they had rented in the city came without air conditioning, and the temperature indoors was often higher than it was outside. It made working in the apartment during the summer vacation almost impossible.

A great advantage of the Lowell Street apartment was that it had a balcony of sorts and was on the top floor of the building. Both Isaac and

Gertrude took advantage of this. Isaac would often set up his typewriter in the shade and work in the open. During the latter stages of her pregnancy, when the temperature in the shade shot into the nineties, Gertrude often took naps on a cot Isaac had set up at the opposite end of the balcony.

David was premature and small at birth. For the first four days of his life he had to be kept in an incubator. He was often ill as a child and his parents were constantly worried about his weight. He remained thin into childhood and developed into a rather shy, retiring boy who found it difficult to communicate with others of his age and to join in their games. With the arrival of Isaac and Gertrude's second child, Robyn, when David was three, he began to come out of himself a little and to open up with other children. Robyn was a boisterous and energetic child, the complete opposite of her elder brother.

As the family grew, Isaac was busy creating most of the science fiction for which, in later years, he became internationally famous. Gertrude had typed *I, Robot* during 1950 and it had been published at the end of the year, around the time of David's conception. Between Gertrude becoming pregnant with David and the birth of Robyn in February 1955, Asimov wrote and had published *The Foundation Trilogy; The Stars, Like Dust;* two of the Lucky Starr books, *The Currents of Space* and *The Caves of Steel.* During Gertrude's pregnancy with David, Isaac was preparing the Foundation stories for publication in book form with Gnome Press, while *Pebble in the Sky* was selling well in the shops, and just before Robyn's birth Asimov wrote *The End of Eternity.*

This time clearly marks the transition period during which Asimov's writing became critically and financially consistent. By the early 1950s his earnings from writing began to so significantly outstrip his college salary that he could seriously consider leaving his academic position and taking up writing full-time.

During the years 1950–55, Asimov's earnings from writing climbed from 4,700 to 15,000 dollars, while his college income remained almost constant. It was apparent that Asimov could earn even more from writing if he were to take it up full-time rather than fitting it around his college commitments. But even then he was not sure that he wanted to leave the college. He enjoyed the long, paid vacations, and the demands of teaching and his minimal research responsibilities were not too stressful. Above all, he enjoyed the prestige of being a college professor.

In the event, the decision to leave Boston University was protracted and fraught with arguments and bitterness.

During the first couple of years of his employment, Asimov was skating on thin ice, but he always managed to stay on the right side of the head of department, Professor Walker, in part because back in 1950, Bill Boyd had approached Asimov with the idea of collaborating on a biochemistry textbook. The team had quickly grown to include Walker. This helped Asimov ingratiate himself with his boss and at the same time provided him with a weapon. If his position at the college were ever to be at risk, he told himself, he could threaten to withdraw from the project.

After a while, it was clear to Asimov that in taking on the biochemistry book, he had not thought of the downside of the deal. He ended up doing most of the hard work, and from an early stage, despite the encouragement of the publishers, the book was doomed to failure. It finally appeared in May 1952 under the title *Biochemistry and Human Metabolism* and was old-fashioned before it was published. It was also full of errors that required correction before a second edition appeared.

The major difficulty the authors faced was that two other, far superior, books had been published almost simultaneously and instantly cornered the market. The Asimov, Boyd, and Walker text consequently sold only a few hundred copies and ended up as a bit of a fiasco. Asimov had labored hard over the book, including taking responsibility for creating the tortuously complex index, and all it really achieved was a little artificial security at college. For him the book looked extra pale in comparison to the glamor of having *Pebble in the Sky* published and writing *The Stars, Like Dust* and *The Currents of Space*.

Asimov seriously considered the idea of looking for another academic position during 1951 and 1952. He felt the college was not treating him well. He wanted a pay raise provided by the college rather than one taken from Dr. Lemon's grant, and was simultaneously angling for a promotion to assistant professor.

With Walker's help, by the end of 1951 Asimov was successful in escaping the financial dependency placed upon him by Lemon's grant.

However, it took another eighteen months of constant pressure for Asimov to succeed with his demand for a promotion.

In order to make the college put him on their payroll he had to threaten them with resignation. Although Asimov was unpopular with some of the academic staff, Walker knew what a good teacher he was, and some of those in superior positions to Walker, including the top man, Dean Faulkner, had the foresight to realize that Asimov's growing fame was an asset to them.

On the negative side stood Dr. Lemon and Professor Walker's boss, Dr. Charles Keefer. On the plus side were the dean and some of his immediate underlings, Bill Boyd, who had no real power, and Professor Walker, who had precious little sway.

For a few years an unspoken truce was called. Indeed, in the summer of 1955 Asimov realized a new and hard-fought-for ambition at the college when he was finally promoted to associate professor of biochemistry. This was an important milestone in his academic career because it gave him tenure. It also meant that unless he committed some gross misconduct, he would retain his academic position at the college for life.

Things would have continued in this favorable way for Asimov if it had not been for the fact that in November 1956 Professor Walker resigned from the department and was succeeded by a young outsider called F. Marrott Sinex.

Sinex turned out to be a pleasant man but inexperienced and unwilling during his first year to really stand up to his immediate superior, Dr. Keefer. By the time of Sinex's appointment, Keefer and Lemon were demonstrating an open hostility toward Asimov and making it abundantly clear that they wanted him out. Walker, thanks partly to the biochemistry book, had always interceded and supported Asimov whenever Keefer had flared up over some minor problem. Now there was no one to stand between Asimov and Keefer. With Lemon fighting a rearguard action, the battle lines were drawn.

Meanwhile, with the promotion and the accompanying tenure, the Asimovs had been talking about the possibility of buying their first home.

Naturally, it was Gertrude who first suggested the idea. Isaac would probably never have considered the possibility of buying a house, no matter how much money they had in the bank. However, once the concept had sunk in, he found the idea thrilling. After all, he reasoned, despite the conflicts with Keefer and Lemon, with his promotion his position was secure, and with his writing career in full swing he was earning a substantial sum.

Even then, the idea was not put into practice for some time. The Asimovs halfheartedly began looking at properties and thinking about the price bracket they could afford, but somehow they never seemed to find the right place or to really commit themselves.

Isaac only realized he had been dragging his heels when his younger brother Stanley bought a house *before* his marriage in 1955 and their parents had retired to live off the earnings from their properties. In early 1956 the Asimovs finally settled on a house in West Newton, a very neat, middle-class suburb favored by academics and businesspeople. The house cost them twenty-three thousand dollars.

Quite out of character, Isaac suggested that they buy the house outright from their savings. By this time they had over thirty-five thousand dollars in the bank. Gertrude advised against cutting their savings by two-thirds at a point in their lives where they had two babies and Isaac's career at Boston University was not exactly on an upswing. Instead, they acquired a mortgage for fifteen thousand dollars and put down the rest in cash. The family moved during February 1956.

Strange as it may seem, Isaac had never before lived in a house. He had always shared apartments or rooms above a shop or lived in lodgings and digs. At the age of thirty-six, married and with two children, an associate professorship and a succession of published novels behind him, he had finally managed to buy his first home.

It was a three-bedroomed house with a living room-cum-dining room, a large kitchen, and a sizable garden. Best of all, the attic had been converted into two rooms that were just perfect for an office. Soon after the family moved in, Isaac began to get the attic into shape. He set up his typewriter on a stand at one end of the room with his desk making up one side of a U-shaped arrangement and his filing cabinet the other. He had built a set of bookcases in which he kept his reference books as well as the growing collection of his own books in their different editions. He also had his collection of bound volumes containing his magazine pieces. By 1957 he had reached volume twenty-seven.

Asimov soon realized that he no longer need wait for the mail to arrive in the morning. The post office was only a mile away. By taking the car he could be there when the mail room opened at 8:00 A.M. and save at least an hour of working time by taking any returned manuscripts and letters back to the office himself.

Among his neighbors, this habit soon gained Asimov a reputation for being a workaholic. The fact that he turned up at the post office every morning whatever the weather was a favorite anecdote for journalists.

As much as his domestic life was settling into a cozy pattern and his writing work was progressing well during the mid-1950s, the situation at the college continued to go from bad to worse. The loss of Walker, and Asimov's exposure to Keefer, soon set the scene for a decisive battle between the two men.

In 1956, the National Heart Institute had approached Asimov to do an academic, limited-edition book about blood. They suggested that they pay him for the task by means of a grant. Asimov asked that the grant be paid to the college, for him to draw upon as he needed it. The Institute was quite happy to pay Asimov directly, but he had already decided that his research for the academic book would enable him to simultaneously write a commercial book on blood for a mass-market publisher, thus maximizing his output. The Institute did not object and agreed, too, that the money should be funneled through the college. Asimov also reasoned that because it was a highbrow academic book that would obviously enhance the name of the college, he would be allowed to work on the project during his spare time at the college.

Thanks to Asimov's obsession with honesty, problems arose almost immediately. Believing that he was profiting from the project by doing his own book on a similar subject at the same time, he felt that he could not allow himself to draw on the money the Institute had sent to the college—a sum of 2,500 dollars for his first year's grant. Then, toward the end of 1957, after the money had been in the college coffers for nearly a year, the head of the project at the National Heart Institute phoned Asimov on a matter concerning the book. He was gratified to hear that the project was going well, but horrified when Asimov let it slip that he had not drawn out any of the money. Asimov's overhonesty, the official informed him, would cause the Institute all sorts of complex problems involving tax thresholds and the like. He then told Asimov that he must, for the Institute's sake, immediately draw the money.

Asimov then went straight to Keefer to ask for the release of the funds for the book. To his astonishment, Keefer refused. He was instantly incensed. He did not need the money, but it was his if he wished to use it. The issue immediately became a point of principle.

Keefer argued that Asimov was working on the book during college time. This was in fact untrue, and Asimov quickly realized that Keefer was using the matter to antagonize him and to force him into resigning, an action that would have lost Asimov his tenure. He was not going to fall for it. He knew that as an associate professor he could not be sacked without a very good reason and that he was not going to be pushed into anything as rash as resignation.

The battle raged for the best part of a year. Asimov argued that if he was forced to resign, then the college and Keefer would be made to look totally ridiculous; that he was an internationally famous writer and that he could do a great deal to enhance the public image of the university by the simple fact that he was affiliated with it. Not only that, Asimov argued, but Keefer's action was immoral, even unlawful; the money was his, not the college's, and if Keefer insisted on making an issue out of it, then he, Asimov, would make the matter very public.

By 1957, Asimov no longer needed Boston University and no longer wanted the job. But he did want to keep his associate professorship and his tenure. He relished the prestige value of his university affiliation and also saw it as a secure fall-back in the unlikely event that he should ever fail with his writing career. Consequently, he set about the task of maneuvering Keefer into a position where his resignation would be accepted but he could retain his tenure.

After a lengthy battle he succeeded in getting his way. It was touch-and-go for a time. Keefer set his face against Asimov's demands and even held out for a while against the influence of his superiors (who, unbeknownst to Asimov, were keen to keep his name associated with the university). After months of stalemate and as the end of the 1958 academic year approached, Asimov thought that he would have to resort to taking legal proceedings against Keefer and the university, but in the end they backed down. It was just as well, Asimov later admitted, because at the time he did not have a lawyer and did not even know one. It really boiled down to a personal war between Keefer, who wanted to get rid of Asimov altogether, and Asimov, who was invoking the letter of the university rule book to keep tenure.

The academic year 1957–58 was his last as a teacher and a researcher at Boston University or anywhere else. By cleverly emphasizing his importance in the larger world outside the ivory tower of Boston University, Asimov managed to leave teaching but retain his tenure and title.

It was only after the battle had been won, during a ceremony at the college attended by the dean, that Asimov realized that he could have saved a lot of time merely by pulling strings. If Keefer had insisted on pushing Asimov out, the dean told him, he would have intervened on Asimov's side.

By the spring of 1953, after almost eleven years together, cracks were beginning to appear in the Asimovs' marriage.

Isaac had always been a flirt. He made no bones about it and most people found it an amusing and endearing aspect of his character. In later years he definitely cultivated a "lovable dirty old man image" with which he felt entirely comfortable. Yet his attitude toward sex took a far more serious route from 1953 and led finally to the disruption of his marriage.

I have said elsewhere that Gertrude was uninterested in sex. Reading between the lines of Isaac's own statements on the matter, and piecing together information drawn from a number of people who knew the couple, it is clear that Gertrude's disinterest actually ran to inertia. It is highly probable that she was unable to achieve sexual satisfaction and that consequently the Asimovs' sex life was pretty much a nonevent. The reasons for Gertrude's inertia are difficult to pinpoint and it is unlikely that she shared her feelings on the matter of sex with anyone else. It could simply have been a question of incompatibility. Isaac was typical of his generation and upbringing in that sexual feelings were not openly discussed except perhaps in clinical, scientific terms. Unable to talk about it, growing mutual resentment must have made the situation worse.

In April 1953, Isaac took a young woman whom he had met at the college to lunch. She brought along a female friend, and he and the friend instantly hit it off. Over lunch he flirted outrageously and in his accustomed way he came out with one suggestive remark after another. What made the situation unusual was that the woman returned Isaac's salvos shot for shot. Isaac was immediately impressed.

After lunch he dropped off his friend at her apartment, and the other woman asked him to drop her off at her apartment some miles away, in Cambridge. She invited him in for coffee, one thing led to another, and they ended up in bed.

Isaac claimed that *he* had been seduced and that after the event he had been instantly guilt-ridden and ashamed of himself. He had never strayed before and felt that he had been drawn into a situation that had grown out of control. Maybe he had, but he also loved it.

Isaac pulled no punches in admitting that the experience opened his eyes. For the first time in his life he came away from a sexual encounter feeling that he was a successful lover. He quickly concluded that either he and Gertrude were ill-matched or else Gertrude disliked sex so much that it had always been a mechanical process. Isaac and Gertrude had both been virgins when they married and their sexual relationship had started off on a clumsy footing on their wedding night. It seems to have improved little during their eleven years of marriage.

Despite the guilt and the feeling of shock, Asimov was elated by the fact that he had satisfied a woman. Until that point he had not realized what he had been missing.

He claimed not to have immediately embarked on a campaign of seduction and extramarital sex, but there is plenty of evidence to suggest that from 1953 onward, Isaac was sexually liberated and that he had a large number of extramarital relationships as increased opportunities for infidelity arose. Gradually his feelings of guilt and anxiety over his behavior evaporated.

Although Isaac did not tell Gertrude of his sexual encounter in Cambridge, she was not entirely unaware of the change in her husband. Isaac described a time, shortly after the incident, when the family were driving to New York to visit relatives for the weekend. He noted that Gertrude seemed unhappy with him and was inexplicably snappy. Further evidence that Gertrude was wise to what was going on comes from the fact that, for the first time in their marriage, the word *divorce* was mentioned. It seems reasonable to assume that Gertrude was willing to put up with Isaac paying her little attention and being totally absorbed with his work, but with the additional problem of infidelity, she was beginning to feel that their marriage was going nowhere. In his autobiographical writings, Isaac dates this first fissure in his marriage around 1953, shortly after his first dalliance with the young woman in Cambridge.

In almost all other respects the Asimovs gave the impression of being a happy family, and it is evident from the fact that they did not divorce at this time that Gertrude came to the conclusion that the positive aspects of their marriage outweighed the problems. Either Gertrude decided to accept her husband's infidelity or else she pretended that it was not actually happening. Isaac's own description of the time shows that he believed Gertrude was unaware of his secret relationships and he was perpetually terrified that she would find him out. He went to great lengths in later years to present to the world in general, and his wife in particular, the image of the "lovable (but nonpracticing) dirty old man." The chances are he fooled no one, least of all Gertrude.

It is also clear that even then, with his marriage in such a rocky state, Isaac did not devote enough time to Gertrude; he was too concerned with beginning the book race that would remain the cornerstone of his reputation in later years. Nonetheless, he was an attentive father and he doted on Robyn in particular. As Gertrude tried to cope with the domestic realities of family life, Isaac dealt with his problems by submerging himself in his work. On many occasions he admitted that he often used writing as a form of escape.

Problems at the college during the fifties were certainly a source of stress for Isaac, and at the same time he was always busy trying to place new ideas and getting started on the next project. It is likely that his sexless marriage was the main reason he needed to find solace in his work. Not being able to satisfy his wife was bound to have lowered his self-esteem. Liberation came firstly through the typewriter and a collection of sexless universes, then later through the embraces of a young woman in a Cambridge apartment.

Isaac believed that this single experience did indeed open up a whole hidden side to his character, giving him renewed self-confidence. This in turn manifested itself in his prodigious writing output and what he considered to be the peaking of his talents as a science fiction writer.

Asimov thought that his robot detective novels, *The Caves of Steel* and *The Naked Sun,* were the pinnacle of his work up until the end of the 1950s. I see his masterwork as *The End of Eternity.* Whichever book is taken as his greatest achievement, they were all written within this same narrow time period in his life, the point at which he became sexually liberated.

Curiously, little of Asimov's sexual feelings appeared in his writing of the period. He always professed an amazingly prudish attitude toward sex in fiction. When asked by a friend why he had never attempted to write a sex science fiction story, Asimov replied gruffly that he had never chosen to. When the friend then said that some people thought he did not know how to, Asimov naturally rose to the bait. Within weeks he had written the rather lame short story "I'm in Marsport Without Hilda."

Even then, Asimov gave the story to the writer friend who had set up the challenge, claiming that he did not want to publish the thing under his name. Several years later, when Asimov perhaps considered the times had changed, he allowed "I'm in Marsport Without Hilda" to be put into a collection of his short stories.

The single change that appeared in Asimov's fiction, post-extramarital sex, was the element of romance in *The End of Eternity* and a single, almost nonexistent sex scene between the lead characters (discussed in depth in the next chapter).

It is quite apparent that, although Asimov attributed his increased output of fiction and his greater powers of imagination to his sexual awakening of 1953, he deliberately chose not to interlink his real-life experience with his writing.

This is in fact a general criticism often leveled at Asimov's fiction—he almost never makes a link between the real world of emotions and relationships and the world of techno-dynamics his characters inhabit. In Asimov's fiction there is little depiction of the life around the characters; they seem to exist in a void cluttered up with machines and images of the past and the future.

Asimov very powerfully conjures up a sense of historical perspective, of grand temporal and spatial vistas, but the personal or emotional aspects of fiction are underplayed. There is little sense of the characters' surroundings, little depth to their lives. Often they are cardboard cutouts playacting on a galaxy-wide stage. We only sympathize with them because we are made to care about the overall panorama, the sweep of history, the enormity of this thing called humankind that permeates into every corner and orifice of the galaxy but that has no reported soul. It is Asimov's particular skill as a storyteller that enables him to powerfully evoke the reader's concern about the grand scheme rather than the individuals who are playing out their roles in the story. This may be said to be a clinical, scientific form of writing, but it can still motivate the reader to stick with a story.

So, was Asimov too ashamed of his sexual side to include even a shadow of it in his writing, or was he simply incapable of doing so? It is likely that once he began writing science fiction and established his style, he realized that he could not suddenly change it. He could not simply write a novel full of sex. Even Asimov, with his charming lack of subtlety, could hardly have imagined he would get away with that, even if he had wanted to.

I think the reason Asimov hardly ever included sex in his novels was simply that his upbringing ran deeper than his sexual liberation. Until 1953 he was unaware of the potential of sex, and after 1953 the mold had been altered slightly but not totally changed.

Asimov has gone on record as declaring that he does not enjoy pornography. "Every time I've read it, it just embarrasses me," he claimed.[1] Friends and colleagues would support this. The one time he went to a burlesque show was in New York soon after he married Gertrude, and he found the whole experience dull and boring. Once confronted by a prostitute on 42nd Street he later claimed to have been unaware he was being propositioned and, when he was, he panicked and ran off.

Against the odds, the Asimovs survived. Robyn was born in 1955 and Isaac and Gertrude stayed together for a further fourteen years until their separation in 1969. Yet it is obvious that from the mid-fifties onward, their marriage was largely one of convenience. They thought first of the children and their comfortable lifestyle. Gertrude merely

---

[1] "The Amazing Asimov" by Herbert Kenny. *Boston Sunday Globe Magazine,* October 12, 1969.

accepted her position as the wife of an increasingly successful author, a man whose popularity was spreading throughout the world, a man she loved, but nonetheless a man with whom she could not enjoy a total relationship. The couple were good together, in the sense that they made an efficient team.

By the end of the fifties, Asimov had entered the happiest phase of his life. He left his teaching position at Boston in the summer of 1958, but retained his title. He became a full-time writer the day he left the college and immediately embarked on his most commercially successful period of writing.

Financial success did not come instantly, but the Asimov family were very comfortably off. They had cleared the mortgage a little over a year after moving in, and they had a bank balance in a healthier state than it had been before making the initial purchase. By the time he left Boston University, Asimov's writing earnings had already exceeded the twenty thousand dollars a year mark, and they increased enormously during subsequent years.

Before taking a look at the decade in which Asimov became an international writing celebrity, I will look at the work that really catapulted Asimov's science fiction career from successful pulp magazine writer to author of a body of work still selling and widely read today, almost half a century after the publication of his first novel, *Pebble in the Sky*.

8

THE SCIENCE FICTION NOVELS

The 1950s were the decade for the science fiction novel, and at the head of this new, innovative genre was Isaac Asimov.

Aside from the Foundation Series, six adult Asimov novels and six juvenile novels in the David (Lucky) Starr series were published between 1950 and 1958.

After his final Lucky Starr book in 1958, Asimov took a fourteen-year break from science fiction. This was only interrupted by one piece in the genre—*Fantastic Voyage*, which was an adaptation of a screenplay. However, it was fiction that made Asimov his name (primarily from the robot and Foundation books). This success was consolidated by his collection of adult novels of this era—*Pebble in the Sky*; *The Stars, Like Dust*; *The Currents of Space*; *The Caves of Steel*; *The End of Eternity*, and *The Naked Sun*.

Asimov's first novel was originally written under the title *Grow Old with Me*, which was supposed to have come from the Robert Browning poem "Rabbi Ben Ezra." Asimov had not bothered to check the exact line, which was in fact "Grow old along with me," and had tried for two years to get the novel accepted before he realized the embarrassing error and corrected the title.

Although Asimov claimed never to be superstitious, he thought that this mistake over the title had been a jinx. When he did change the name he felt altogether better about the book and, by the merest coincidence, he soon after found a publisher for it. It was finally renamed *Pebble in the Sky* shortly before going to press.

Pebble in the Sky began life in May 1947 at the suggestion of the editor of the pulp magazine *Thrilling Wonder*, Sam Merwin, who wanted a 40,000-word lead novel for a sister magazine called *Startling Stories*.

Asimov was inspired by the idea of writing 40,000 words at two cents per word and collaring a check for 800 dollars. He immediately set about starting the project and dashed off over 12,000 words in little more than a month. He worked steadily on the project throughout the summer, and as the words flowed from his typewriter, he took in parts of the novel to show Merwin. The editor was always pleased with what he read and each time encouraged Asimov to keep up the good work and to deliver the finished novel as soon as he possibly could.

Then, at the end of September 1947, Asimov took the completed manuscript into Sam Merwin's office. Merwin was in a bad mood. There had been a change of direction at the magazine and his boss had decided that they should change the type of stories they were publishing. *Startling Stories*, the boss decreed, was to contain more blood-and-thunder stuff rather than the gentler, more cerebral, *Astounding*-type stories they had been running.

Asimov was not really worried by this because he had a firm commitment from Merwin. Then, a week later, after constantly trying to get in touch with Merwin, Asimov was told over the telephone that the story had been rejected.

He was furious and stormed over to the offices of *Thrilling Wonder* and *Startling Stories* to confront Merwin's boss, Leo Margulies, over the matter. Asimov was intercepted by Merwin, who tried to placate the angry author by telling him that the story might be accepted if he were to completely rewrite it. Merwin began to describe some suggested changes, but Asimov considered his new plot inferior to the original.

Quite out of character, Asimov snatched back the manuscript from Merwin's hand, told him to "go to hell," and stormed out of the office. The two men did not speak for some years, and Asimov never submitted anything to Merwin again.

Asimov later admitted that he had overreacted to the situation and that it was, of course, the editor's prerogative to accept or reject pieces. But he did feel aggrieved at the fact that Merwin had encouraged him to spend his entire summer writing a novel that was then rejected out of hand.

In 1947, at the time Asimov was writing the first draft of what would later turn into *Pebble in the Sky*, there were very few full-length science fiction books. Despite the fact that the general science fiction readership was growing older and the subject matter more mature, the genre was almost exclusively restricted to the pulps. Publishers had not begun to fully appreciate the possibilities science fiction offered to the adult literature market.

It was Fred Pohl who helped resurrect the story and to open up the possibility of Asimov moving into the novel-writing business.

After the debacle with Merwin, Asimov had tried *Grow Old with Me* with Campbell. He said it was too long for them and that he would need to split it into two parts. Neither Asimov nor Campbell could find a natural break point in the story and so, after much deliberation, Asimov had reluctantly consigned his first attempt at a novel to the bottom drawer.

Pohl began to get things moving in early 1948. He passed on the manuscript to his friend Martin Greenberg, who at the time was starting up Gnome Press. Greenberg liked it, but, for a variety of reasons, nothing happened and it languished in his office for almost a year.

In early 1949, Asimov hit one of the lowest points of his career. Nothing seemed to be moving and the story he was working on—the final installment of the Foundation series—"And Now You Don't"—was giving him little in the way of inspiration. Progress with his academic work was slow, and his hopes of moving away from the pulps and into the more grandiose world of book publishing seemed to be going nowhere. Greenberg was sitting on Asimov's first attempted novel and doing nothing with it.

The lucky break came in February 1949, and was again thanks to Pohl. A new science fiction list was starting up at the giant publishing house Doubleday. Initially Asimov and Pohl toyed with the idea of submitting "The Mule" to them, but in the end they settled on *Grow Old with Me*. Pohl claimed it back from the inert Greenberg and submitted it to Doubleday.

By the end of March 1949, the same week Campbell accepted the final story in the Foundation saga, Asimov finally heard news from Pohl that Doubleday was going to accept *Grow Old with Me*. They would pay him 150 dollars for the option, on the condition that he rework it and lengthen it to 70,000 words. If they liked his revision, Doubleday would pay him a further 350 dollars and the standard royalty on sales. Asimov naturally jumped at the chance.

Pebble in the Sky is a rather naive story, which appears almost childishly simplistic when compared to Asimov's later novels. In spite of the fact that "first novel" flashes out at you from every page, it is entertaining and often a more exciting read than some of Asimov's later science fiction. Despite the many weaknesses of the book, *Pebble in the Sky* is still on sale today and continues to do well.

In Joseph Schwartz, the lead character, Asimov chose a most unconventional hero. Schwartz is a nobody, a retired tailor projected by the purest accident into a world tens of thousands of years in his future.

Throughout the book, Schwartz is in a perpetual state of bewilderment over the situation in which he has found himself, and until the final pages, it is the subsidiary characters who do most of the work.

All the action in *Pebble in the Sky* takes place on Earth in the year 927 of the Galactic Era. The planet is suffering from the aftermath of a global nuclear war; much of the land area is radioactive and uninhabitable. The Earth is viewed as a leper planet by the rest of the galaxy, and the people of Earth call all who live beyond the planet "outsiders." The population is kept in equilibrium by voluntary euthanasia at the age of sixty, and the planet is held under uneasy dominion by the Galactic Empire, who deal savagely with any form of resistance.

Following a minor nuclear accident in a Chicago laboratory in the late 1940s, Schwartz is projected thousands of years into the future. He immediately finds himself embroiled in a convoluted plot involving a power-hungry government official, Secretary Balkis; a scientist, Dr. Shekt (who has developed a device that increases the intelligence of humans); and a tall, handsome academic called Bel Arvardan, who is on a crusade to prove that the human race began on a single planet and that the world in question is Earth.

Schwartz finds himself in Dr. Shekt's clinic in the city of Chica—the burned-out, depopulated shell of what was once his hometown of Chicago. Here he is used as a human guinea pig in experiments conducted by Shekt using his mind machine—the synapsifier. When Schwartz is also mistaken for an underground spy by the evil Balkis, the plot begins to take on a multidimensional aspect.

Asimov's editor at Doubleday, Walter Bradbury, thought that the plot needed a romantic element, something rarely required in pulp stories. Asimov then wrote in a relationship between Dr. Arvardan and Dr. Shekt's daughter, Pola.

The climax of the novel is reached when Dr. Shekt, Pola, Arvardan, and Schwartz are all captured and held by the corrupt Balkis, who is about to unleash an Earth rebellion using germ warfare that will wipe out most of the population of the Galaxy and leave the Earth immune.

Naturally it is Schwartz, the most unlikely character in the story, who saves the day. Because of a side effect induced by the synapsifier, he now possesses amazing mental powers, in particular the ability to kill and injure with his mind.

However, as far as Schwartz is concerned, all the people he has encountered are in some way using him. Confused and still totally disorientated by his experiences, he hardly knows which way to turn and has to be persuaded to use his talent on the side of the good guys—Arvardan and the Shekts.

Of course, we have seen almost all these characters and much of this plot before. Dr. Shekt is an amalgamation of Ebling Mis and Dr. Darell from "And Now You Don't," the final section of the Foundation series, a story that Asimov was working on at almost exactly the same time as *Pebble in the Sky*. Balkis is a clichéd baddy, a blend of Brodrig, Cleon II's favorite in the Foundation story "The General," and Wienis from Foundation ("The Mayors"). The entire concept of a corrupt underling scheming to obtain power is in essence the same plot device used several times in *The Foundation Trilogy*. Asimov clearly had a penchant for creating the victor from the underdog, so that Schwartz may be superimposed on Bayta Darell, Lathan Devers, and indeed the Foundation itself.

Asimov was also clearly interested in mental powers and mind-altering devices at this time. The synapsifier is a device from the same area of science as Dr. Darrel's Mind Static Device, and Schwartz's artificially induced mental talents are modeled on the natural powers of the Mule.

However, a much deeper connection between *Pebble in the Sky* and *The Foundation Trilogy* lies in the choice of setting. If one is to survey Asimov's fiction output as a whole, there is clearly an overall structure to his stories. This has led to the idea of "Asimov's galactic novels," as advertised on the jackets of the relevant books, a term used to describe those novels and short stories that take place within the structure of the Galactic Empire.

The links between Asimov's stories grew more intricate with each publication. Initially he had no master plan, but the idea of a succession of interlinking stories grew more conspicuous each time. In *Pebble in the Sky* we have references to Trantor, and it is clear that it is set in the very early days of the same Galactic Empire as that of the Foundation stories.[1]

In *Pebble in the Sky*, we also, once again, have the concept of the galactic civilization losing its roots and forgetting the fact that it originated on one planet. This was an idea Asimov explored at length in a number of his novels and short stories of the 1950s (and indeed returned to during the 1980s).

Throughout Asimov's fiction of the 1940s and '50s we have three independent threads. There are the robot short stories and novels, set either in the near future, as with the Susan Calvin, Powell, and Donovan stories; those set in the not-too-distant-future, as in the case of *The Caves of Steel* and *The Naked Sun*; and thirdly, the Empire novels. The first group have no link with the empire; those in the second category are linked only tenuously.

The Galactic Empire books are all set amid a pangalactic civilization where thousands of worlds are solely inhabited by the human race. Humanity has forgotten where it originated. It possesses highly advanced technology but no robots.

On more than one occasion, Asimov clearly stipulated that his Galactic Empire was not based on robot technology. The reason for this was not made clear until the Foundation books of the 1980s, which will be discussed in the final chapter.

The only real connection between the two robot novels of the fifties,

---

[1] Confusingly, in an afterword tacked to the end of the Granada edition of *Foundation's Edge* in 1982, Asimov asserts that "the events in *Pebble in the Sky* take place when the First Galactic Empire was at the height of its power." This is misleading because in the early Foundation books we are repeatedly told that the First Galactic Empire had endured for tens of thousands of years before Hari Seldon, and that it was only during the era in which he lived that the Empire had begun to wane.

The most important consequence of the positive reception given to *Pebble in the Sky* was the fact that it opened the doors for further projects with Doubleday.

Even before the publication of *Pebble in the Sky,* as early as October 1949, Asimov had approached Walter Bradbury with the idea for another novel. Interested, Bradbury asked Asimov for an outline and two sample chapters. Asimov had always hated working with outlines and had avoided them if at all possible. He knew that with his novel in the shops, he had reached a crucial stage in his career, and that he was not merely proposing a short story for Campbell. He was with a large international publisher and he had to play by their rules—at least for the time being.

He immediately set about writing an outline and the sample chapters and delivered them to Bradbury a few weeks later. Within a week Bradbury had read them and was not impressed. He invited Asimov to lunch and explained his reasons for rejecting the first samples. Asimov was overwriting, he was being overdescriptive, and there was far too much exposition. He had hit the classic "second novel syndrome": naiveté could be excused in a first novel, but by the time of the second, such errors were no longer acceptable—Asimov had to now consider himself to be a professional novelist.

Asimov went away with his tail between his legs and had a second try at the new novel. Bradbury had said that he wanted Asimov to start from scratch and write six new chapters. This Asimov did, and the second attempt was finished in February 1950—a month after *Pebble in the Sky* was published.

By early March, this second draft was back on Asimov's desk. It was still overwritten. This time the script was covered in red ink. But there was a note attached to the manuscript asking Asimov for a third try.

Asimov was shaken. After the fantastic beginning to the year 1950, he now felt like, as he put it "a fired science fiction writer."[1]

On April 1, he tore up the second version of what was to become *The Stars, Like Dust* and began a third version. A week later he took the first new chapter to Bradbury. He liked it and urged Asimov to continue along the same lines. By May 7, Asimov had finished the first third of the book as requested by Bradbury and mailed it. A week later, he heard from

---

[1] *In Memory Yet Green* by Isaac Asimov. Doubleday, New York, 1979 (p 586).

The Caves of Steel and *The Naked Sun*, and the Galactic Empire of *Pebble in the Sky, The Stars, Like Dust, The Currents of Space*, and *The Foundation Trilogy* is that the two robot novels give accounts of the very earliest days of colonizing the galaxy.

The two robot novels are set mere hundreds of years in the future, when the Earth has colonized a mere handful of planets. This is a time during which the isolation of the Earth is starting as the colonists sever their links with the mother planet. *Pebble in the Sky* is set several thousand years later when the separation is complete and—I feel, quite unrealistically—the human race has forgotten from whence it came. *Foundation* begins over eleven thousand years later when the great empire is beginning to crumble.

It is clear that Asimov had no great master plan before he began to write his Galactic Empire stories and novels. Unlike Tolkien, there was never a time when Asimov sat down and carefully organized his mythology; Asimov did not work like that. The mythology simply grew and became increasingly elaborate, reaching its logical conclusion with the final four Foundation novels written during the last ten years of his life.

Asimov began the revision of *Grow Old with Me* requested by Doubleday in April 1949, almost two years after he had started the first version. On April 6, he realized that he had titled the book upon a misquote and immediately changed it to *Grow Old Along with Me*.

The reworking of the novel was difficult and time-consuming, coming at a troublesome time for Asimov. Not only did he feel ill with abdominal pains, he and Gertrude were in the process of moving to Boston. It took him over six weeks to finish.

It was Walter Bradbury at Doubleday who suggested that the title should be changed. He thought *Grow Old Along with Me* had an over-romantic ring to it, and Asimov agreed. Asimov took a line from the text, and his first novel, earmarked for January 1950 publication, was at last christened *Pebble in the Sky*.

In the autumn before publication, Doubleday asked for a jacket picture of the author and Asimov gave them a holiday snap of him and Gertrude, taken some five years earlier when he was only twenty-five. They cut it in two and used the Isaac Asimov half for a number of his future books. Asimov was very pleased with the picture—it was flattering and gave him what he liked to think of as a Cary Grant, matinee-idol look. As late as the 1970s Asimov claimed that he would like to still use the picture, but acknowledged the fact that he had aged considerably while his picture had not. During the 1950s he was beginning to receive an increasingly large quantity of mail from admiring women readers, and it was Gertrude who pointed out, toward the end of the decade, that he could not carry on using the same picture taken when he was twenty-five, especially as any female admirers meeting him for the first time at an SF conference would be terribly disappointed.

Although amusing, this story is also revealing. Asimov's vast ego and his thinly veiled vanity went hand in hand. He was clearly self-conscious of the fact that he was aging, and must have been increasingly insecure about his own looks as he grew older. Ironically, to the majority of women who expressed interest in Asimov, his most attractive qualities were his intellect, his sense of humor, and, later, his fame and wealth. His looks would have come far down the list. Asimov had never considered himself to be a physically attractive man, so when he found a highly flattering picture of himself, he milked it for all it was worth.

Pebble in the Sky was published on January 19, 1950. It received a number of reviews, most of which were favorable, and it began to sell well from day one. Asimov, unaware that there was such a thing as a clippings agency or that the publishers automatically forwarded reviews to authors, rushed out to buy every newspaper and magazine he could find for the first two weeks the book was on sale.

Asimov's friends within science fiction, including those whose opinions he most respected, Robert Heinlein and Sprague de Camp, wrote to congratulate him and to praise the book. Even the dean of Boston University Medical School, where Asimov was teaching at the time, told him that he and the college were pleased to be identified with the book.

Then, much to Asimov's surprise, the book was accepted by a book club. Admittedly, it was a tiny outfit called the Unicorn Press, but they paid a thousand dollars for the book club rights. The money was to be split evenly between Doubleday and Asimov. Until then, Asimov had had no idea that a book made money from serialization, syndication, and foreign rights sales after it was initially signed to a publisher.

Fred Pohl, who was once again acting as Asimov's agent, that Doubleday wanted this version and that they would pay an advance of 750 dollars. Asimov gave a deep sigh of relief—not only did Doubleday want it, but they were offering an advance half again the size of that given for *Pebble in the Sky*.

Once over this hurdle, things moved quickly. Asimov had the book finished by September. Even before it was completed, Horace Gold, the editor of a new magazine to rival *Astounding*, called *Galaxy Science Fiction*, had heard about it and wanted to serialize it. However, there was a catch. Gold wanted to introduce another element into the story—a character who was looking for a secret document that would eventually turn out to be the United States Constitution.

Asimov instantly rejected the idea, complaining, quite accurately, that this twist was totally unbelievable. The setting of the novel was in the distant future, tens of thousands of years away. What chance was there that such an obscure document would be discovered in such a time, and more importantly, who would give a damn about it anyway? But Gold was insistent and made the addition a provision of acceptance. He pointed out that it could be added to the magazine version and taken out again for the book.

Asimov considered selling it to Campbell, but at that time, Campbell had entered the most extreme phase of his interest in mysticism, and *Astounding* was full of articles about the new pseudoscience of Dianetics, of which Asimov strongly disapproved. Instead of telling Gold what to do with his ridiculous idea and passing it on to Campbell, Asimov capitulated and wrote in the subplot as requested.

When Asimov next met up with Bradbury, he told him about Gold's offer. Smiling, he related the fact that Gold wanted to make his silly addition to the tale. To Asimov's horror, Bradbury thought the suggestion a good one and pushed Asimov into including the new twist in the novel version as well as the magazine copy.

Asimov has said that *The Stars, Like Dust* is his least favorite novel. He cited two reasons for this. Firstly, it was a devil of a book to write (and the last book for which he ever agreed to do an outline). Secondly, he always hated the fact that he was forced into adding the Constitution subplot.

By the time the first part of the serialization of *The Stars, Like Dust* had appeared in the December 1950 issue of *Galaxy*, and prior to its publication in book form, Asimov had already begun to think of the next novel.

Meanwhile, his earlier works were beginning to appear in book form. Martin Greenberg's Gnome Press published *I, Robot* in 1950, and early in 1951 he had accepted the Foundation stories that had appeared in *Astounding*.

In March 1951, Asimov sent Walter Bradbury a sample chapter of his new novel. It was to be a pangalactic thriller, full of intrigue and entitled *The Currents of Space*. Bradbury immediately liked the sample and signed the book to Doubleday without further ado. By now he had sufficient confidence in Asimov's ability to dispense with an outline. He also realized that writing outlines and endless sample chapters was not the way Asimov worked best. Being a good editor, Bradbury played up his author's strengths and tried to circumvent his weaknesses in the best way he could.

This time, Asimov gave the serialization rights to *Astounding* and was relieved that Campbell only required minimal alterations to the novel version. By April 1952, the book was finished and bought by Campbell. At three cents per word, the 70,000-word novel earned Asimov the largest check he had ever seen—1,890 dollars (after Pohl's deduction)—and the story was serialized later that year.

Asimov himself was now gaining confidence as a novelist. By early 1952, he had had four novels published—*Pebble in the Sky* and *I, Robot* in 1950, and *The Stars, Like Dust* and *Foundation* in 1951—and *The Currents of Space* was completed and scheduled for December publication. As well as writing for *Fantasy and Science Fiction* and Gold's *Galaxy*, he was continuing to write short stories for a number of magazines, including his regular contributions to Campbell. Finding the writing of science fiction novels easy, he decided he would branch out a little.

At about the time he created the plot for *The Currents of Space*, Asimov decided to try his hand at a juvenile science fiction novel. He had heard *The Lone Ranger* radio series and thought that there might be an opening for a television series called *Space Ranger*. He put the idea to Fred Pohl and Walter Bradbury, who both thought it had possibilities.

Nothing ever came of the television idea, but as a result of that first suggestion Asimov did create the Space Ranger series. These became immensely successful books for the young teenage market and established Asimov as a writer who went beyond the adult science fiction field.

During the 1950s Asimov wrote six Space Ranger novels, all of which involved the hero David Starr. They were all set within the Solar System, hence titles such as: *Lucky Starr and the Pirates of the Asteroids* and *Lucky Starr and the Moons of Jupiter*. Initially Starr was given the name David— a name clearly prominent in Asimov's mind at the time. During that summer of 1951, Gertrude was heavily pregnant with their first son, whom they called David. However, soon after the first book appeared and Asimov had begun to work on the second, he decided that the name David was a little too pedestrian for a space ranger. He could not change it but he could give him a nickname—"Lucky."

The Space Ranger books were unique in that they were the only ones Asimov ever wrote under a pseudonym. It is unclear exactly why he decided to do this, but it can only be supposed that he was anxious to keep his adult and juvenile fiction separate so as not to mislead fans. After much deliberation over the choice of a pen name, Asimov chose Paul French. He wanted a name that had little color and would not compete with his real name. Later, he realized that there was, after all, no need for a pseudonym and dropped the idea.

Walter Bradbury thought that *The Currents of Space* was Asimov's best book up until that time, and even before it had gone to press in the summer of 1952 he had asked Asimov to think about a fourth novel for Doubleday.

Asimov was finding that he had developed a neat working routine with his books and their serializations. He had a verbal agreement with Gnome Press that they would publish alternately with Doubleday. So Gnome had *I, Robot* and the Foundation series while Doubleday published the other novels. Asimov established the same pattern with Campbell at *Astounding* and Gold at *Galaxy*. Gold had had *The Stars, Like Dust*, and so *The Currents of Space* went to Campbell. Thinking about beginning a new novel, in April 1952, Asimov visited Gold and suggested the idea of tackling a robot novel as opposed to a short story. Gold immediately liked the idea and suggested that Asimov try writing a robot detective novel centered on a human-robot police duo.

After working through the idea, Asimov eventually came up with the plot of what became his fourth novel with Doubleday, *The Caves of Steel*.

It was during the writing of this that Asimov was becoming more and more disillusioned with Gnome Press. Asimov and Martin Greenberg had been on very friendly terms during their entire partnership, but Asimov was beginning to grow frustrated with Greenberg's inefficient business system. In May 1953, Asimov received advance copies of *Second Foundation*, the last in the series of Foundation books, and to celebrate, Greenberg invited Asimov out to lunch with a view to discussing their next publication.

Asimov liked Greenberg on a personal level, but when Gnome was compared to the ultraefficient Doubleday, he began to realize that he would be foolish to give Gnome any more of his books. Greenberg did not provide proper statements, so that Asimov never knew how many copies each of his books had sold. Consequently, he never knew for sure what was owed him. Gnome was forever in murky financial waters and paid Asimov in an ad hoc manner, just managing to keep their heads above water. At this stage in his writing career, such a mess was the last thing that Asimov needed. He told Greenberg that *Second Foundation* would be the last book he would do with Gnome.

Angered, Greenberg declared that Asimov was breaking their agreement. Instead of pointing out the fact that their agreement—alternate books between Gnome and Doubleday—only extended to the four books Gnome had already published, Asimov simply asked for the latest statements on the three books already in the shops. Greenberg was caught; he had obviously done nothing about them, and gave in. Despite this fissure over future works, Greenberg and Asimov remained friends, and the writer finally secured all the money owed him without unpleasantness. Greenberg operated honestly; it was merely his gross inefficiency that rattled the ultraorganized and clear-minded Asimov.

Everyone involved was delighted with *The Caves of Steel*. Asimov was always very proud of this, his first foray into the detective genre. Even Gold suggested only minor alterations before handing over a check, which, after Pohl's commission, provided Asimov and Gertrude another 2,520 dollars to add to their swelling bank account.

While working on *The Caves of Steel*, Asimov had not neglected his magazine writing. It is a common misconception that Asimov gave up short story writing when he began to make a name for himself as a novelist. In fact he wrote as many short stories during the fifties as he had done when the medium had been his only outlet.

By the middle of 1952, Asimov realized that he really ought to try to use his position with Doubleday to maximize the potential of his shorter pieces, and suggested to Bradbury that he would like to have a collection published. To Asimov's surprise Bradbury immediately accepted the idea and asked for a sample story.

Asimov already had an idea for the first story in the collection. Although he was never politically active, he had always voted for the Democrats and was particularly incensed by the rise of McCarthyism, a political stance that Asimov saw as rapidly eroding the fabric of the U.S. democratic system. He decided that he wanted to write a story that would portray his feelings on the matter without being overtly political. From this idea came "The Martian Way," a tale centered upon the interaction between a reactionary and powerful Earth government and a small group of Martian colonists who make their living from scavenging the discarded hulls of Earth spaceships. Asimov used the story as an allegory of McCarthyism, taking the side of the persecuted colonists in their struggle to overcome the extremism of the Earth government.

Asimov was very pleased with the story, which became the lead in *The Martian Way and Other Stories,* but was amazed that no one ever wrote to him about the symbolism of the piece. The allegory, he later concluded, must have been too subtle.

A frequently criticized aspect of Asimov's writing was highlighted in "The Martian Way" in its original form: it did not involve a single female character. When Walter Bradbury pointed this out, Asimov dutifully went away and worked in a subplot involving the wife of one of the Martian colonists. Typically, this character turned out to be a moaning, nagging housewife, overdone and stereotyped.

In November 1953, as *The Caves of Steel* was in production, Asimov tried to formulate an idea for the next novel but found nothing would come. Any other author would perhaps have been content with the fact that he had had seven works of fiction published in the space of four years, with another about to be published; not so Asimov. Someone had mentioned to him that the Boston University Library had a complete collection of *Time* magazine dating back to 1928. Thinking they might just provide the seed for the next project, he began to work his way through the archive, month by month, starting with the first issue in the collection and working up to November 1953.

Asimov became such a frequent user of the collection that before long he had earned the nickname among the library staff of "the *Time* professor." But the astonishing thing about the exercise was that it worked. Asimov had only reached the second volume, editions taken from the second half of 1928, when he saw a tiny advertisement that immediately sparked off an idea.

He was glancing through the ads section and his eye was caught by what looked like the shape of the mushroom cloud produced by an atomic bomb. Bearing in mind that the magazine was from the late twenties, Asimov was taken aback by the image. It was, of course, merely an initial impression, and when he looked closely he realized it was the Old Faithful geyser of Yellowstone National Park, but it got him thinking: What if an advertisement using the mushroom cloud had really been there? What could it mean?

The answer, in what became *The End of Eternity*, was time travel.

Asimov had written about time travel before. In fact, his very first serious attempt at science fiction had been "Cosmic Corkscrew," which related the story of a time traveler who had journeyed into the distant future and found the Earth totally empty. Time travel also provided the opening to *Pebble in the Sky* and transported Schwartz into the Chicago of the future. But, in *Pebble in the Sky*, it is merely a device and discarded after its primary use. *The End of Eternity* was different and a first for Asimov in that it dealt *exclusively* with time travel and created an entire universe, past, present, and future, built upon the principle.

The first version of *The End of Eternity* was of novelette length and was written in two months, from the beginning of December 1953 to the first week of February 1954. Asimov tried to sell it to Horace Gold at *Galaxy* and, within days, received a surprising rejection. Gold did not like the story but suggested that Asimov completely rewrite it. Asimov totally disagreed, told Gold so, and instead tried it as a sample for a novel with Doubleday.

Here it received a very different reception. Bradbury liked the story straightaway and immediately offered Asimov a contract for the complete, full-length novel.

Asimov's advances from Doubleday had been steadily growing since *Pebble in the Sky*, and Bradbury confidently offered 1,250 dollars for *The End of Eternity*. Asimov was naturally encouraged by the fact that Doubleday was becoming more aware of his talents. The house obviously now viewed him as one of its more important writers.

Asimov never did manage to place *The End of Eternity* with *Astounding, Galaxy,* or any other magazine of the time. Gold was eventually persuaded to accept the novel version, but then declared that publication in *Galaxy* would have to be delayed for a year. Because, under the terms of the contract with *Galaxy,* the book version could not be published until after it had appeared in the magazine, this would mean a wait of over a year before the novel could be put into the shops. Bradbury was not interested in this, and so the deal with *Galaxy* fell through.

Asimov then turned to *Astounding,* but Campbell rejected it because he was oversubscribed with novels at the time. As a consequence Asimov had to accept the loss of around three thousand dollars and launch his novel without prior serialization.

The End of Eternity is, I believe, Asimov's most complete and most entertaining novel up until that time. In almost all of the author's other work there was invariably a missing element—love interest.

Despite the fact that Asimov was an incorrigible flirt and in later years made no bones about the fact that he was a practicing ladies' man and adulterer, until *The Gods Themselves* in the 1970s, he seems to have been embarrassed about including sex or romance in his fiction. This mold was almost completely broken with *The End of Eternity*. I say "almost completely" because, although the framework of the story is built around a personal relationship between the hero and heroine, the one "sex scene" is a mighty disappointment.

Hearing that Isaac had included a "sex scene" in his latest novel, Gertrude excitedly asked if she could read it. She read the passage, looked at her husband, and said: "I thought you said there was a sex scene in this? I couldn't find it." She reread it, and smiled when she reached the appropriate section:

. . . He did not know what she meant, but suddenly he didn't care. He seemed in flames. He put out his arms clumsily, gropingly. She did not resist, but melted and coalesced with him . . .[1]

"Well, where's the bedroom scene?" she said.

"You've just passed it,"[2] replied a red-faced Asimov.

In some ways this incident tells us more about Gertrude than Isaac. If, as Asimov repeatedly told his friends (and after Gertrude's death, his readers), Gertrude was completely uninterested in sex, why would she be so keen to read a sex scene in *The End of Eternity*? Perhaps she was simply amazed that after so many years of writing, her husband had at last attempted to tackle the subject, but it also begs the question: Can the blame for the Asimovs' almost sexless marriage be placed entirely with Gertrude? After all, we only have Asimov's word that he discovered his own sexual prowess as a consequence of his first adulterous encounter. He would say that. Asimov had the voice to express his case, but we can only speculate about Gertrude. On the one hand, we have Asimov's declaration that he only really discovered sex outside his marriage, and on the other is the fact that he could never express his supposed seductive talent in his writing, which, after all the reasons have been taken into account, still niggles as an oddity. Because we do not have any written or verbal account of Gertrude's side of the story, we will perhaps never know the truth.

If we put aside Asimov's clumsy attempts at fictionalizing sex ("coalesced with him" is so typically clinical and scientific of him, and heaven only knows what "gropingly" means), *The End of Eternity* has everything else a popular novel needs. It has a well-thought-out and convincing plot, adventure, suspense, and the reader immediately identifies with the main protagonists, backing them all the way, not merely, as with so much of Asimov's fiction, because they are good, wholesome, or correct in their actions, but because they are in love with each other.

[1] *The End of Eternity* by Isaac Asimov. Panther, 1959 (p. 56). Originally published by Doubleday, New York, 1955.
[2] *In Joy Still Felt* by Isaac Asimov. Doubleday, New York, 1980 (p. 116, slightly paraphrased).

The story revolves around the hero, Andrew Harlan, who lives in Eternity—this is the "nowhen" outside time, where time travelers, "the Eternals," live and work. The purpose of Eternity and the job of the Eternals is to monitor human history and to make changes in time to steer humanity along what they deem to be the most desirable path. Eternals journey into different eras and make subtle calculated changes to perfect the future according to their master scheme.

Of course, the problem is that by trying to create the path of least resistance, the Eternals merely succeed in producing stagnation to the point where humankind never explores space and eventually dies out. The Eternals do not realize the damage they are causing and see themselves as taking the moral high ground. They will do anything possible to preserve the status quo—undo lives, destroy what would have been great artistic or scientific achievements, "unmarry," kill, create changes so that living people are never born, all for what they perceive to be the greater good.

Before long the reader becomes aware that the system is rotten to the core. At the same time it is clear that such a gargantuan entity as Eternity cannot be brought down, nor, according to Asimov, can humanity be readjusted to anything like a normal evolutionary path by anything less than the power of love.

Enter on the scene the beautiful Noÿs Lambent. Noÿs is not an Eternal, but a normal mortal, a "Timer." Despite the fact that personal relationships between Eternals and Timers are strictly forbidden, Harlan falls in love with her, and this is the central premise of the story.

Noÿs is to be involved in a Reality Change, a rearrangement of the present to suit the calculated plans of the Eternals. If the change occurs, Noÿs, Harlan discovers, will no longer exist. Naturally, he is horrified by this idea and decides to interfere with Eternity to save his relationship.

As the plot unfolds we learn what the Eternals know of the history of humanity. It turns out that time travel was first developed in the twenty-fourth century by a scientist called Vikkor Mallansohn, who created a thing called the Temporal Field. This is accepted as part of Primitive History. But our hero Harlan, who happens to be an expert in Primitive History, discovers a paradox. Mallansohn could not possibly have developed the Temporal Field because the mathematics needed to work it out were not invented until the twenty-seventh century.

At the same point as he realizes this, he is given the task of teaching a new junior Eternal, a "cub," who has just appeared on the scene. The cub's name is Brinsley Cooper, and he was born, we learn, in the seventy-eighth century.

Harlan's job is to teach the young man Primitive History—Harlan's specialty. Before long, Harlan has put two and two together. The trouble is, he makes it three. He concludes that Brinsley Cooper is to be taught Primitive History so that he can be sent back to the twenty-fourth century to teach Mallansohn the twenty-seventh century mathematics he needs to create Eternity in the first place. In other words, the whole of Eternity, this huge edifice that is working to help man by traveling through hundreds of thousands of centuries, is built on a paradox.

As the story progresses, intermingled with the increasingly complicated relationship between Noÿs and Harlan, we learn that Harlan's theory is wrong in only one crucial detail. His job is not to teach Brinsley Cooper so that he can educate Mallansohn. Cooper *is* Mallansohn.

We soon learn that Cooper, who was indeed born in the seventy-eighth century, has to return to the twenty-fourth, where he encounters a man called Mallansohn. He tries to teach him the theory of time travel, but before he succeeds, Mallansohn dies in an accident. In desperation, Cooper, unable to travel back to his own century, adopts Mallansohn's identity and eventually develops time travel himself. The big problem is that Harlan, Cooper, Mallansohn, and, by implication, Noÿs Lambent and the entire cast of Eternity are involved in a time loop that must never be broken. Harlan has to keep teaching Cooper, who has to keep traveling back in time and developing time travel so that Eternity is created and Harlan is born to teach Cooper, who travels back in time . . .

Needless to say, with the interference of Noÿs Lambent, the loop breaks, Cooper is sent back to the wrong century, and Eternity is threatened with nonexistence.

Harlan and the reader learn all about the time loop from another crucial character in the story—Senior Computer Laban Twissell. It is he who decides, after Cooper returns to the wrong century, that the only chance Eternity has of surviving is for Harlan to go back to whenever Cooper has mistakenly ended up and to put him to rights. Harlan agrees, on the conditions that Noÿs goes with him and that once the mission is completed, they may be together. Twissell can do nothing but agree to the terms, and so the search begins for the location of Cooper lost somewhere in the primitive era.

Having narrowed down the time period to which Cooper could have been sent to the first third of the twentieth century, Harlan soon realizes that the only way to find Cooper's exact location is by looking through his specialist collection of magazines from the twentieth century.

So we have come full circle, back to the original inspiration for the plot. Harlan spends weeks going through his vast collection, searching for a clue, and eventually he finds it, an advertisement that reads:

> ALL THE
> TALK
> OF THE
> MARKET[1]

Not only do the first letters read down the page spell ATOM, but the real giveaway is that the entire advertisement is surrounded by, you've guessed it, a line drawing of a mushroom cloud.

Even now, close to the end of the book, we still have one more twist to go. Harlan takes Noÿs with him to intercept Cooper. They arrive in 1932. Cooper is nowhere to be seen. Suddenly, Harlan draws a blaster on Noÿs. He has concluded that she is from the far "upwhen," a little-known region in Eternity that has cut itself off from the Eternals and will not allow them into their time. Her purpose all along, Harlan believes, was to bring about the destruction of Eternity. He cannot face that prospect even though he loves her, and so he has reached the conclusion that Noÿs must die.

Naturally, Asimov gives us a happy ending. Harlan was right again—almost. Noÿs *is* from the far upwhen and her people do want to destroy Eternity. They perceive it as being the crucial factor that eventually destroys humanity. From overprotection, the human race never innovates and eventually suffocates on its own single, dried-up world—a scenario completely opposite to the concept of the Galactic Empire,

[1] *The End of Eternity* (p. 169).

which lies as the cornerstone of the Foundation books and other "Empire" novels.

Of course, Noÿs convinces Harlan that they should leave Cooper alone. Stuck in an era three hundred years before the birth of Vikkor Mallansohn, Cooper is powerless and cannot create Eternity. By the nature of time itself, as soon as Harlan decides not to kill Noÿs and to stay with her in the twentieth century, Eternity instantly vanishes, leaving the hero and heroine unaffected and safe in a time before Eternity was created.

There are a number of critics who think that *The End of Eternity* is Asimov's most satisfying novel and rightly see it as his most complex work.

Soon after it was completed, Asimov began working on a sequel to *The Caves of Steel* entitled *The Naked Sun,* which was published two years after *The End of Eternity,* in 1957. Aside from juvenile fiction (*Lucky Starr and the Rings of Saturn* was published in 1958) and his novelization of *Fantastic Voyage* in 1966, the publication of *The Naked Sun* marked the beginning of a fourteen-year hiatus in Asimov's science fiction writing.

With the exception of Asimov's later novels, including *The Gods Themselves,* two more robot detective novels and four more Foundation books, the titles I have discussed in this chapter constitute Asimov's entire collection of science fiction novels. They are all still in print and have sold countless millions in their various editions and translations during the past four decades. *Pebble in the Sky* sold over 13,000 copies in hardback during its first eighteen months in bookstores.

The work Asimov returned to during the last ten years of his life sold in phenomenal numbers, but because his first eleven major works of fiction (including the first three Foundation books and the first two robot collections) have been selling consistently for decades, it is upon these that his reputation rests and it is these books that turned him into a household name. Even as early as 1950, Campbell had called Asimov "one of the greatest science fiction writers in the world."[1] In 1974, the critic Joseph Patrouch Jr. declared: "For many people the name Isaac Asimov *is* science fiction."[2]

[1] *In Memory Still Green* (p. 613).
[2] *The Science Fiction of Isaac Asimov* by Joseph Patrouch Jr. Doubleday, New York (1974).

So what is it that makes Asimov's novels of the fifties so incredibly popular? There are many who are vocally dismissive of a lot of Asimov's work. They complain that his books are overlong, the characters wooden, that his novels contain too much talking and not enough action, that the plots are, at times, simply unbelievable. Yet, despite these comments—all, in degrees, true in one book or another—Asimov's novels continue to sell and to appeal to new generations of avid fans. Science fiction has changed enormously since the days in which *Foundation* was first conceived. But the old guard of Clarke, Heinlein, Herbert, and, most importantly, Asimov, has still maintained its premier position, not only commercially but also in the hearts of the science fiction readers.

I believe that Asimov's success lies in his rare and great talent as a storyteller. His plots are intricate but entirely believable. His ability to use dialogue as a plot driver is peerless. But probably Asimov's greatest quality is his skill in creating an alternative reality that is scientifically self-consistent, logical, and entertaining to read about.

Asimov's short stories are often frivolous, constructed upon a single idea or a throwaway final line. The notable exceptions to this are "Nightfall" and a few of the robot stories. The latter are, of course, based on the grandiose construct of the Laws of Robotics rather than a cast-off one-liner.

In the best of his novels, Asimov creates a perfect pace, unraveling the plot as though he were peeling back the levels of explanation of a scientific principle. He also has a powerful voice, one that is instantly friendly and attractive.

One journalist described Asimov's writing in the following way:

> Why do I find his writing style so special? I'll tell you. He talks to you, not at you. He is there in the living room, sitting on the divan, drinking a cup of left-over supper coffee. He just dropped in to say hello. An old friend. A good listener. You know, that nice guy with the firm handshake and the friendly, crinkly smile.[1]

---

[1] "Thelma's Thoughts" by Thelma Zimmerman. From the *Boston Globe*.

Certainly, Asimov's writing can be pedestrian, workmanlike, even, at times, obtuse. His gift for describing the various ways in which his characters speak is unparalleled; no other writer has used so many adverbs in this context—a range extending from "screechingly" to "boomingly." Yet, despite these faults (faults that never seemed to be ironed out in later work, as similar awful adverbs crop up in *Forward the Foundation*, published in 1993), Asimov is simply one of the most readable writers who ever committed words to the page. It is his old-fashioned storytelling ability and his warmth of expression that make his books so successful; no matter how techno-based or dehumanized the plot may be, the reader is instantly drawn into the Asimovian landscape.

In the same way that Asimov never really improved his use of English, he also never lost his voice. It is interesting to observe that editors seemed to appreciate that Asimov's writing should, within reason, be left alone, and the sometimes terrible use of English was kept in deliberately. Without such phrases, they realized, much of Asimov's fiction would no longer be "Asimovian."

At the pinnacle of his powers, he managed to thread together all the aspects required in a novel. The book that demonstrates Asimov at his peak is *The End of Eternity*, and even as he was writing it during 1954, he was beginning to realize that the rich creative vein of science fiction he had tapped since he was eighteen was fast running dry.

Luckily for Asimov, he had other writing talents, and as one area of work began to fade, a new one opened up. Turning from science fiction, he began to explore the possibilities in the world of nonfiction.

9

FANTASTIC VOYAGE TO DIVORCE

From his very first day as a full-time writer ensconced in the attic office of his suburban home, Asimov set about changing the course of his career. According to his diary, the date was July 1, 1958. From that moment he never looked back.

The sixties mark the era during which Asimov wrote very little fiction, but it was the period during which he launched his career as a highly successful nonfiction author and blossomed as a public speaker.

Back in 1957 Asimov had joined a small agency run by an entrepreneur called Harry Walker. It specialized in placing public speakers for functions at venues along the East Coast. Within days of joining the agency Asimov had his first engagement. It was a few miles outside Boston and the fee was seventy dollars.

Asimov loved talking at meetings, taking on the role of an after-dinner speaker or lecturing on popular science. He quickly realized that this could provide another string to his bow and a further source of income. He was also aware that his public appearances would certainly not harm his book sales and might even enhance his profile within the publishing world.

The relationship with Harry Walker did not last long. Even before leaving Boston University, during the early spring of 1958, Asimov and the Harry Walker Agency went their separate ways—after Asimov was booked as a comic when he thought he was required to deliver a talk on space exploration. The evening was a fiasco and Asimov immediately severed all contact with the agency.

This did not appear to hamper his progress as a speaker. He had already gained a considerable reputation in the Boston area and sometimes traveled as far afield as New York or Philadelphia to deliver a talk. By the end of the fifties and little over a year after embarking on his writing career full-time, Asimov was commanding a fee of five hundred dollars for a speech and had no need to hand over any agency commission.

According to popular mythology, every adult alive at the time remembers what they were doing the day President Kennedy was assassinated. Thanks to his public speaking, in later years Asimov could clearly remember where he was. On November 22, 1963, he had been booked to talk in New York. Upon hearing the tragic news from Dallas, he and the organizers automatically assumed that the hall that night would be empty. Asimov offered to forgo the fee and return home. The organizers suggested that he wait to see what happened. To their complete amazement, come 7:30 P.M. the hall was packed and a number of people had to be turned away at the door. It appeared that everyone wanted to get out and do something to take their minds off the calamitous events of the day.

Asimov began the talk by saying that he had been planning to deliver a lighthearted speech but because of the shooting he felt that he ought to speak on a more serious subject. Detecting disquiet at this and realizing that what they really wanted was a lighthearted talk, he rapidly changed his mind and, instead, launched into a lively rendition of one of his favorite semicomic talks. The audience loved it, and years later Asimov recalled the evening as being the perfect antidote for the morbid mood of that day.

By then Asimov was delivering an average of two or three talks per month and regularly receiving one thousand dollars a time. When he accepted a talk in New York he usually tied it in with a visit to his publishers. He called these visits "doing the rounds."

At this stage in his career, Asimov was deeply involved with nonfiction writing (discussed in detail in the next chapter). He still occasionally wrote short stories, which were snapped up by the science fiction magazines, and he had a regular column in the magazine *Fantasy and Science Fiction.*

In New York, Asimov's closest work colleagues and friends were Walter Bradbury at Doubleday, who left the company at the end of 1964, and Larry Ashmead, Bradbury's successor. Ashmead later played an important role in furthering Asimov's relationship with Doubleday and became a close personal friend.

Ashmead remembers with fondness the first time he ever met Asimov. During his first week working at Doubleday as a young trainee editor in 1961, he was given Asimov's manuscript of *Life and Energy* and asked to check through it and write to the author with any suggested changes. With the keenness of a young graduate new to the job, Ashmead composed a twelve-page letter and mailed it to Asimov. A couple of days later Asimov called the Doubleday office and spoke to Ashmead. They arranged to meet up during the author's next visit to New York. A week later Asimov arrived in Ashmead's office, and in the space of half an hour he corrected the editor on all seventy-six points of his letter. "He did it with such grace and humility," Ashmead recalls. "It taught me a valuable lesson, and from that moment on we were friends." During the next fourteen years the two of them worked on forty-four books together before Ashmead left Doubleday in 1975.

Asimov was a very popular man who had a vast number of acquaintances and friends during his lifetime, and a handful of very close personal relationships. Apart from Larry Ashmead and Walter Bradbury in publishing, his closest friends were in science fiction and science circles. In his twenties and early thirties, the most important of these were John Campbell, Professor Dawson, and Robert Heinlein. But in later years, Asimov drifted away from Campbell, very rarely saw his old supervisor, Dawson, and only bumped into Heinlein at the odd convention.

From the 1960s, Asimov's closest friends were the writers Harlan Ellison, Ben Bova, and Lester del Rey, the editor Judy-Lynn del Rey, the astronomer Carl Sagan, the anthologist Martin H. Greenberg, and Larry Ashmead. With each of these close friends Asimov had a natural, easy-going relationship, and the witty banter they worked up together was a joy to witness. The Ellison–Asimov double act was particularly popular at science fiction conventions, and these occasions would not be complete without at least one memorable quote or a public verbal duel on the platform before the gathered fans and friends.

Sometimes the jokey vitriol between them could be so intense that fans left the convention under the misapprehension that the two men were deadly enemies. The truth was they loved each other and understood each other so well that they could act up with incredible conviction.

Harlan Ellison was considered to be one of the leading writers of the new wave of science fiction of the mid-sixties. He is a very different writer from Asimov, and for most of his career he has specialized exclusively in the short story form—with award-winning titles such as "I Have No Mouth and I Must Scream" and "The Beast That Shouted Love at the Heart of the World." He is an extrovert who loves to be center-stage at conventions, a man with an acerbic tongue and a rapier wit.

Ellison set the tone of their relationship at their very first meeting at a science fiction convention held in Philadelphia in 1953. Ellison sidled up to Asimov and said:

"Are you Isaac Asimov, sir?"

"Yes, young man," Asimov replied.

"Really? The great Isaac Asimov?"

"Yes," Asimov replied, beaming. "I am."

"Gee. No kidding. You're Isaac Asimov?"

"Yes."

"Well," says Ellison. "I think you're a . . ."—and his voice suddenly changed to one of contempt—"a nothing."[1]

For a moment Asimov was totally devastated, but then when he heard everyone around him laughing loudly, he realized he had been set up. Thus began a beautiful friendship.

Asimov's favorite story about his friend recounted the only known time anyone got the better of Harlan Ellison. Asimov was never sure that the story was true, but he liked to believe it was.

Approaching a particularly beautiful woman at a science fiction convention, Ellison put on his best macho pose and said: "What would you say to a little fuck?"

To which the lady replied: "Hello little fuck."[2]

[1] *Asimov Laughs Again* by Isaac Asimov. HarperCollins, New York, 1992 (p. 86, slightly paraphrased).
[2] Ibid. (p. 283).

Asimov loved the company of intelligent people. He once claimed, with typical Asimovian immodesty, that he had only met two people more intelligent than himself. They were two of his friends, the artificial intelligence expert Marvin Minsky and the astronomer Carl Sagan. In company, Sagan delighted in reminding Asimov of this comment and endeavored to get the maximum embarrassment factor from it. On one occasion, Asimov became so tired of Sagan's constant reminders that he turned to the astronomer and said with fake annoyance, "Carl, I may have said that you were more intelligent but I did not say you were more talented."[1]

Some have claimed that Isaac was unable to have a proper fatherly relationship with his only son, David. It is certainly clear from his own writings and comments that he absolutely doted on Robyn, while sparing little talk or ink on his son. Close friends of the family have suggested that Isaac found his son too mundane a character, that he lacked intellect and therefore had become almost an embarrassment to the world-famous polymath and internationally acclaimed writer.

Father and son did not see much of each other in later years, and some friends believe that Isaac did not care about his son simply because he was not his intellectual equal. Isaac certainly never had the sort of relationshp with his son that he enjoyed with his own father, Judah Asimov. According to some accounts, David has never been interested in having a regular job or in leading a conventional life. He has spent much of his adult life living in California and, with the exception of Robyn, he has had little to do with his family. Friends of the Asimovs have stated that Isaac continued to send his son money upon request until his death in 1992 and that he never once asked for a cent to be paid back. Whether or not this generosity was a reaction to any sense of belated guilt on Isaac's part is debatable. His readiness to support an adult son into his forties seems contrary to his own sense of responsibility and at odds with his own relatively tough childhood years working in his father's candy store. The most likely reason for Isaac's support is that he grew to accept his son's character and was happy to keep him at a distance. Perhaps he reasoned that he was, in a sense, "paying off" David.

---

[1] *In Joy Still Felt* by Isaac Asimov. Doubleday, New York, 1980 (p. 302).

If this is true, then it displays a darker side to Isaac's character and is a further demonstration of his deep-rooted insecurity. If Isaac was truly comfortable with himself he would not care what people thought of his son. I have speculated elsewhere that Isaac's manner, particularly with women, was a sign of his inner lack of confidence. His need to remain isolated from a son he considered a failure is perhaps another sign of this. It is certainly true that David did not want to have much to do with his family, but by all accounts, Isaac himself was happy with this arrangement.

By the mid-1960s, Isaac was spending an increasing amount of time away from Gertrude and the children. He was never away for very long, a week at the most, but, with increasing numbers of talks, frequent trips to publishers in New York and science fiction conventions around the country, he was often out of Boston.

Isaac did not like traveling and never flew to any engagement, no matter how urgent or important it was. At some point after his one and only flight during his days in the army, he developed a fear and mistrust of flying, which meant that he could never attend science fiction conventions held outside a radius of two to three hundred miles from Boston. It also meant that he could have no personal contact with friends and business colleagues in, say, California.

In later years his hatred of flying meant that he had to turn down numerous lucrative offers to act as consultant for films in Hollywood, to write film scripts, or to visit some of his dearest friends who had moved to distant parts. It meant that after his parents moved to Florida in the late sixties, he did not manage to visit them before his father died in 1969, and when Robyn went to college in Vermont, Isaac was extremely unhappy because he knew that he would not be able to easily visit her.

Every domestic aspect of Isaac's life had to fit around this flying phobia. It was not a case of "Oh, well, when Robyn goes to Vermont, I'll just have to force myself onto a plane." Instead his attitude was, "I won't be able to see Robyn unless she visits Boston."

With so many visits away from home, Isaac and Gertrude began to drift apart. As early as the mid-sixties, Gertrude had become increasingly suspicious that Isaac was having an affair with a woman in New York. In fact he was having numerous extramarital relationships. As one of his friends has said: "During his first marriage, Isaac only had sex with about ten percent of the women who made themselves available to him!"

The facts are simple. Isaac had both the opportunity and the motive. As his celebrity grew, he soon discovered that there was no shortage of women who wanted to leap into bed with such a famous, successful, and rich intellectual. Asimov had sampled the fruits of infidelity and had discovered that there was far more to sex than the pale image it presented within his marriage. When opportunity knocked, he answered.

It is clear that Isaac continued to do his best to keep the facts from Gertrude. Friends have said that her suspicions would flare up on occasion and then calm down after she had been reassured that nothing was going on behind her back.

During the mid-sixties, Asimov was coming under increasing pressure to deliver a vast plethora of books he had taken on. He loved writing to the exclusion of almost everything else and wrote books for the sheer pleasure it gave him. Writing paid the bills, but that was a secondary factor. If a publisher offered a contract for an exciting project, Asimov could not turn it down. As his reputation for speed and versatility increased and his growing fame meant that almost any Asimov book would automatically sell, he was finding himself completely inundated with work. This meant that he had little time to devote to his family.

As Asimov himself put it in the introduction to his one hundredth book, *Opus 100*:

> Being the wife of a compulsive writer is a fate worse than death anyway, since your husband is physically home and mentally absent most of the time, and that is the worst possible combination.[1]

Isaac doted on Robyn, but his work always came first. He did not like to travel and loathed being dragged away from his typewriter to go on holiday. He did agree to go on vacation with the family, but there were always two conditions. Firstly, the journey had to be overland, and secondly, he had to be left alone to work while the others sunbathed or went

---

[1] *Opus 100* by Isaac Asimov. Houghton Mifflin, Boston, 1969 (Introduction, p xiv).

sightseeing. It is easy to imagine the frustration Gertrude must have felt increasingly throughout the sixties as their marriage fell apart. On the one hand there was the obvious but hotly denied fact that her husband was having at least one affair, and on the other she and the family could not enjoy the rewards of Isaac's success by living in a larger house in the smartest district of the city.

By the mid-sixties, the Asimov family were very wealthy. Isaac was earning in the region of 100,000 dollars a year and they had savings of at least 250,000 dollars, but they still lived in an average family home in a very ordinary suburb of Boston and never traveled abroad.

Despite Gertrude's constant protestations, Isaac refused to move to another part of Boston. Even as early as the first few years of the sixties, not long after leaving Boston University, he had tired of the city and desperately wanted to move back to New York. He had moved to Boston to take up an academic position that he had long left behind him. Almost all of his business dealings were in New York, and it was the city in which he had grown up and in which he had always felt most at home. Furthermore, once entrenched in his comfortable attic office in Newton, he had no desire to uproot, move his library and all his manuscripts-in-progress, simply to reestablish himself in another part of Boston.

Gertrude was miserable. They could afford a large house with plenty of land. She wanted to play the role of wealthy Jewish wife and mother, socialize with the rich and famous, and live out the dream of every poor immigrant from Brooklyn, but this was constantly denied her. All Gertrude could do was to look after the children while Isaac went off to conventions, meetings, and, as far as she believed, the embraces of another woman.

It appears that Isaac and Gertrude called an unspoken truce for most of the sixties and agreed that they would separate when the children had both left home and could look after themselves. In the meantime they would give the appearance of being a happily married couple; they would stay in Newton and Gertrude could enjoy as many little luxuries as they could manage without moving house. They had a wide network of friends in Boston and New York, and Isaac socialized as frequently as he could. He did this both to please Gertrude and to maintain a number of friendships that had grown increasingly important to him.

The worst period of the Asimovs' marriage, apart from the burst of venom that finally destroyed it at the end of the sixties, was between the summer of 1965 and the spring of 1966, when Asimov was working on *Fantastic Voyage*.

The episode began in April 1965 with a request from Bantam Books. They had acquired the rights to the novelization of the Hollywood film *Fantastic Voyage*, which was already in production. They offered Asimov a five-thousand-dollar flat fee to write the book version of the screenplay. Naturally he turned it down out of hand. Bantam kept pestering him to reconsider and requested a meeting to discuss it further. Asimov finally agreed to have lunch with them and to chat about the idea.

Over lunch the Bantam executives upped the offer and even considered the possibility of a royalty for the author. By the end of the meal Asimov had agreed to at least look at the script.

The plot of *Fantastic Voyage* involves a machine that is able to miniaturize objects. Using this device, a submarine and crew are injected into a patient, and the rest of the story follows the adventures of the crew as they travel around the body. They only have a limited period in miniaturized form before the effects of the device reverse and the submarine begins to grow back to normal size. Naturally, unless they want a very messy conclusion to the project, they have to be out of the patient's body by then.

It was a great idea—in theory. However, when Asimov read the script he noticed a number of fatal flaws in the plot. The worst of these was the fact that although the crew of the miniaturized submarine escaped the patient's body, the submarine was left behind. Asimov argued, quite correctly, that the submarine would expand and kill the patient. The Hollywood scriptwriters argued that the submarine would be digested by white blood cells. Asimov then stated that white blood cells could not digest metal and that even if they could, the individual atoms that had made up the submarine would expand and cause the patient irreparable damage.

The mistake Asimov made was reading the script because, aside from the scientific inconsistencies, he loved the story and did not want anyone else to do the novelization. He later declared, with typical immodesty, that he felt that no one else would make such a good job of it.

Finally he managed to persuade the filmmakers and Bantam that he would only do it if he had the submarine out of the patient by the end of the book. He also stipulated that Hollywood could do what they wanted with the film but would not be allowed to change anything in the novel version.

Friends claim that the deal Asimov did eventually strike with Bantam and Hollywood was very lucrative and earned him a lot more than five thousand dollars. Nonetheless, Asimov hated the project. For almost a year during the writing of the novel and the production of the film, he was engaged in an endless stream of arguments with the producers and the original screenplay writers. He, of course, did not travel, so he could not go out to Hollywood to argue his points properly and had to do it all thirdhand or over the telephone. He also felt stifled by the fact that he was reworking someone else's story and that it had little to do with him.

When the film did finally appear after the publication of the book, Asimov did not receive a credit or even a mention in the movie titles. The Hollywood people also turned down an offer to serialize the story in *Fantasy and Science Fiction,* for which Asimov was a regular columnist. This annoyed him because he had secured the offer, but Hollywood felt there was not enough money on the table to make it worth their while.

He was even more humiliated when, a few weeks later, he learned that the original scriptwriters had landed a very good deal for the serialization of the story in the *Saturday Evening Post,* which paid an undisclosed but substantial sum for the serialization rights. But Asimov could hardly complain—he was given a very reasonable cut of the money.

All in all, the *Fantastic Voyage* project was very rewarding on a financial level but incredibly frustrating and, on occasion, humiliating for Asimov. Friends said they had never known Isaac to be so bad-tempered as he was during that period, and it is certain that this greatly damaged his relationship with Gertrude and disturbed the whole family. While Isaac was spending a lot of time in New York working on the novelization, Gertrude's suspicions of infidelity were at their most acute.

The Asimovs hobbled on. Isaac found solace in his other writing work and in his close group of friends. But the single most important character in his life during the mid-sixties was the woman who was to help him totally change his life when the final breakup with Gertrude came—his future second wife, Janet Jeppson.

Isaac had first met Janet in 1956 at a science fiction convention held in New York City. She had been a science fiction fan for several years and cited

Arthur C. Clarke's *Childhood's End* as the book that had initially sparked her interest. As with many people who go on to become lovers and sometimes lifelong partners, Janet and Isaac did not hit it off at their first meeting.

Isaac claimed that he could never remember their first encounter, but this was probably an example of selective memory—Isaac was usually loudly boastful of his perfect recall. Janet remembers Isaac at that first meeting as being quite obnoxious.

Offered a copy of *Foundation and Empire* to sign, he scrawled his name on the inside flap and, without lifting his head to look at her, asked what she did, to which Janet replied, "I'm a psychiatrist."

"Good," Asimov instantly responded. "Let's get on the couch together."[1]

Janet slammed shut the book and turned on her heel. For years after she simply thought of Asimov as a contemptuous lech whom she had no desire to see again.

Isaac's sense of humor and flirtatious manner did not work on everyone, and this time it certainly did not work with Janet. Some women found his manner offensive, and as he grew older, what he saw as his innocent, mock passes to women often drew quite the wrong reaction. A friend's wife once whirled on him at a party after he had pinched her bottom.

"God, Asimov," she snapped. "Why do you always do that? It is extremely painful and besides, don't you realize, it's very degrading." Suitably chastened, Asimov learned his lesson and never pinched her again, but it did not stop him pinching other women's bottoms.

One New York editor recalled how, even by the early fifties, among the secretarial staff at Doubleday he was known as "the man with a thousand hands."

Despite this, Asimov was very proud of what he naively considered his adept treatment of women and his effortless ability to flirt with any half-attractive female he encountered. Once asked by a waiter if he was Italian, Asimov replied, "Only with women."[2]

Why was Asimov like this? Some have suggested that beneath his brash exterior lay a basic insecurity. It is likely that, in order to make

[1] *In Joy Still Felt* (p. 66).
[2] Ibid.

himself, the physically unattractive boffin, seem more attractive to women, he deliberately acted up and played the unlikely role of gigolo. It seems clear that he stumbled upon this formula in his early twenties around the time he first met Gertrude and realized the power of flirtation. After he was rich and famous he had no need for such displays, but the up-front approach had become integral to his character decades earlier and he could not easily have discarded it, even if he had wanted to. Besides, by the early fifties Asimov had an unhappy marriage, especially on a sexual level. He may have been rebuffed more often than he was accepted and he may have antagonized a great many women along the way, but if the testimony of some of his closest friends is to be believed, then he also met with considerable success.

Once it began properly, Isaac's relationship with Janet seems to have been based on genuine friendship. After their initial encounter, they did not meet again for two and a half years, and then it was only by chance, at a Mystery Writers Association dinner, held once again in New York.

On this occasion, they talked animatedly. Isaac told Janet he had no recollection of their first encounter, and in later years put his mood down to a painful attack of kidney stones at the 1956 convention. Kidney stone pain was a genuine recurring problem throughout his adult life and landed him in the hospital on more than one occasion.

At this second meeting they got on famously and found each other such invigorating company that they spent almost the entire evening speaking exclusively to one another, ignoring the other guests. Isaac even ended the evening by holding Janet's hand, and she made no effort to stop him.

The romance that grew between Isaac and Janet during the sixties was a purely platonic one. They became great friends and helped each other through difficult patches. Janet is an intelligent woman who is full of the joy of learning, appreciative of nature and history, steeped in literature and the arcane. Isaac could not believe his luck in finding a female companion who was so bright and responsive, and also able to allow him to express himself in her company. Once he dropped the annoying playacting and engaged her in a proper conversation, she was very taken with him. Gertrude was not in the least bit academic, and although she was bright and lively socially, she did not have a natural appreciation of anything intellectual. Isaac had never been able to talk to Gertrude about anything other than domestic matters and their family life. In the early days of their relationship, he had been so totally besotted with Gertrude's good looks that he had pushed aside any notion that he did not really get along with her on a fundamental level.

Janet did not have the beauty of the young Gertrude, but she had many desirable qualities he felt were lacking in Gertrude. By the sixties Gertrude was beginning to lose her looks, and because Isaac had ostensibly married her for her beauty, there was nothing underpinning their relationship when they grew older. Coupled with this was the fact that Isaac and Gertrude's relationship was more or less sexless. It is therefore easy to see how their marriage began to falter.

Isaac, of course, was not immune to the aging process himself, and had also grown fat. Ironically, this gave him a "cuddly" look, which many women liked. They saw Asimov as a harmless teddy bear, and those who wanted sex with a teddy bear usually found him amenable. Gertrude had been slim during the war, but as she entered her mid-thirties she began to put on a lot of weight. In her forties she was definitely fat.

A further difficulty in the Asimov marriage stemmed from the fact that Gertrude smoked, and Isaac hated smoking. No matter what he said, he could not persuade her to give it up. Isaac increasingly saw this attitude of Gertrude's as a reflection of the fact that she no longer loved him. If she could not give up something he hated so much, he reasoned, then she could not care about him.

Isaac's anger over this matter can be seen in retrospect as a way for him to pass the blame for the failure of his marriage onto Gertrude. Whether she smoked or not, the fact was, it was he who was being unfaithful, and the notion that her inability to give up smoking was a sign that Gertrude no longer loved him was simply childishness on his part. Gertrude was unhappy in the house in Newton; she wanted to expand her horizons and to lead a fuller life. Small wonder she could not give up a habit of a lifetime. In this we can perhaps see a sign that Gertrude was at least subconsciously aware of her husband's infidelity and saw her habit as a last vestige of free expression in a life otherwise totally dominated by her husband's wishes and drives.

Nonetheless, Isaac was genuinely repelled by the fact that the house in Newton constantly smelled of stale cigarette smoke, which even drifted up to his personal sanctuary in the attic. Although he should have become used to it and perhaps accepted it as a foible, there was also the fact that Janet did not smoke and hated the habit as much as Isaac did. If Gertrude was using her habit as a final vestige of individuality, it was eventually to backfire on her.

Although she was naturally unaware of the facts, the odds were certainly stacked against Gertrude. Isaac and Janet saw eye to eye on almost all aspects of life—politics, music, food, science fiction. Janet was more literary in her tastes than Isaac and was well-read in contemporary fiction as well as the classics. Modern writing had largely passed Asimov by.

Janet was a bit of a health freak—something Isaac had little interest in. While she really cared about her diet, Isaac was never concerned about what he ate as long as it tasted good. In other ways Janet and Isaac were simply made for each other, and both of them knew it. With her, Isaac did not have to play the Italian. He felt secure when he was with her, and their friendship was a source of emotional as well as intellectual support.

Despite hitting it off so naturally, Janet and Isaac did not see much of each other. He visited her when he was in New York, and they met up at a number of conferences and meetings. Janet's brother John was a medical student at Boston University, so she sometimes had occasion to visit the city, and when she did, she and Isaac would get together for dinner and conversation.

Things came to a dramatic head for the Asimov family in August 1969. As Asimov expressed it, in that month, "things fell apart."[1]

Realizing their marriage was on a knife edge, in the summer of 1969 Gertrude decided that she would take Robyn on a holiday to Britain. By this time David, now eighteen, was in high school, and Robyn was fourteen. It was clear that unless something was done the marriage could not last to see both children through college; a trip abroad and a lengthy separation might just pull them together enough to make a go of it.

Gertrude and Robyn left on August 2, 1969, and Isaac settled himself into working flat out on his latest project, which was, ironically, *Isaac Asimov's Treasury of Humor.*

---

[1] *In Joy Still Felt* (p. 498).

Isaac once again found solace in writing. He was fully aware of this response and on a number of occasions used it as a protective device. There is also no doubt that when it came to problems with Gertrude, he often escaped to the typewriter rather than face trouble head-on. Gertrude's escape was the family and a limited social life, one she found unsatisfactory. At least for Isaac his haven was energizing.

Two days after Gertrude and Robyn left, and as Isaac was sitting in his office thinking up the next joke for the book, the telephone rang. It was Stanley, informing Isaac that their father had died.

Isaac had an enormous respect for his father and had always cherished his close relationship with both his parents. For decades the old man had struggled in America to build a comfortable life for his family, and he had been amazingly successful. Having arrived in America with hardly a penny, he had established himself in a successful business and found financial rewards and a standard of living far beyond his wildest dreams. Isaac had never failed to appreciate that.

His parents had retired to Florida in 1968, but they had never felt entirely at home there. It was immediately decided that Anna Rachel should be brought back to New York at the same time as Judah Asimov's body was flown home for burial. The only members of the immediate family to attend the quiet and private service were Isaac and Stanley, who took care of all the details. Isaac decided not to break the news to Gertrude and Robyn. He wanted them to enjoy their trip abroad in peace. Curiously, he also decided not to contact David, and only told him after the funeral had taken place.

The next day, Stanley and Isaac used their influence to have their father's obituary placed in a couple of New York newspapers.

In this uniquely emotional situation Isaac was confused over the correct way to behave. The night of the funeral, Isaac was due to give a talk at Brandeis University in Massachusetts. At Stanley's insistence, on the day Judah died, Isaac canceled his talk.

"I've never had to cancel a talk before," Isaac had protested.

"Yes, but you've never lost a father before either," Stanley had replied coldly.[1]

---

[1] *In Joy Still Felt* (p. 499, slightly paraphrased).

Naturally, the college found a replacement, but nonetheless, straight after the funeral service, Asimov dashed to the university to see if he could give a quick talk to make up for the cancellation. His replacement made a very good job of it. At the beginning of the speech he announced the reason for Asimov's absence. He then declared that he was giving his fee to the college in order to start a Judah Asimov Scholarship. After the talk, twelve hundred dollars was raised to start the fund used to educate students who could not afford the college fees. Judah would have been very proud and more than a little astonished.

Gertrude and Isaac knew that the trial separation was really the last hope for their marriage, yet when they did call each other across the Atlantic, the conversation was full of divorce talk.

Gertrude and Robyn were staying with friends of the family in England. Over two decades later, the Asimovs' hosts could still recall how Gertrude and Isaac would have blazing rows on the telephone, arguing about the division of the estate. Despite the pain Isaac must have felt over the recent loss of his father and his self-imposed inability to tell his wife and daughter about it, he still fought his corner over the planned financial arrangements. "The ironic thing though," remarked the family friend, "was the fact that there they were, the two of them, discussing the division of literally millions of dollars, and yet they were arguing about who was going to pay for the telephone call!"

"Isaac's attitude," the friend continued, "was that *he* had earned all the money so why should Gertrude have half of it?"

It was a thoroughly miserable time for both Gertrude and Isaac. Although he was convinced that the marriage was all but over, and although part of him wanted to make a clean break of it, he could not help but be affected by it. They had, after all, been married for twenty-seven years.

Salvation from total depression came from two sources. On the one hand Isaac always had his work to turn to. Unlike most people who go through marriage breakups and have to return on a Monday morning to a job they no longer care for, Isaac could put down the telephone and abandon himself in the world of his latest project, albeit a joke book. The other, unexpected relief came from his friend Janet Jeppson.

A few days after his father's funeral, Isaac called Janet and they went out for lunch. They then drove to New England and spent a wonderful afternoon together, walking through the woods in the August sunshine, visiting historical sites around the town of Concord, and standing at Emerson's grave.

The trip really cemented their relationship and came as an enormous relief from the multiple pressures of bereavement and marital catastrophe. Isaac found Janet the perfect companion: intelligent, witty, and continually fascinated by the minutiae of life as well as the broader canvas of politics, art, science, and literature. Isaac was beginning to feel that he had been with the wrong woman for the past twenty-seven years.

But, against the odds, when Gertrude and Robyn did return to Boston, she and Isaac managed, for a short time, to salvage something of their marriage.

It is fair to suggest that when Gertrude discovered that Isaac had been suffering terribly from the loss of his beloved father, her antagonism mellowed. All through the remainder of the summer, the autumn, and early winter of that year, their marriage stayed intact. But it was precarious, and by early 1970 things began to fall apart again.

New Year was a disaster, and although the whole family attended a superficially merry party thrown by Asimov's Boston publisher, Houghton Mifflin, to celebrate Isaac's fiftieth birthday, the writing was on the wall.

In early February Asimov appeared on the *Dick Cavett Show* and made a fool of himself on air by making some crass, sexist remark about a beautiful young actress who was also a guest on the show.

Asimov had half-jokingly asked the young woman what she was doing after the program, and the station did not cut the comment before transmission—even after Asimov, seeing what he had said on the playback, specifically asked for the sequence to be deleted.

Gertrude was used to her husband's flirtatious manner and knew as much as anyone that it was an intrinsic aspect of his character, but there is a big difference between flirting at parties and doing it in front of millions of viewers around the country.

Robyn had been watching the program at a friend's house and was embarrassed and furious with her father. Gertrude was quietly embittered.

It turned out to be the final straw as far as the Asimov marriage was concerned. From February onward, Isaac and Gertrude hardly spoke; Isaac buried himself further in his work and began to make plans for the future.

Isaac talked to friends and to Stanley. He discussed his marital problems with Janet and tried to formulate a plan whereby he and Gertrude could separate with the least possible pain all around.

By early June 1970, after living in the same house but hardly sharing a word with his wife for several months, Isaac decided that he had had enough. He felt caged living in Boston, and separation from Gertrude gave him the perfect opportunity to move back to New York. He had clearly hankered after his old home almost from the moment he and Gertrude had moved to Boston twenty-one years earlier. His lawyer's advice that a divorce would be easier if Isaac moved to New York was all the excuse he needed.

On July 3, 1970, the movers arrived at the house in Newton to take away Isaac's bookcases and desk, books, and papers. Twenty-five days short of his and Gertrude's twenty-eighth wedding anniversary, he said good-bye to his wife and left the house for the last time. He had finished *Isaac Asimov's Treasury of Humor* on June 13.

10

SCIENCE, GOD, AND EVERYTHING

With the exception of *Fantastic Voyage* and a handful of short stories, Asimov spent the 1960s concentrating on nonfiction. Before the decade was out, he had reached and passed the magic figure of a hundred books. The majority of these were published between 1960 and 1970 and covered a wide variety of nonfiction topics.

Asimov did not really miss writing science fiction. He was very excited by the idea of writing popular science books and then allowing himself to be led into a plethora of different subjects ranging from analyses of the Bible to joke books.

In many ways Asimov's hiatus from science fiction came with unintentionally good timing. During the 1960s, science fiction underwent a complete change. Out went the more mechanistic approach, the fascination with hardware and space travel, and in came a more introspective form of writing.

Science fiction became more concerned with the exploration of the human psyche, the interaction between fantasy and the drug culture, introversion rather than extroversion. It was in such an environment that the new wave of science fiction writers, epitomized by Harlan Ellison, Ray Bradbury, Robert Silverberg, and Philip K. Dick, became famous. In this new mindscape, Asimov could well have been submerged and even dismissed as a dinosaur.

Asimov himself, almost before anyone else, began to realize that the world of science fiction was undergoing a radical change. Although by the early sixties he was only rarely writing in the genre, he continued to attend science fiction conventions when they were held near home, and many of his friends were successful in the field.

Asimov was so keenly aware of the new environment that in an atypically modest mood, he often declared to close friends that he did not dare take up the pen and try his hand at science fiction again because he felt that the field had left him behind. "I felt that I didn't measure up any longer and I didn't want to prove it,"[1] he once said.

Even after the success of *Fantastic Voyage*, in 1967, when Harlan Ellison tried to persuade him to write for an anthology he was editing called *Dangerous Visions*, Asimov refused, saying that his style would not fit in with Ellison's image of the project.

Asimov does not appear to have been too depressed by the notion that science fiction had left him behind. Perhaps he never really believed it. Perhaps he realized that, as with many areas of the creative world, fashions within writing are often cyclical.

It was Evelyn del Rey, first wife of the writer and publisher Lester del Rey, who finally lifted Asimov's spirits. When she asked him why he no longer wrote science fiction, he replied that he thought that the field had moved on, to which she replied; "Isaac, when you write you *are* the field."[2]

Such comments made him feel good, but aside from the odd short story it was to be another four years before Asimov began another science fiction novel, *The Gods Themselves*.

Asimov's nonfiction career began quite naturally with science books. The first of these was the doomed biochemistry text *Biochemistry and Human Metabolism*, published in 1952 and cowritten with William Boyd and Burnham Walker. His first nonfiction book for the general public was *The Chemicals of Life*, published two years later, in 1954.

This initial inroad into the nonfiction market was largely through the publishers Houghton Mifflin and Abelard-Schuman, and included such titles as *Realm of Numbers* and *The Clock We Live On* (both 1959). Asimov dashed off literally dozens of such titles, often completing them within a

---

[1] *In Joy Still Felt* by Isaac Asimov. Doubleday, New York, 1980 (p. 417).
[2] Ibid (p. 418).

few weeks of signing the contract. In this way he could count on a large number of relatively small advances (in the thousand-dollar region), thereby grossing a respectable yearly income.

Naturally, as he churned out more and more titles, not only did his reputation grow and his name spread, but he began to receive royalties from an increasing number of books.

Asimov's science fiction novels of the early fifties have never stopped selling and collectively provided him with a substantial annual income for the rest of his life. His royalty statement in the summer of 1969 from just one of his publishers, Doubleday, came to forty thousand dollars.

His record for finishing a nonfiction book was *Realm of Numbers*, which took him thirteen days from first word to final copy. The facts were all in his head and it was simply a question of putting pen to paper.

Asimov's speed did slow when he expanded his repertoire beyond biochemistry and started to write books for adults on any subject that took his fancy.

For research he relied heavily upon his growing reference library, which included the *Encyclopaedia Britannica,* scientific and medical dictionaries, astronomy atlases, tables, maps, and foreign-language dictionaries. Even though he had written several nonfiction books on subjects with which he was comfortably acquainted, he admitted approaching his first serious nonfiction book outside his area of specialist training with some trepidation.

Ignoring his first mathematics book, *Realm of Numbers,* which was very basic, his first real departure was into the subject of astronomy. He decided on this because he felt that it was the area of knowledge most closely associated with science fiction, and was also of great interest to him. By this time he was a full-time writer, not an academic, and could risk plunging into a subject in which he had no formal training. His first attempt at an astronomy book was *The Clock We Live On,* which became a great success.

Encouraged by this, Asimov then went head-on into a series of projects that created his image as polymath extraordinaire, and also made him a great deal of money.

Asimov was genuinely interested in almost any area of knowledge. He had realized as a child that he had no aptitude for economics, and his mathematical training stopped at calculus and the mathematics necessary to his biochemical research. Apart from that, the entire realm of knowledge was his playground.

With his typical immodesty he shunned any criticism that he was delving into subjects of which he knew nothing, and wrote about anything he chose—as long as a publisher was willing to pay for it. On occasion he even wrote entire books without any form of commitment from a publisher.

Because of his voracious appetite for writing, Asimov often overstretched himself and ended up in a mad panic to finish a book by the agreed deadline. He hated the thought of delivering late and often completed a book ahead of the promised time. He certainly never delivered a manuscript after the deadline and would rather work all the hours he could find than renege on an agreement. He saw the art of writing several books at once as employing the juggler's rhythm and he thoroughly enjoyed it.

Although he sometimes made slight errors in his writing and had to correct factual problems pointed out by observant readers, Asimov was a very meticulous man. He loved indexing, and was scathing of professional indexers employed by his publishers against his will. He forever found fault in their work, and once he was famous, he insisted on doing his own indexing.

Word of Asimov's mastery of nonfiction traveled fast. As early as 1961 one reviewer, the internationally renowned paleontologist George Gaylord Simpson, described Asimov as "a national wonder and a natural resource."[1] Asimov was very proud of that comment.

Amazingly, Asimov's work also reached the desk of J. Edgar Hoover. Although Asimov was never aware of the fact, as early as 1960, the FBI had a file on him. The file was opened because a reader had been annoyed by a statement in Asimov's *Inside the Atom* (1956) in which the writer supported the view that the Russians had nuclear power plants before the USA. The anonymous reader sent a copy of the book to the FBI, along with a letter pointing out that Asimov had been born in Russia. Documents released in 1993 under the Freedom of Information Act suggest that Hoover was sufficiently interested to carry out electronic surveillance

---

[1] *Science,* April 23, 1961. George Gaylord Simpson reviewing *Wellspnngs of Life.*

of Asimov's home and bug his telephone lines. The material gathered from this surveillance is still classified and exempt from disclosure. It was only after Asimov's death that the file was unearthed and a copy sent to Janet Jeppson. She found the whole matter laughable.

In 1965 the FBI discovered that Asimov's name appeared on a list in the possession of the Communist Party. Presumably, unknown to Asimov, he had been targeted by them as a potential member.

In reality, Asimov had little real interest in politics and was certainly not sympathetic toward communism. However, this incident does show the level of fame he had acquired by this stage in his career.

Asimov's most successful nonfiction book of the sixties was *The Intelligent Man's Guide to Science.* The offer to do the book originally came in May 1959, from Leon Svirsky of Basic Books. Throughout the late fifties Asimov had been gaining a steadily growing reputation as a generalist within the science field. Svirsky visited the author at his Newton home and suggested that he might like to attempt a general science book for the intelligent and interested layman. Asimov thought it was an ambitious idea, but nonetheless liked it. He had always been a sucker for flattery; Svirsky had done his homework and knew this. He took great care in complimenting Asimov and his many science efforts, making it clear that he thought Isaac Asimov was the only man in America for the job. Svirsky offered a fifteen-hundred-dollar advance for the book—the largest Asimov had ever been offered up until that time. That did the trick.

The contract arrived a couple of days after the meeting, and Asimov was about to sign it and return it to Svirsky when he had a sudden fit of nerves about the prospect of covering so many scientific disciplines in one book. It nearly terminated the whole project, and he took almost two months to get up enough courage to sign the deal.

It is significant that the person Asimov turned to for advice about the book was Janet Jeppson. He phoned her in July to tell her about the offer and to explain the source of his trepidation. She told him that she thought it sounded like a good idea and that he would be perfectly capable of writing it. He signed the contract within minutes of hanging up, and it was back with Basic Books by the end of that week.

The title of the book remained an area of contention in the early days. Svirsky had chosen the title because it reminded him of George Bernard Shaw's *The Intelligent Woman's Guide to Socialism and Capitalism.* Asimov thought that *The Intelligent Man's Guide to Science* sounded elitist and that this would lower sales. He suggested changing the title to *Everyone's Guide to Science.* When he mentioned this to Svirsky, the publisher disagreed, claiming that *his* title would actually increase sales because everyone who bought it would think of themselves as intelligent even if they were not. Asimov conceded.

The real surprise is that no one at the time suggested that the title might be sexist. Today a title like *The Intelligent Man's Guide to Science* would be laughed out of the publishing house, but in the late fifties it did not occur to anyone that the title was at all chauvinistic. Several years later Asimov started to get a stream of complaints about the title, and cleverly dodged the issue by claiming that the intelligent man of the title was in fact the author.

At the beginning of October Asimov finally settled down to work on the new project.

Svirsky's original idea had been for an overview of science starting from 1901 and ending in 1960. Asimov immediately realized that this would not be the best way to approach the book. The first rule of chronological science writing is that work of previous centuries must be discussed rather than leaping to an arbitrary date and pretending that science in all fields began then. Starting in 1901 would have been meaningless.

Asimov decided the only way to approach the entire scientific field was to begin with the universe and work his way down through the various levels of human knowledge, ending with the brain. Along the way each subject could be dealt with in historical form, starting with the initial discovery or first application of a concept and moving on through history to the present day. Asimov's reasoning was that all science is simple in its early stages, and writing about the beginnings of each topic allowed him to gradually introduce more and more sophisticated levels of knowledge and understanding as he approached the present day. It was a highly successful formula, which Asimov utilized again and again in his other books.

In order to make the book as exciting as possible, and to inject a sense of awe, he treated ignorance as the villain and the good scientist as the hero struggling to understand the universe in which we live.

As usual, Asimov worked amazingly quickly, and by November he had written the first sections of the book. Despite his earlier trepidation, he found it easy to write and managed up to ten thousand words per day. Almost unbelievably, Asimov had the first draft of *The Guide* finished by his fortieth birthday, on January 2, 1960. He had written over four hundred thousand words in less than three months.

Although Asimov had not approached the book as he had been instructed, when Svirsky read through the small section delivered to him in November, he was enthusiastic. Presented with Asimov's clear and logical format, Svirsky quickly saw the folly of his original approach. However, what did cause a tremendous problem was Svirsky's input in *The Guide*.

Trouble began soon after Asimov delivered the final draft of all but two chapters of the book, in February 1960. Svirsky wanted to cut the text in half because, as it stood, it could not be put into a single volume. Asimov was incensed and stood firmly against the decision. He had two more chapters to complete and decided that he would not deliver these to Svirsky, he would not return the advance, and he would not talk to the publisher in case he was forced into a compromise. Instead, he would simply sit and wait to hear from him.

It took the editor two weeks to come around. Finally he gave in and called Asimov. He was not going to cut the book after all and agreed to publish it in two volumes.

That was not the end of the story: two further disagreements ensued. When the final draft of the entire manuscript was delivered and Asimov received the galleys, Svirsky announced that he had commissioned an introduction for the book. For some unexplained reason, Asimov hated the idea of anyone else writing an introduction to one of his books and protested loudly. But this time Svirsky got his way. And when Asimov heard that it was George W. Beadle, he was vocal in his appreciation of this choice. He had a great respect for Beadle and was flattered that the eminent geneticist was willing to write the introduction.

No sooner had this dispute passed than another, more serious problem arose concerning the editing of *The Intelligent Man's Guide to Science*. Svirsky had stuck to his word that he was not going to cut the book in two and reduce it to a single volume, but when Asimov received the edited galleys, to his horror he discovered that at least 30 percent of the material had been cut out.

Being used to editing the work of scientists rather than professional science writers, Svirsky had adopted the habit of discarding superfluous material in the text. The fact that Asimov's nonfiction writing is incredibly lean and carefully structured without a wasted word meant that Svirsky's heavy editing cut the text to ribbons and in most places made its original meaning quite unintelligible. If Svirsky had got his way, the book would have to have been retitled *The Unintelligible Guide to Science*.

Asimov immediately contacted Svirsky and demanded that all the cuts be reinstated. He then went through the text and put everything back, with clear and concise reasons why they should not have been omitted in the first place. However, he found he could not put back what had been cut quickly enough. Consequently, the book went to press with numerous errors, inconsistencies, and weak explanations.

Because of Svirsky's clumsy interference, instead of feeling due triumph with the book, Asimov ended up ashamed of *The Intelligent Man's Guide to Science* and always considered it his least favorite book. He would not even open the cover when he received his author's copies. Luckily, the public and the critics did not see the book in the same light. It was a massive critical and financial success.

During the week of publication of *The Guide* in October 1960, Asimov had his first interview with *Newsweek*. It appeared in the December 5, 1960, issue. The book received rave reviews throughout the country and a nomination from the National Book Awards. It immediately began to sell. Before long Asimov could justifiably refer to the book as "his nonfiction 'Nightfall.'"

The advance for the book was soon paid off, and in November 1961, when the second royalty check arrived, Asimov was staggered to find that it was for 27,600 dollars, a sum four times his old college salary and by far the largest check he had ever seen in his life.

There is no doubt that Asimov was thrilled by the fact that *The Intelligent*

Man's Guide to Science had met with such fantastic and immediate success, but, strangely, at the same time he felt depressed by it. He thought that with this check he had peaked and that things could only go downhill from then on. He had absolutely nothing to worry about; *The Intelligent Man's Guide to Science* continued to sell well, and although he did not receive such large checks for that particular book again, his writing earnings continued to increase year after year.

In 1964, Asimov was delighted to be asked to reedit the book, as it provided him with the opportunity to make good all the problems with the first version. This new edition was called *The New Intelligent Man's Guide to Science* and was published as a single volume. That was a book Asimov was always proud of. It, too, sold well and helped to provide the increasing income Asimov enjoyed throughout the 1960s.

By the time he began *The Intelligent Man's Guide to Science,* Asimov had developed a working system for his nonfiction books and managed to find an enviable rhythm in his work. He was, of course, obsessive about writing, a fact that continued to cause friction within the family but that also enabled him to maintain his amazing output.

Asimov found the crucial factor that allowed him to work at such a phenomenal pace was his ability to switch from one subject to another at will. He almost never suffered from writer's block, partly because he loved the process of writing, but also because, if he tired or became bored with a particular piece, he could easily switch to something else he was working on.

He also found that with little more than a quick perusal of what he had been working on days or weeks earlier, he could return to a project almost as though he had never left it. But this was only true for nonfiction. He always insisted on working on a fictional piece with as few breaks as possible, to avoid spending a lot of time reimmersing himself in the story and getting the feel of the characters back.

Asimov was not only astonishingly fast at writing but he also delivered revisions at top speed. He had a rule that unless it was for something very special or there were very good reasons, he would never rework anything more than once. The reasoning behind this was twofold. The first and quite justifiable reason was that if a piece was revised too often it lost its spontaneity. The second reason I cannot defend, which was that reworking a piece took time away from the next piece of writing.

His immediacy was one of Asimov's greatest gifts. His writing has a consistency rarely found in fiction or nonfiction and his "writing voice" is always clear and unmistakable, but he could be slapdash in other ways. Considering the sheer volume of his work and the breadth of the nonfictional subject matter he covered, Asimov made remarkably few factual errors; but there are many points in his books where a little more discipline would have made them better products. Asimov's domineering attitude to many of the editors he worked with also meant that they could not really exert as much influence over the quality of his writing as they would have liked.

There is no doubt that Asimov was an unparalleled master of science popularization, not simply because of the number of books he wrote but because of his natural teaching ability. Asimov was a superb explainer. He loved to teach and found that he could combine this talent with his other, greater love, writing. To his delight, he found that this combination could also make him wealthy.

Even after he had achieved international fame and fortune as well as respect as a science popularizer, Asimov still had a kernel of guilt that he had left academia to become a writer. He knew he was not a true academic and never would be, but deep beneath the surface he still believed that he was, in some odd way, taking the easy option by writing about science rather than actually doing it. The clearest indication of this was the sheer delight he always showed when he received the praises of scientists who had read and appreciated his work. By the end of the 1960s, Asimov was receiving dozens of fan letters each week but none gave him as much pleasure as those from working scientists.

Asimov enjoyed the research stage of writing a book, but it was the actual process of writing that gave him the biggest thrill. He once said, ". . . it is the writing I live for. Nothing else."[1]

This could be interpreted as amazing eccentricity, but it is possible to see his point. Research can be enjoyable, and on many occasions Asimov found it immensely rewarding, but, for him, it paled into insignificance beside the joy of actually putting ink on the page.

As for the root cause of Asimov's writing obsession, many theories have been suggested. I believe we have to look no further than his own

---

[1] *In Joy Still Felt* (p. 275).

explanation—that working on his writing in such a regimented fashion was the only way he could justify to himself that he was doing a "proper job." In essence, it was the only way in which he could show that he was working as hard as his father had done in running the candy store for so many years. It was also this powerful work ethic that drove him to care so much about the number of books he had written and where he would find the next title.

By the mid-sixties, if Asimov had not written another word, he could still have provided a very comfortable lifestyle for his family. By then money was no longer a prime motivation. But the fear of poverty instilled in him from a very early age never left Asimov and he continued to be very careful with money for his entire life.

After completing *The Intelligent Man's Guide to Science,* he began writing a vast number of smaller books on an increasingly varied range of subjects, while at the same time beginning work on a vast collection of scientific biographies.

This volume, published under the title *Asimov's Biographical Encyclopedia of Science and Technology,* took him three years to write and ended up being the longest book he had written up to that point. At almost half a million words, it was longer than the original draft of *The Intelligent Man's Guide to Science* and considerably longer than the published version of that book. It consisted of just over one thousand short biographies of the most important scientists in history as well as those of the current time. Published in 1964, it immediately sold well and stayed in print well into the 1980s. As a scientific biographical text it remains unsurpassed, and is still used as a reference book in major libraries around the world.

It is an indication of Asimov's fame that Doubleday put the author's name in the title of the book. Asimov's working title had been *The Biographical History of Science and Technology,* but Tom Sloane, his editor, had not liked it, claiming that "the word *history* was poison at the box office."[1] (How times change! I think Tom Sloane would have been perfectly happy with the box-office performance of *A Brief History of Time* if it had been one of his books.) The Doubleday salespeople had noticed Asimov's name carried weight in the marketplace, and suggested the new title. They were absolutely right. By the mid-sixties Asimov was widely known

[1] *In Joy Still Felt* (p. 306).

as a science spokesman on radio and television, and there is no doubt that this helped to make the book a big seller.

From a collection of scientific biography, Asimov went on to write an analysis of the Bible, called, predictably, *Asimov's Guide to the Bible*. Again it was a two-volume work, which Asimov worked on alongside *Fantastic Voyage*. Volume I was published in 1968 and Volume II the following year.

Following his treatment of the Bible, and without the slightest twinge of concern that he might be overstretching himself, Asimov turned to a critical analysis of Shakespeare, which resulted in yet another mammoth two-volume book, *Asimov's Guide to Shakespeare*. And he did not stop there. Throughout the sixties, alongside his larger projects, Asimov wrote several books about history, beginning in the summer of 1962 with a book about Benjamin Franklin, which he called *The Kite That Won the Revolution*.

This was another book that caused Asimov a great deal of trouble with an editor. It had originally been signed up by Houghton Mifflin, the Boston-based firm with whom Asimov had a very good working relationship and for whom he had already written a number of successful books. The trouble with *The Kite That Won the Revolution* was that it was meant to be part of a series of books for the juvenile market, and Asimov's draft manuscript simply did not fit the bill.

Almost immediately after receiving it, the editor of the series, Stirling North, returned Asimov's manuscript covered in editor's blue ink. Fearing a repeat of the problems he had faced with Leon Svirsky, Asimov straightaway decided to withdraw the manuscript and called up the editor at Houghton Mifflin with whom he had the closest relationship, the adult nonfiction editor Austin Olney. Olney immediately realized the problem had nothing to do with Asimov's writing; it was just that his text did not fit the stylized approach of the other books in the series. Instead of losing it forever, Olney made the decision to publish it as an independent title.

For this reason, *The Kite That Won the Revolution* was one of Asimov's favorite books. It made very little money and is one of the least well known of his titles, but he was particularly proud of it. It was entirely his own work and free of any editorial influence—a commodity perhaps inordinately important to Asimov.

The fact that he was so keen to have a large degree of editorial control of his work is another reflection of Asimov's excessive belief in himself. Although he referred to this powerful faith in his own ability as "immodesty," it was a very real facet of his personality. In his eyes, no one could write science as well as he. He was therefore resentful of what he often perceived as editorial interference in his science writing. After the experience with Svirsky, he found it very difficult to place any faith in nonfiction editors again. When it came to fiction, Asimov was more relaxed. He realized that fiction was more subjective and was willing to concede that outsiders' comments could be valuable.

Although *The Kite That Won the Revolution* was not a great financial success, it was an important book in another sense. Asimov had enjoyed writing it so much that he suddenly became very interested in writing a series of history books along similar lines.

First on the list came *The Greeks*, again published by Houghton Mifflin. Asimov was fond of recounting the story of how Austin Olney accepted the idea of doing *The Greeks* and gave Asimov a contract. He then made it clear that he only wanted a book about the Greeks, not two books, one on the Greeks and one on the Romans. He might consider another book if *The Greeks* did well.

Two months after *The Greeks* was published, Asimov went along to see his editor. Olney was delighted with the book and satisfied with the initial sales figures. Encouraged, Asimov reminded him that he had wanted to see how *The Greeks* did before he could consider a book on the Romans.

Olney remembered, and reassured Asimov that he could start a book about the Romans anytime he wanted. Whereupon Asimov reached in his bag, pulled out the finished manuscript of *The Roman Republic*, and dumped it on Olney's desk in front of him. After Olney had recovered from the shock, he burst out laughing and accepted the book.

Asimov simply could not resist the temptation of writing about the Romans at the same time as he was completing *The Greeks*. By this time he was confident enough in his own abilities and clout in the marketplace to take the risk. However, even if it had not been accepted by his publisher or any other, he would have still loved writing the book, as he had done it simply for pleasure.

Asimov's history books and his literary critiques did not sell as well as his science books, but they did healthy enough business to encourage his publishers, particularly Houghton Mifflin and Doubleday, to continue publishing them.

After *The Roman Republic,* Asimov went on to write *The Roman Empire, The Egyptians, The Near East, The Dark Ages,* and *The Shaping of England,* all before the end of the decade. Others followed in the early 1970s, ranging from French history, through the early history of the United States, to the history of Constantinople.

For Asimov in the late sixties, history was becoming something of an obsession. He told a journalist writing for *Newsday*:

> From 1939 to 1949, I thought of myself as a science fiction writer. From 1949 to 1958, I thought of myself as a bio-chemist. From 1958 to 1965, I thought of myself as a science writer. Now I don't know what to think of myself; my current interest is history.[1]

At the same time that Asimov was writing a series of history books, his enormous encyclopedias, *Fantastic Voyage,* the occasional science fiction short story, and other miscellaneous nonfiction books, he was also contributing a regular column to *Fantasy and Science Fiction Magazine,* commonly known as *F & SF.*

This new task began in 1958, after Asimov had written four articles for a short-lived magazine called *Venture Science Fiction.* The editor, Robert P. Mills, was also involved with the long-established *F & SF,* and after the folding of *Venture,* he asked Asimov if he would like to write a monthly column of up to four thousand words on any subject he liked. Naturally, Asimov jumped at the chance.

The first essay was about meteoric dust on Earth and on the moon; in the hundreds of columns that followed, he wrote about almost anything, ranging from mathematical conundrums to feminism—the choice was Asimov's. The new magazine did well and is still going strong today. Asimov continued to write his column until ill health prevented him

---

[1] *Newsday,* March 18, 1967 (Harvey Aronson).

from writing the four hundredth essay in 1991, a sad fact that, combining Asimov's obsession with numbers and his delight in writing, caused him a great deal of pain.

It was through this regular column that Asimov developed his friendly, open style of addressing the reader directly, a device he frequently used in his books. It was also the first time he was addressed as "the good doctor" in the introductory blurb to his articles, a term Asimov then, endearingly, applied to himself.

One of the great benefits of his regular column was the fact that it enabled Asimov to keep open a crack in the door of science fiction. The magazine catered primarily to the science fiction market, and so it kept his name in the minds of readers.

A further spin-off from the *Fantasy and Science Fiction* column, unforeseen at the time he started to write it, was Asimov's canny idea of periodically collecting the essays into books, which were then published by Doubleday. The first of these was *Fact and Fancy*, which was published in 1962. It contained Asimov's favorite seventeen articles, culled from the thirty-one he had contributed to the magazine up until that time. Over the years, collection after collection of his columns appeared, almost one for every year until after his death, the latest being *Frontiers II*, published by Truman Talley Books in 1993.

In contriving these collections, Asimov managed to accomplish two things at once. On the one hand he genuinely felt that the essays should have a broader circulation and deserved to be collected under headings like *Asimov on Astronomy* or *Asimov on Numbers*, but at the same time his obsession with the number of books he published was already taking over. The *F & SF* collections added dozens of titles to his total, and although the final tally of his books appears to have been 467 by the time of his death, this is a bit of a cheat because they include many anthologies, collections, and rearrangements of science fiction collections. (The exception to this was *Triangle*, published by Doubleday in 1961, which was a collection of *Pebble in the Sky*, *The Stars, Like Dust*, and *The Currents of Space*. Because he had not added a word to the text, much to his chagrin Asimov felt that he could not justify adding this to the list as a new book.) Because he had done so much work on the rewrite in 1964, Asimov did include *The New Intelligent Man's Guide to Science* as another title on the list.

Asimov's absorption with the number of books he had published was a very odd characteristic of the man, and also a great source of publicity. Relatively early on in his career, after perhaps forty or fifty titles, his prodigious output was already attracting the attention of journalists. By 1969, one journalist on the *New York Times* summed it all up by heading an interview with Asimov: "Isaac Asimov—Man of 7,560,000 words."[1]

Others could not really understand Asimov's obsession with figures. As early in his career as December 1957 and before leaving Boston University, Asimov had had twenty-four books published, and it was at this point that the first notion of reaching one hundred titles occurred to him. He mentioned this to Gertrude, who, tellingly and quite bitterly, was not impressed.

> "Someday Isaac," she said, "when you feel your life drawing to a close, you'll think back on how you spent it at the typewriter and you'll feel sorry you missed all the pleasures you might have experienced. You'll regret all the years you wasted just so that you could write a hundred books and it will be too late!"[2]

From the early 1960s onward, Asimov became as famous for his literary output as he was for his science fiction and science popularizations. Attending a gala dinner in New York in the mid-seventies, Asimov bumped into the star of M*A*S*H, Alan Alda. Asimov introduced himself. Alda looked at him and quipped, "Hello there. Why aren't you at home writing a book?"

Asimov's phenomenal tally of books has even reached the pages of a science fiction novel. In *Valencies* by Rory Barnes and Damien Broderick can be found this playful lampooning of Asimov's obsession:

> "Have you ever read of the early proleptic poems of Asimov? Prediaspora, about two thousand years ago?"
>
>   "Child, I make it a firm rule never to vid classics. The only

[1] *New York Times,* August 3, 1969 (by Lewis Nichols).
[2] *Opus 100* by Isaac Asimov. Houghton Mifflin, Boston, 1969 (Introduction, p. xiv).

Asimov I've ever heard of is the fellow who directed the com-
pilation of the rather arrogantly titled *Asimov's Encyclopedia
Galactica.*"

"That's the chap. I can't see why you think it's arrogant, he
wrote the bloody thing."

The gene-sculptor jerked violently, and managed to get his
hand up her skirt. "What, all five thousand volumes?"

"Easy with those fingernails. Yes, he's a demon for work,
poor old bugger. There's nothing much else for him to do, he
was eighty-nine when they perfected the immortality process.
If you're interested, he has a retrospective in the DATA-
BANK called *Opus 6000.*"[1]

Asimov may never have made *Opus 6000*, but as early as 1969 *Opus 100*
had been published.

The idea for a retrospective of Asimov's first ninety-nine books first
arose in the autumn of 1968 over lunch in Boston with Austin Olney and
other editors from Houghton Mifflin. They began to talk about the tally
of his books, and he pointed out that he had just received the advance
copy of his ninety-second book, *The Dark Ages*, and that seven more were
in press. Austin Olney then suggested that the hundredth should be something special, perhaps a collection of excerpts from the first ninety-nine,
with some personal discussion about the author to interlink them.

Naturally, Asimov loved the idea; as he put it: "Any writer who is a
monster of vanity and egocentricity—like myself, for instance—would
love to write a book like that."[2]

The book was published in October 1969, by which time Asimov had
already written several books over the hundred, some of which were in
press, ready for publication immediately after *Opus 100*.

Houghton Mifflin threw a launch party in Boston, and as Asimov cir-
culated happily with his Boston friends, he must have secretly wondered
how many more books he could possibly write in his lifetime. He was

---

[1] *Valencies* by Rory Barnes and Damien Broderick, as quoted in *Trillion Year Space* by
Brian Aldiss with David Wingrove. Paladin, London, 1988.
[2] *Opus 100* (p. xv).

approaching his fiftieth birthday and had written over one hundred titles in nineteen years. Secretly, he may have harbored dreams of doubling the number and perhaps, in a decade or so, attending another party to mark the publication of *Opus 200*. But I'm sure that not even Asimov in his most immodest frame of mind would have imagined that he might, in his lifetime, witness the publication of over 360 more of his books.

11

DIVORCE AND NEW LOVE

A simov arrived back in New York on the Friday evening of the Fourth of July weekend 1970, alone. He checked into the Cromwell Hotel, a place with which he had grown familiar during his frequent visits to the city. The difference this time was that he was intending to stay there for a lot longer than his usual one or two nights.

The first night in his new home was incredibly lonely. He knew he had done the right thing and that he had to get away from his stagnating life with Gertrude and the claustrophobia of Boston; but what was he to do next? There was always his writing to escape to, but his library had been boxed and transported to New York by a haulage firm and would take several days to arrive. He could not visit the publishing houses on a weekend, and most of his friends who lived in the city had gone away for the national holiday. That first Friday was, he later claimed, the most frightening night of his life. He had not felt so low since his first night in the army, twenty-five years earlier.

Once again, he was saved from abject depression by Janet Jeppson. With a wary eye to the fact that Gertrude's lawyers might question her role in the Asimovs' marital situation, she nonetheless offered Isaac the use of her apartment at 80 Central Park West during the transition period of his settling back into New York life. Isaac decided not to accept the offer immediately and spent his first night alone at the Cromwell. But after a mostly sleepless night tossing and turning and worrying about

the future, he took Janet up on her offer and was at her door early the
next morning.

It was this move that really sealed their future together. After the bleak
loneliness of Friday, Isaac spent a wonderful weekend with his closest
friend. They strolled around Central Park and talked all day and all Saturday evening. On Sunday they drove to Westchester (where Janet's parents lived but were away at the time). It was the perfect antidote to the
trauma of separation and divorce. By the end of the weekend Isaac felt
refreshed and confident, ready to face the world and the problems that
lay ahead, and Janet, who ran her own psychiatry practice, had to return
to her patients.

Realizing that he could not work on any large-scale projects straightaway, Asimov began to fret. He was anxious that he might never be able
to write again because of the traumas he was facing. Overcoming this
illogical superstition, he forced himself to work on an optimistic science
fiction story. He called it "The Greatest Asset," and although it was
rejected by the magazine for which it had been originally written, Asimov
sold it to Campbell the very same day. He was back in business.

Isaac and Janet began to spend more and more time together, and
Isaac found himself staying at Janet's apartment more than at the
Cromwell. After a few months of flitting between the two, Janet finally
suggested that he move into her apartment and use his hotel room solely
as an office. The Cromwell could be his mailing address and he could set
up his library there. Janet's apartment was close by, and there was plenty
of space for the two of them. Isaac quickly realized that he could keep one
of his two typewriters at the Cromwell and the other at Janet's apartment
in case of sudden inspiration. It made perfect sense and he took her up
on the offer straightaway.

As the summer of 1970 progressed, Isaac and Janet realized that they
were falling in love, and before August was out, within two months of
Isaac's arrival in New York, they made their relationship public. Isaac
took Janet out to dinner with his friends, some of whom she already
knew, and they were soon to be seen out socially with the del Reys, Ben
Bova, Larry Ashmead, and others. Isaac's friends all immediately
accepted the new arrangement and got on very well with Janet.

Lester del Rey and Isaac had been friends from the early days of

Campbell's editorship of *Astounding*, when they had both written for the magazine. Lester's first wife, Evelyn, who had been very close to Isaac, had died in a car crash early in 1969. Del Rey remarried in 1971 and his new wife was Judy-Lynn Benjamin, with whom Isaac had been good friends for several years. She worked for some time on the science fiction magazine *Galaxy* before moving to Ballantine books, so her relationship with Isaac, like so many of his friends', was both professional and personal.

In the early seventies, Isaac began to blossom again. Friends began to notice how much happier he appeared to be. He had, of course, always been very good at concealing his true feelings—smothering any signs of depression with a puff of ebullience—a mask that he imagined was more effective than it really was. His close friends had realized how jaded his relationship with Gertrude had become and how much he needed to escape the restrictions of his life in Boston. With Janet, Isaac was once again his old self.

Isaac found a great personal happiness in his relationship with Janet, but black clouds were gathering on the horizon. As much as the seventies were a time of liberation for Isaac and a period in which he finally realized contentment with his partner, it was also a time plagued with troubles.

It began in July 1971 with the death of John Campbell. Although Campbell and Asimov had drifted apart during the late fifties, they still corresponded, and their personal relationship had survived despite their falling out over philosophical opinions. Asimov had always hated pseudoscience, and Campbell reveled in it, dabbling with cults such as Dianetics, created by the onetime pulp writer Ron Hubbard. Asimov also strongly disapproved of Campbell's politics and social theories. There was Campbell at one extreme with his anglophilic jingoism, and at the other end of the spectrum the Nixon-loathing liberal Asimov. But none of these differences of mere opinion diminished the pain Asimov felt upon hearing the news of his friend's death.

Campbell died at the age of sixty-one, after his aorta burst while watching television. He had been a heavy smoker his entire adult life and knew that as he was suffering from severely hardened arteries, it was only a matter of time.

The memorial service was attended by a small group of Campbell's close friends and colleagues. Asimov read the Twenty-third Psalm and the party returned to the Campbells' home for a quiet drink.

Asimov said that his emotions at the death of Campbell were second only to those he experienced at the death of his father, Judah, two years earlier. He was the first to declare that he owed his literary career to the great editor and that Campbell was "my literary father."[1]

Asimov had met Campbell thirty-three years earlier, and although he had sold very few stories to him for the best part of fifteen years, Asimov knew that he was deeply indebted to *Astounding*'s editor. If it had not been for Campbell's guidance and inspiration when Asimov was young, his road to literary and financial success would have been a great deal rockier.

Less than six months passed before the next crisis arose in Asimov's life. In January 1972, after a routine medical examination, it was discovered that he had a cancerous growth in his thyroid gland and needed an urgent operation.

For the first time, at the age of fifty-two, he confronted the prospect of an early death. He had no fear of dying, except that, most oddly, he was scared of what he saw as posthumous embarrassment, believing that people would ridicule him for living only to the age of fifty-two, as though he were some sort of medical freak.

The operation was a complete success (even after he had given the surgeon the jitters by reciting amusing doggerel about his throat being cut minutes before the first incision was to be made). He was out of hospital and back at his typewriter within three weeks. The doctor who had performed the operation insisted that he take it easy. But Isaac, being Isaac, could not resist his greatest pleasures in life—writing and sex. He was back at the Cromwell four days after being discharged from the hospital and would have been there sooner had he not been physically restrained by Janet.

Isaac did not consider sex a health risk after the operation and jokingly told his doctor that sex did not cause him any stress. The jokes fell on deaf ears, and it was only after the doctor became angry that he agreed to behave himself.

---

[1] *In Joy Still Felt* by Isaac Asimov. Doubleday, New York, 1980 (p. 572).

Although Isaac often passed off his anxieties with a joke or a funny story (even at the point of undergoing a dangerous operation), he had been very ill and would probably have died if the thyroid growth had gone unchecked. The operation also came at a bad time—in the middle of the arguments surrounding his divorce. Isaac claimed that the divorce process should have gone smoothly and that the last thing he wanted was to have a protracted battle with his estranged wife.

Proceedings began almost immediately after Isaac moved out of the family home in Newton. Early on, things appeared to be going smoothly. Isaac had made Gertrude an offer that apparently both she and her lawyer thought reasonable. Then, for some unknown reason, Gertrude suddenly decided that the original offer was not good enough, sacked her lawyer, and hired a far more aggressive attorney. Things turned nasty when Gertrude's lawyer froze Isaac's earnings from Houghton Mifflin, pending settlement.

Isaac fought the ruling and eventually had it reversed. He was not desperate for money but resented the action as a point of principle. He had always argued that *he* should retain the majority of the Asimov family fortune because it was he who had earned the money. He did not seem to consider that Gertrude had a serious claim to half the total value of the estate as she had been keeping the family home together and raising two children while he wrote books.

The battles went on. After Isaac's financial and legal details had been placed in evidence, the press got hold of his personal documents, and it was revealed in a Boston newspaper that the author earned over 200,000 dollars a year. The media made much of the fact that a "mere" science fiction writer could command such a staggering income. It even made the radio station news in Massachusetts.

The proceedings meant that Isaac had to travel to Boston on numerous occasions, taking him away from his work and disrupting his routine. It was bad for his career and he loathed the fact that while the wrangles with Gertrude continued, he could not keep up his normal prodigious output. But then, Isaac always did love a fight and would move heaven and earth over a point of principle. In this respect he appears to have had a very strange moral code. He did not seem to think that cheating on his wife was immoral, but if he was given a penny too much change at a drugstore he would immediately return to hand it back.

Isaac claimed that there was no question of adultery involved in the divorce case. This was simply because Gertrude could not prove it. Doubtless, her lawyers wanted to use a claim of adultery to strengthen her case and obtain a larger settlement, but Isaac must have covered his tracks so well that there was no chance of using this allegation against him. There is also the possibility that Gertrude disliked thinking that her husband had been unfaithful to her before their separation and therefore refused to push the point.

During the many months of arguments, claims, and counterclaims, Gertrude's lawyers were playing a childish game. Their favorite pastime was to call for a hearing that Isaac had to attend, and then cancel it at the last moment so that his five-hundred-mile round trip would be a waste of time. This happened so often that when the hearing actually did take place on November 16, 1973, Isaac was caught unawares and was unprepared. On that date a settlement was reached and Isaac and Gertrude were finally divorced.

Isaac made great claims regarding his quixotic approach to the divorce. He publicly stated that he wanted to give more to Gertrude than his lawyers actually thought fair and that he even stopped them arguing further to reduce the alimony. He declared that, acting against the advice of his lawyers, he insisted that his original and very generous offer be accepted.

This all sounds quite out of character and totally unbelievable. Indeed, these claims are the exact opposite of what close friends recall about the fights and arguments between the Asimovs. The most telling fact is Isaac's own revelation that the legal fees for the divorce process cost him fifty thousand dollars, surely a ridiculously high sum if, from the start, he had so magnanimously insisted on giving Gertrude more than was reasonable.

During the three and a half years of the divorce process, legal and financial wranglings were not the only traumas Isaac and his new partner had to face. No sooner had Isaac undergone the thyroid operation than Janet found what turned out to be a cancerous lump in her left breast. In July 1972, she was taken into the hospital to undergo exploratory surgery. The doctors found the growth and performed a mastectomy.

When she came around after the operation, Janet was naturally devastated by the news. Isaac insisted that he be at her bedside as she awoke and that he should be the first person she saw. It was the most traumatic thing that had ever happened to her and she was naturally obsessed with the notion that such a disfigurement would mean that Isaac would leave her for a younger, more healthy woman.

Isaac reassured her that she was talking absolute nonsense and that he would do no such thing, that he loved her very much and planned to marry her just as soon as he could; but his words had little effect. It was only after realizing that kind words and comfort were getting him nowhere that he turned his famous humor on her. Being so upset would be understandable, he claimed, if she had been a showgirl; the removal of a breast might mean that she would lose her balance and it would affect her career, but what did she have to worry about?

It did the trick; Janet laughed for the first time in days and slowly began to come to terms with the situation.

Overcoming the trauma of the operation and the psychological and physical pain that went with it undoubtedly brought Isaac and Janet closer together and reassured both of them of their feelings for one another. However, it was not the last emotional battle to be fought alongside the divorce case.

In June 1973 Janet was again seriously ill, this time with subarachnoid bleeding—internal bleeding centered on the outer membranes of the brain.

Isaac had been in Boston on the day the bleeding occurred. He called Janet in the afternoon and thought she sounded very vague and a little confused. She reassured him that she had just had a bad night and was tired. Taking her at her word, Isaac thought no more of it. It was only after a patient of Janet's found her to be totally incoherent on the phone that the alarm was sounded. The patient managed to elicit her doctor's name from Janet, and telephoned for help. She was immediately admitted to the hospital, and a call was put through to Isaac. Naturally, he rushed back to New York to be with her.

It was touch-and-go as to whether or not Janet would need brain surgery, but in the end the doctors decided against it. She was kept in the hospital for nearly three weeks to undergo extensive tests and it was almost six weeks before she felt her old self again.

Even this incident was not the end of the traumas. In August, two months after the scare over Janet, Isaac's mother, Anna Rachel, died, just short of her seventy-eighth birthday and almost exactly four years after her husband had passed away.

She had never really overcome the loss of Judah and had, in a sense, wanted to die for some time. Although Isaac was deeply saddened by the death of his mother, it did not affect him as badly as his father's in 1969. Isaac knew that it was really a release for her.

To complete what had in many ways been one of the worst years in Isaac's life, November of 1973 brought more bad news. Days before the final settlement and the ending of Isaac and Gertrude's marriage, Robyn fell seriously ill.

She had gone to Windham College in Vermont in the summer of 1973 and seemed happy there. But in late October she contracted what she thought was a bad dose of flu. The illness became worse and she was admitted to the college infirmary, where they discovered that she had a low white blood cell count.

Gertrude visited the college and took Robyn to the Children's Hospital in Boston, where they carried out diagnostic tests. Naturally talk of low white blood cell counts made Isaac think that his daughter had leukemia; but after extensive tests the doctors ruled out that possibility. Robyn was given heavy doses of penicillin, and within a few days of being hospitalized, the illness began to subside.

She had to stay at home for some time to convalesce and was unable to complete the academic year at Windham College. After talking the matter over with her father and having several months to work out what to do, she eventually decided against returning to Windham and instead went to Boston College in 1974.

Toward the end of 1973, after riding out a whole series of family problems with Janet, Isaac began to seriously consider the possibility of remarrying. At the end of November 1973, he proposed to Janet and she accepted. Within days they were planning the wedding. Neither had any interest in a religious service, but they did not like the idea of a rather clinical civil service at the Municipal Building. Instead they decided to be married in Janet's apartment and set the date for November 30, 1973.

Isaac recalled the occasion fondly. It was a romantic setting, the sun was sinking over the towers of Manhattan, clearly visible from Janet's living room, and the wonderful red light cast bright bands across the room. They were married by Edward Ericson of the Ethical Culture movement, with which Janet and Isaac were associated, and they had two friends, Al and Phyllis Balk, as witnesses.

Janet had taken the phone off the hook immediately before the service. As soon as she had replaced the receiver when the formalities were over, the phone rang. It was Austin Olney at Houghton Mifflin in Boston, calling with the happy news that they were going to accept a science fiction novel Janet had written called *The Second Experiment*. It was her first attempt at placing a novel and she was overjoyed at its acceptance. To the gathering it was a positive omen and a wonderful start to the couple's future life together.

Janet was remarkably good for Isaac. She did not interfere with his working pattern, respecting the fact that he was a workaholic and needed to be at his typewriter for ten hours a day in the same way that he needed oxygen and food. Janet brought Isaac out of himself; she encouraged him to socialize more; and, above all, she cured his travel phobia.

But even Janet did not manage to get Isaac onto a plane, although together they did discover the next best thing—travel by ship.

Isaac had begun to realize the potential of traveling around the world without the use of the dreaded airplane some time before. He had taken a cruise on board the *Canberra* to the coast of Africa during the summer of 1973 to witness a solar eclipse. Then, before the year was out, Janet and Isaac found themselves on board the *QE2* to observe the comet Kohoutek. But the breakthrough for Isaac was his visit to Great Britain in 1974.

The trip was organized by Mensa, which saw it as an opportunity for Asimov to speak about the organization and at the same time allow him to promote his books in Britain. *The Gods Themselves* was his latest novel and marked his return to science fiction after a lengthy break. Asimov's phobia about flying had always been the stumbling block as far as visiting Europe was concerned, but now with his newfound liking for travel by sea, there was nothing to stop him.

The *QE2* docked at Southampton on June 5, 1974, and the couple were met by Steve Odell from Mensa, who was to act as their guide for the duration of their stay. They visited the famous tourist sights, taking in Stonehenge, driving through the Cotswolds, staying in Oxford, and going on a guided tour of London. Asimov did a book-signing session at Foyle's on Charing Cross Road. At the book signing, the representative from Panther, Asimov's paperback publisher in Britain, astonished the author by revealing the fact that Asimov books sold more than any others on their list in *any* genre. In Birmingham, Asimov delivered a Mensa talk, which was introduced by Arthur C. Clarke.

Asimov had for some time privately questioned the value of the IQ concept, but he enjoyed the camaraderie and the friendliness of the organization, particularly at the British end of things.

Unconsciously anglophilic his whole life, during this trip Isaac realized how at home he would have felt if he had been born an Englishman. He was always a great city person and loved the excitement of life in New York City, yet beneath the surface he felt equally comfortable with the slower pace he experienced in Europe. Both Isaac and Janet were fascinated by history. Isaac had studied and written about it without experiencing the Old World firsthand, and Janet had always gone out of her way to find history in her home country. To both of them, Britain was a fund of many of the things they found so stimulating, and they left wishing that they had arranged to stay longer.

It was during this period that Asimov first began to take an interest in humanism, a school of thought that puts human culture and achievement at the apex of philosophical considerations and totally dismisses the notion of religion or the supernatural.

The first of these notions sounds a little like the Campbellian ideal of man, the superman; but not so. Humanism does not see humans as superior to other forms of life or other races that may exist in our universe, but it places the greatest emphasis on human creativity and thought. It dismisses any notion that humankind is a creation of some nebulous deity and it supports the view that the destiny of humanity is in our hands alone.

Asimov took humanism very seriously and frequently gave talks about it as well as devoting essays and entire books to the subject. In later years he became the president of the American Humanist Association and was still holding that office when he died.

All of Asimov's work is naturally influenced by his political and philosophical opinions. Although his views developed in subtle ways as he grew older, the substance of his social, political, and philosophical views was remarkably consistent throughout his adult life.

Asimov placed education and knowledge at the pinnacle of his beliefs and was strongly of the opinion that the ignorance of those in political power lay at the root of the world's problems. Like many of his friends and colleagues, he lamented the appalling scientific ignorance of most people. This ignorance was all the more scandalous, he believed, in those who were otherwise highly educated. Asimov was a natural teacher, and at the root of his pleasure in teaching was his desire to educate the people he spoke to in the things that mattered most to him.

A constantly recurring theme in Asimov's talks and in much of his nonfiction writing was his belief that the world was already overpopulated, and that the continuation, or not, of this trend would be the key to a future blackened with plague and starvation—or a world that could grow and provide a stable, comfortable life for its inhabitants. He also placed a great emphasis on these themes in his fiction. *The Caves of Steel* was a nightmare scenario of global metropolises and computer-controlled discipline necessitated by the overpopulation and food supply crises he saw as an almost inevitable feature of the future.

Asimov's power to alter the thinking of people was limited, but as the world's most famous and successful science writer, he did as much as he could. Through his work with the American Humanist Association, his writings and his frequent television and lecture appearances and his talks on radio, he constantly discussed and analyzed the important issues concerning the future of the world and offered possible solutions to the problems ahead. In this way he was following the lead taken by such luminaries as Albert Einstein and Bertrand Russell. He shared the ideal of a world government, global disarmament, and the application of science to help society to cure its ills and prevent new ones.

While Asimov did not become publicly involved in politics, he was a vigorous armchair Democrat. He hated Nixon above all politicians, and once claimed that if Satan had been running on the Democratic ticket, he would have voted for him before turning to Nixon. Asimov was suspicious of Nixon many years before Watergate and absolutely reveled in what he saw as the man's deserved political destruction.

Although he did not speak along party political lines, Asimov was political in a broader sense. He took part in Non-Parents Day, which was a demonstration designed to highlight the problems of overpopulation, and he participated in several battles against fundamentalist groups in Tennessee when they tried to ban the teaching of evolutionary theory in public schools. He believed it to be his duty and purpose in life to defeat ignorance wherever he saw it and with whatever weapon lay at his disposal.

Soon after arriving back in New York in the autumn of 1974, the Asimovs began to think about moving out of Janet's apartment.

Janet had her eye on a property on West 66th Street. It was an ideal location, close to the museums, with spectacular views of Central Park. It was spacious and quiet, a penthouse on the thirty-third floor of one of New York's most exclusive apartment blocks.

One New York publisher described how, when he was viewing a far more modest apartment in the same area of the city during the late 1980s, the estate agent showing him around had pointed out the roof of a penthouse building across the street but many floors beneath them. "That's the Asimovs' apartment," he said. The publisher stared at it in amazement. "I thought it was an indoor football arena," he said.

Isaac was not terribly keen on moving but accepted that it was becoming necessary. Janet wanted somewhere bigger and the new neighbors on the floor above them were incredibly noisy. Isaac still traveled to the Cromwell every day, but the place was changing. The owners were converting it to an apartment block and the constant building work going on all around him in the once peaceful hotel was becoming annoying.

The move to West 66th Street didn't get arranged until the spring of the following year, by which time Asimov was once again working on a new science fiction story, which proved to be one of his most famous, "The Bicentennial Man." Finished at the Cromwell on the eve of their move, it was the last piece of writing he completed at the hotel before dismantling his office and having his beloved library and the collection of irreplaceable manuscripts moved to his new home.

Asimov soon settled into his new environment. It was to be the last move of his life; he lived and worked on 66th Street until his death almost twenty years later—the longest period he remained living in one place.

By the mid-seventies, Asimov was a science celebrity around the world. He could command large fees to talk at banquets and scientific meetings, and he was frequently asked to appear on television. His first time on network TV was in 1957, and during the sixties and seventies hardly a month went by without "the good doctor" being called upon to talk about anything scientific in the news. By 1974, he had even made the *Encyclopaedia Britannica*. His name appeared under ASIMOV, ISAAC, and was included in the SCIENCE FICTION entry as well, entry along with other luminaries of the genre such as Heinlein and Clarke.

Asimov was also attracting the attention of Hollywood. Over the years a number of movie options had been taken out on Asimov's stories, including *The Caves of Steel*, *The Naked Sun*, and *I, Robot*, but they had all come to nothing. At the time, the closest any of Asimov's stories came to the silver screen was *I, Robot*, which would not hit cinemas until 2004, starring Will Smith.

In 1977, Hollywood producers John Mantley, Edward Lewis, and Mildred Lewis set things in motion. They bought an option on the robot collection and commissioned Harlan Ellison to write the screenplay. The purchase came shortly after the huge global success of *Close Encounters of the Third Kind* and *Star Wars*, films that had made science fiction very fashionable in Tinseltown.

The project was given an estimated thirty-million-dollar budget and Ellison wrote a two-hundred-page screenplay, but things soon fell apart over arguments between Ellison and the producers. Ellison hated the new spate of science fiction films of the *Star Wars* variety; presumably Hollywood wanted more of the same rather than Ellison's rather avant-garde version of the Asimov stories. Asimov himself loved what Ellison had done with *I, Robot*, but Hollywood dropped the idea as quickly as it had been picked up.

Asimov had not become involved in Hollywood since his novelization of *Fantastic Voyage*. But by the 1970s anyone becoming involved in the field of science fiction for the first time naturally gravitated toward Isaac Asimov. He was not only the most visible author in terms of shelf space in the bookshops of the world, but he was also frequently on TV and in the newspapers because of his science popularization, sociopolitical arguments, and fame as an almost absurdly prolific writer.

He frequently accepted offers to advise on the making of science fiction films, but because he would not uproot himself to travel to California and never entertained the idea of staying there temporarily, his involvement never went much beyond preliminary chats with producers.

Gene Roddenberry, the producer of *Star Trek,* became a friend of Asimov's during the early sixties and often consulted him during the making of the series. Roddenberry constantly had to fight battles with film executives who knew absolutely nothing about science but frequently questioned the feasibility of a scientific idea he had used in the script. Roddenberry would then call on his famous friend for support. It is easy to imagine the fury and frustration Roddenberry must have felt when his ideas were questioned by people he perceived as clerks. Asimov was his very effective secret weapon and always won the day.

Asimov loved *Star Trek* and attended many conventions during the seventies. These "Trekkie conventions" grew increasingly popular during the decade, and Asimov would occasionally appear as the star speaker and do his turn for sometimes tens of thousands of fanatical Trekkies.

Woody Allen was probably the first filmmaker to approach Asimov. A lunch meeting was organized during the planning stages of Allen's film *Sleeper.* The director was interested in testing the science in the script to make sure that his ideas were feasible. Asimov reassured him that they were. The two men chatted for an hour, and that was the last Asimov ever heard. He did not even receive a thank-you letter.

Paul McCartney approached Asimov for the same reason. They met in New York and McCartney discussed the ideas for a film proposal he was working on. The story concerned a group of extraterrestrials who were impersonating the members of a famous pop group. McCartney asked Asimov if he could prepare a preliminary treatment for the screenplay. Asimov agreed, and delivered the piece long before the suggested deadline—and it was rejected. This time Asimov received a fair payment for his efforts, and that was the last he ever heard of the project.

The closest Asimov came to becoming deeply involved with a movie was in 1975. Steven Spielberg asked him to be technical adviser for his new project, *Close Encounters of the Third Kind*. At their first meeting in New York the two men immediately got along well, but while Asimov liked the idea of the film, he nonetheless turned Spielberg down.

Some people have been surprised by Asimov's attitude to the film industry, but it is not as odd as it initially seems. He had, after all, experienced great frustration during the novelization of *Fantastic Voyage*. Asimov never was a team player and collaborated very rarely during his career. More important was the fact that he really had no need to get involved in filmmaking.

By the mid-seventies, Asimov was a multimillionaire who had no wish to totally disrupt his life by moving across the country or traveling between California and New York. He did not need the money; the effort would not do anything to add to his already highly esteemed position in the world of science fiction; and he did not find the medium particularly exciting to work in.

He once declared: "I detest Hollywood and stay clear of it just as much as possible."[1] On another occasion, he said: "The visual media are not my bag, really."[2] He claimed to have had no regrets about never getting involved in films.

After the health scares of the early seventies, Isaac, prompted by Janet, agreed to take better care of himself. He began to watch his weight and to generally show his body greater respect. At Janet's insistence they began to take frequent holidays together. They traveled to the Caribbean on board the *QE2* in 1976 and spent two much-needed weeks away from New York. Naturally, Isaac did not leave work behind entirely and wrote for at least two hours each day, but gone were the days when he would lock himself away for the entire duration of a vacation and behave the same way as he did at home.

Despite this greater awareness of the passing years and the need to slow down, Isaac's health took a dramatic turn for the worse toward the end of the 1970s. His first serious health problem since his thyroid operation in 1971 was a coronary in 1977.

---

[1] *Asimov Laughs Again* by Isaac Asimov. HarperCollins, New York, 1992 (p. 50).
[2] *In Joy Still Felt* (p. 717).

This first attack was really a warning, and, amazingly, Isaac did not even know that he had had a heart attack until after the event.

It came during a particularly intense period of public talks in Pennsylvania during May 1977, and at first he thought that it was another attack of kidney stones, a complaint that had plagued him from time to time over the past twenty years.

Isaac believed that the attack was precipitated by eating a giant slice of creamy cheesecake in his hotel room during the late evening, just before going to bed. Whatever the cause, the pain he woke up to in the early hours of the next morning was so intense that he thought he was going to die. He even gave Janet instructions concerning his funeral and the form of memorial service he wanted.

By dawn the pain had subsided, and against Janet's protestations, Isaac decided to carry on with his schedule even though he was feeling breathless and unusually tired. He continued with the program, claiming, "I have no time for angina."[1]

Back in New York a few days later, Isaac finally submitted to Janet's protests and visited his doctor to undergo tests. An ECG was performed and the results stunned him. The intense pain he had experienced a few days earlier had indeed been a heart attack, but luckily only a mild one.

Within hours Isaac was admitted to the hospital for more rigorous tests and observation. He spent three weeks in the hospital, the first few days in intensive care and then in a private room where he was kept under constant observation.

After two weeks of enforced inertia in the hospital, Isaac was starting to go crazy. He finally managed to persuade his doctor to allow him to work for a short period each day under strict supervision. This made his spell in the hospital easier, as Janet visited daily and Larry Ashmead called in several times during the following week.

Isaac was released from the hospital after three weeks and ordered to lose twenty pounds in weight. He was told to slow down his working practices and to take regular, thorough breaks and nonworking vacations. He agreed to the first request and lost the required weight within a month of leaving the hospital. The other demands were only partly met.

---

[1] *In Joy Still Felt* (p. 771).

Despite all the traumas and problems the decade had thrown at him—the depressing scenes of the divorce courts, the frequent hospitalizations for both himself and Janet, and the fears over the health of his daughter—he had fulfilled his dream of doubling his tally of books in little over a decade after *Opus 100*. Late in 1979 he saw the publication of *Opus 200* and entered the record books as one of the top ten most prolific writers in the history of literature.

Throughout the 1970s Asimov had continued to deliver book after book of nonfiction and had reinforced his formidable reputation as the world's leading science popularizer. Yet he had still found time for other interests and new pinnacles of achievement, for it was also the decade in which he delighted his millions of fans by returning to the world of science fiction.

Despite a break of almost a decade and a half, when Asimov did return to science fiction, he showed the world that the old magic was still there and delivered what some consider his best novel in the genre. After its publication, Asimov was lionized within the science fiction community and given the highest honors they could bestow. The old master of science fiction was back with one of his most commercially successful books yet, enjoying both critical acclaim and millions of sales around the globe.

12

RETURNING TO FIRST LOVE

The 1960s were a period of revolution in many spheres of life, and this extended into the world of science fiction. In many respects the writing of the fifties epitomized by Asimov, Heinlein, and the other stars of the Campbell stable reflected the relative innocence of the times. As early as 1964 things rapidly began to change.

The last science fiction novel of Asimov's first wave was *The Naked Sun*, published in 1957. He had stopped writing these novels partly through boredom and partly because he had run out of ideas, finding fresh inspiration in nonfiction. However, he remained a fan of the genre, read widely, and continued to write the occasional short story.

By the early sixties, the science fiction field had begun to undergo a metamorphosis, and according to some of the young writers who were just emerging onto the scene, Asimov's novels were the work of a dinosaur.

This new science fiction was christened the "New Wave" by Asimov's friend, the writer and editor Judith Merril. Catalyst for so many new careers in the field and leader of the movement was the British writer Michael Moorcock. Although during the sixties he established his reputation as a highly respected and successful writer, he could also be seen as the John Campbell of the New Wave.

In 1964, Moorcock took over the editorship of the science fiction magazine *New Worlds* and immediately offered a platform for the avant-garde science fiction writers of the time, writers who have since become gurus of the genre—J. G. Ballard, Brian Aldiss, and Moorcock himself.

The New Wave writers whose work appeared in *New Worlds* wanted to shake up the art of science fiction writing. They were bored with the rather gentlemanly, polite science fiction that had dominated the field from the earliest days. They wanted to give it an edge, to produce work that was more literary and had a strong social conscience.

New Wave was really the antithesis of Asimov's style of writing. Asimov was never particularly interested in literary form, and although he made halfhearted efforts to write political stories such as "The Martian Way," he did not consciously imbue his work with socially aware messages. Asimov had strong liberal principles, but he did not squeeze them into his plots and characterizations. New Wave writers made a virtue out of it.

It has been claimed that Asimov did not approve of much of the work of the New Wave. One author has even suggested that Asimov joined a group of "old wave" writers who tried to stop the New Wave by threatening to withhold their work from publishers who dealt with these new authors.

This may seem unlikely, but Asimov often displayed a strangely disjointed morality. At times he seemed to have one set of rules for himself and another set for others, so it is conceivable that he could be petty enough to act in this way. Asimov was a great believer in personal liberty, he strongly opposed censorship and supported the view that writers should be allowed to express themselves in whatever way they preferred; but at the same time he disapproved of the ethos behind the New Wave and may have felt that it was potentially damaging to science fiction in general. Asimov had nothing in common with the movement, except that some of his friends were New Wave writers. He knew that authors of the stature of Harlan Ellison would not be adversely affected by his protests, but perhaps saw it as his duty to hinder New Wave from going too far.

The most likely explanation is that Asimov probably made a flippant remark at a science convention or during conversation with some colleagues to the effect that he would threaten to boycott his publishers if they continued heightening the profile of the New Wave movement he so disliked. Either way, if he actually did try to interfere in the progress of the New Wave, he was acting in an extraordinarily high-handed fashion and was quite ineffectual.

Asimov said many times during the 1960s that he could not return to science fiction because it had moved away from him. He had no wish to compromise his own writing style; he was happy with his nonfiction work, although he still wrote the occasional short story for *Astounding* and other magazines.

He would certainly not have felt at home trying to write in a New Wave style. Key elements in many short stories and books of the time included explicit sex and language that could be considered obscene. Asimov disliked both of these in science fiction, and he certainly did not approve of many of the views expressed in the stories appearing in *New Worlds* under Moorcock's editorship.

The New Wave was linked with the fashions of the time and expressed the rebellious mood of the period. It was steeped in drug references and ambiguous sexuality, pop culture, and even what would later be known as sword and sorcery—fantasy and mythology-based fiction. Books like J. G. Ballard's *The Atrocity Exhibition* and Samuel R. Delany's *The Einstein Intersection* were a very different breed from Asimov's polite, pangalactic space operas.

The Atrocity Exhibition was written in the sixties but not published until 1972 because of the controversy surrounding its often brutal imagery. When a senior executive at its original publisher took exception to the book, they got cold feet and pulled the plug on the project shortly before publication. Such a fate could hardly have been imagined with something like *The Caves of Steel*.

Yet in 1966, despite having by all accounts left science fiction writing for good, and as the New Wave really began to get a foothold in both Europe and America, Asimov was awarded the most prestigious and coveted prize in science fiction—a Hugo for *The Foundation Trilogy*.

Until then he had not won a Hugo and was fond of letting everyone know it. In September 1966, the twenty-fourth World Science Fiction convention was held in Cleveland—just within Asimov's sphere of movement. The whole family were invited and made the trip in greater excitement because they had missed the twenty-second and twenty-third conventions held in California and London, respectively.

The organizers of the Cleveland convention had created a special Hugo that year to be given to the author of the "Best All-Time Novel

Series." This they defined as a collection of at least three interlinking books.

There were five nominations for the award: J. R. R. Tolkien's *The Lord of the Rings,* Robert Heinlein's Future History series, the Lensman books of E. E. "Doc" Smith, Edgar Rice Burroughs' Mars series, and, of course, *The Foundation Trilogy.* Asimov was convinced that *The Lord of the Rings* would win by a healthy margin and secretly expected to be placed fourth, above either Burroughs or Smith.

Harlan Ellison was chosen to hand out the awards and made a big ceremony of the event, deliberately building up the tension in the main hall, packed with thousands of science fiction fans. After making a series of quips and jokes at the expense of the contestants, Ellison then proceeded to read out the nominations and deliberately omitted the Foundation series.

Asimov was protesting loudly even as Ellison went on to say, "And the winner is . . ." When Ellison announced "The Foundation series," Asimov found himself in what for him was an unnatural and very rare state—he was totally speechless.

For Asimov it was perhaps the greatest triumph of his career. He had grown used to "Nightfall" being perceived as the "best science fiction short story of all time," but because of the poor organization at Gnome Press, he had absolutely no idea just how popular his series had been in both commercial and critical terms.

It was, Asimov recalled, a wonderful evening, full of laughter and great personal satisfaction. He was surrounded by his closest friends and family, all of whom had been rooting for him, and they were delighted that he had finally received an award for his best-known work. John Campbell was there, the man who had initiated the whole venture; even Asimov's colleagues, deeply immersed in the budding New Wave movement, expressed their happiness, for although they did not want to write in the same way as the old school, many of them still had the utmost respect for those they saw as the founders of modern science fiction.

It is difficult to accurately assess the importance placed on the award by the book-buying public, but after receiving the Hugo in 1966, sales of *The Foundation Trilogy* greatly increased. Five years earlier Doubleday had taken over publication of the series from the ailing Gnome Press run by Martin Greenberg, and they really knew how to publicize Asimov's work and get his books into the shops.

Asimov had realized years earlier that he should take the books back from Gnome but had thought that he would have to sue his old friend Greenberg to get them. Luckily for Asimov, Doubleday bought the series from Greenberg without fuss and for what they considered a modest sum. Greenberg emerged as the real loser from the whole affair because the books went on to sell millions and ended up being Asimov's biggest sellers.

An indication of the success of the series is demonstrated by two events. By 1972, Robyn Asimov, who was taking a course in science fiction at high school, found herself in the rather odd position of having her father's most famous work on her reading list. In 1975, a company called Caedmon Records bought the recording rights to the Foundation series and employed the actor William Shatner, who was internationally famous as Captain James T. Kirk, to read the books. Audio books were a relatively rare phenomenon in the seventies.

Despite the adulation of his fans around the world and the great personal success of the 1966 convention, Asimov did not return to science fiction for a further five years. When he did he found that he had yet another blockbuster on his hands, *The Gods Themselves*.

The book that marked Asimov's return actually began life as a short story inspired by a dare thrown out at a literary meeting in January 1971.

Writer Robert Silverberg had been arguing that the human aspects of a good science fiction story should be made more important than any scientific point in the plot. Waving his hand in the air and picking an example at random, he suggested that no one would be interested in reading about . . . say . . . plutonium-186.

During a conversation with Silverberg after the talk, Asimov commented on the statement and said that he could write a short story about the nonexistent chemical plutonium-186 that *was* entertaining. Silverberg declared that if he could and it turned out to be a good story, he would include it in an anthology of original stories he was putting together. Asimov set to work on it straightaway.

As soon as he began, Asimov felt the old thrill of writing science fiction returning and found he could not stop. He had planned to make the story five thousand words in length, and he was an expert at writing to requirements and delivering exactly what was asked of him, but part of his excitement lay in the fact that he could just let this story run away with him if he wanted.

He finished the story on February 28, and it ended up at twenty thousand words. Asimov immediately realized that it would be too long for Silverberg's planned anthology but that he might be able to do something about it because Doubleday was publishing the collection and he could try to talk Larry Ashmead into lengthening the book.

Ashmead read the story and loved it. Within two days he was on the phone to Asimov with the suggestion that the story might be expanded into a novel. Asimov was unconvinced. He believed that the story stood up as it was and that any expansion of the original story would weaken it and make it seem padded. Then, as he was talking, he had the idea of writing a novel in three sections. The story as it stood would constitute the first part. He would then write two more sections, which looked at the central theme from different angles and end upbeat, rather than with the present downbeat conclusion.

This time it was Ashmead's turn to be dubious, but Asimov succeeded in persuading him that it would work, and the deal was agreed. The contract was signed a week later.

The Gods Themselves is certainly the most unusual novel Asimov ever wrote. He was particularly pleased with the middle section, and when it was finished, he thought he had done something truly original and different.

The title originated in the Friedrich von Schiller quotation "Against stupidity, the gods themselves contend in vain." The first part of the book was entitled "Against Stupidity," the second "The Gods Themselves," and the final section "Contend in Vain?"—with the crucial question mark added. These titles fitted the sections perfectly, as did the overall title of the finished novel.

"Against Stupidity" is classic Asimov, a story of one man against the establishment, in the same mold as Hari Seldon or Salvor Hardin. This time the challenge for our hero has arisen over the discovery of an endless energy source that, he realizes, will destroy the world.

In 2070, Frederich Hallam discovers a new "impossible" substance in his lab. After extensive tests he makes the intuitive leap that turns him into a global celebrity: that the substance had originated in a parallel universe. Being an entrepreneurial chap, he eventually builds what he calls an "electron pump," which transfers material between the universes and creates energy.

Hallam's electron pump is built from instructions sent to him by the beings living in the parallel universe. They seem far more advanced technologically and are running the show as far as the transfer of energy is concerned. However, there is no communication between the two universes except for the passage of energy and the information needed to construct the pump.

Our hero, Peter Lament, is suspicious of the whole affair and gathers evidence that the use of the pump will cause an imbalance in our universe that will lead to an overheating of the sun and eventually supernova. Naturally nobody wants to believe him, least of all Hallam, who has become, thanks to his invention, the world's greatest scientist.

"Against Stupidity" ends on the downbeat with our hero seemingly defeated and waiting for the coming conflagration as the sun heats up and threatens to destroy the entire solar system.

Although tightly written and entertaining, "Against Stupidity" is a little too stiff, a little too much like a science lecture. The fact that Asimov had spent the past decade writing nonfiction is all too obvious. This does not quite ruin the enjoyment of "Against Stupidity," because Asimov is skillful enough to hover close to overexposition but pulls back just in time to drive the narrative into action.

The second part of the novel, "The Gods Themselves," is like nothing else Asimov had ever written. The natural route to take after the ending of "Against Stupidity" would have been to deal with the inhabitants of the parallel universe, to see the story from their side of the fence, and this is exactly what Asimov did. But he did not merely describe an alternative universe populated by human beings. For almost the first time in his career he created a totally alien world, complete with its own politics, sex lives, emotions, language, and all the other aspects of society.

Asimov had of course kept well away from aliens ever since the early writing days and his arguments with Campbell. Perhaps it was this self-censorship that resulted in him pulling out all the stops with "The Gods Themselves."

The inhabitants of the parallel universe are semigaseous, nebulous creatures, of three types called "emotionals," "rationals," and "parentals." Instead of living as couples with children, the aliens' family unit is made up of all three individuals, each contributing one or other of their personality aspects to the well-being of the unit and the alien society in general.

"The Gods Themselves" is all about sex. Whereas Asimov had avoided writing about sex as much as he had aliens, here he appears to let his hair down. I say "appears to" because he did not really let himself go. By making sex as alien as possible he neatly avoided describing conventional sex and thus circumvented his personal foibles on the subject.

The three central characters in this section of the story—the emotional, Dua, a vaguely female character, and the two "male" personalities, Odeen, the rational, and Tritt, the parental—engage in what they call "melting" as often as they possibly can.

Sex in the parallel universe is as far removed from sex here on Earth as the aliens themselves are different from solid humans. It also has a slightly different purpose. The three gaseous forms of aliens are not the only types of creatures in their universe. The offspring created by melting are solid creatures that are actually the amalgamation of the three gaseous ones. In other words, the three gaseous creatures of the family unit are a transitory phase in the life cycle of the alien. When they melt they temporarily form what they call "a hard one"; after frequent melting the time arrives when the hard one is "born" out of the three of them and they evolve into this new stage of their physical lives.

It is only at the end of the story that we realize that a fleetingly referred-to character, a hard-one scientist called Estwald, is in fact the leader of the project creating the electron pump and transferring material to Earth.

Things are complicated when Dua, in a parallel to Lamont on Earth, suspects that what Estwald is doing is wrong. Gradually Dua discovers that the transportation of material into the parallel universe will destroy our star system and tries to stop the project. The problem Dua faces is different from that faced by Lamont. In the parallel universe, the scientist Estwald is fully aware of the fact that the pumping of material will destroy our sun, but he has to do it to save his own world, which orbits an old and dying sun. Dua's is not a problem created by the greed of humanity, but a result of the simple need for survival.

"The Gods Themselves" ends in a very similar way to the conclusion of "Against Stupidity." Dua's mission is thwarted by the others around her (her society's establishment). Estwald is fully formed by the melting of Dua, Odeen, and Tritt, and the electron pump project proceeds.

This central section of the novel is the key to the book, and it is with this that the credibility of *The Gods Themselves* rests. For me, it is one of the most interesting pieces of fiction Asimov ever wrote. It is beautifully conceived and executed, complete with all the necessary attendant material to make it believable. With this story Asimov really returned to science fiction with a bang.

Some critics suggested that Asimov was trying, unsuccessfully, to write in a New Wave style, and found his efforts embarrassing. Asimov naturally denied these suggestions and claimed that he was doing as he had always done—writing what he wanted to write. He resented any idea that he was influenced by a form of the genre of which he strongly disapproved.

By the early seventies the New Wave was in full swing, and a writer on the periphery and almost impossible to categorize, Philip K. Dick, had made the theme of parallel universes his own with such works as *Eye in the Sky* (1957) and *Ubik* (1969). Philip K. Dick's style and approach to the parallel universe theme was entirely different from "The Gods Themselves," but simply by dipping into a theme that had been adopted by the New Wave, a theme in which Asimov had never before shown any interest, aroused suspicions. Then there was the fact that Asimov had decided to deal with very alien aliens—again a new approach. Asimov had also tried to tackle sex in an extended piece of writing—another first.

Perhaps the principal cause for raised eyebrows among New Wave writers was not that Asimov was dealing with aliens or parallel universes, but simply that he was writing about sex in such an unusual way, and that his style in the middle section of an otherwise conventional Asimov novel was a deliberate attempt to try to step into New Wave territory. After all, one of the central tenets for the writers of the New Wave was to openly and frankly tackle sexual themes in their work. Then along comes Asimov, the grand old prude of science fiction writing, treading on their toes with a gaseous ménage à trois!

If the New Wave writers were disturbed by this, they were being as petty as Asimov had been in trying to cause them trouble. By the early seventies, the position of the New Wave was so secure that its leading proponents should have had no feelings of insecurity over Asimov's work. There was room for both the old and the new schools of science fiction in the marketplace. It may have been that their behavior was simply retaliatory and came as a result of Asimov's earlier bloody-mindedness toward them.

Asimov was very pleased with "The Gods Themselves" and had his own explanation for the heavily sexual aspect of the piece. When Larry Ashmead had shown the first section of the book to a paperback publisher, they had expressed a keen interest in handling the book but asked the Doubleday editor if Asimov was intending to put any sex into the book. Ashmead had replied rather indignantly that he thought it extremely unlikely. When he mentioned this to Asimov, it was Asimov's turn to become indignant, and he decided there and then to make the section as sexual as he could but in a totally alien way. He quite freely admitted that by this time he was growing increasingly resentful that some people really believed he could not write about sex. His huge ego dictated that he show them that he most certainly could.

With "Contend in Vain?" Asimov returns to the gentle, old-fashioned storytelling Asimov fans had become accustomed to. It is not an entirely successful conclusion to the novel and shows distinct signs that the author, exhausted by his colossal efforts in writing "The Gods Themselves," wanted to get the story finished and over with.

In "Contend in Vain?" the story moves to the moon and the action takes place a few years after the conclusion of "Against Stupidity." Our hero this time is Benjamin Denison, who had almost discovered the electron pump rather than his great rival, the megalomaniac Hallam. Like Lament before him, Denison realizes that there is something wrong with the electron pump. Although embittered because Hallam had made the discovery that changed the world, Denison does not make Lament's mistake and attempt to attack the establishment, nor does he try to snatch back the greatest gift the world was ever given. Instead he has a theory that another type of pump could be set up on the moon that would transfer material from a third universe, thereby counteracting the imbalance created by the original pumps.

With the ending of "Contend in Vain?," *The Gods Themselves* finally concludes on an up note. Denison succeeds and appoints the discredited Lament to head the project. He gets the girl, an "intuitionist" who has helped him set up the pump on the moon, and the world keeps its free energy supply without any universe suffering.

The novel was written fourteen years after Asimov's previous adult work *The Naked Sun* and it is concerned with very different issues. Clearly dominating the whole project is Asimov's awareness of the global concerns faced by mankind.

Many years before most people were aware of the problems of overpopulation, pollution, and depletion of natural resources, Asimov and other scientists and writers were trying to alert politicians and the general public alike to these issues. Asimov had a very pessimistic view of the future of humankind, and this comes across very strongly in *The Gods Themselves*. When it came to analyzing human nature, Asimov was a realist. He was fully aware of the corrupting influence of power, and from his earliest days as a writer one of the central themes in his work was the political intrigue woven around scientific and military matters of the future. In *The Gods Themselves* he succeeds in marrying politics, science, and a strong ecological message years ahead of his time.

Asimov finished *The Gods Themselves* in the beginning of September 1971 and placed the serialization rights with two magazines. Because of a mix-up with changing editors at *Galaxy* magazine, it was eventually decided that "Against Stupidity" and "Contend in Vain?" would be published in the bimonthly *Galaxy,* in their March and May 1972 issues, while the middle section, featuring Asimov's tri-sexed aliens, would appear in the April 1972 issue of *Galaxy*'s sister publication, *If.* Soon after the April issue of *If* hit the newsstands, Asimov was delighted to learn from his friend Judy-Lynn del Rey, who was in charge of the magazine, that the issue containing his first exploration of alien sex had sold out almost immediately.

Although not the most successful of his novels, *The Gods Themselves* was naturally an instant commercial success, and although it received the odd bad review, particularly from hardened New Wave reviewers, it was generally liked by critics. It was also Asimov's personal favorite. Within the science fiction community the book was a staggering success and received both the Hugo and the Nebula Awards for the best novel of 1973.

In Asimov's obituary, the journalist John Clute said of the novel:

> *The Gods Themselves* may be the best tale he ever wrote, superbly lucid in its presentation of the sociology of science and in its description of the mathematics of para-universes.[1]

Surprisingly, Asimov still did not decide to throw himself into writing more science fiction. Instead he returned to nonfiction. But as well as working on a bewildering assortment of projects, including annotated versions of classical literature, collecting together stories for science fiction anthologies, and straight mystery stories, he decided to try his hand at writing humor.

Asimov had written a joke book back in 1969, after it had been suggested to him while on holiday in the Catskills. However, he only got into his stride writing humorous books with a project that was conceived, as was often the case, from a stray comment made by a publisher.

On March 12, 1971, Asimov was at lunch with Beth Walker, who, with her husband, Samuel, ran a small publishing house called Walker and Company. Over dessert they started to discuss the phenomenal recent success of how-to soft porn books such as *The Sensuous Woman.* Suddenly Beth Walker said, "Isaac, why don't you do a dirty book?"

Taking the suggestion too seriously, Asimov declared that he didn't write trash. Then, remembering his penchant for flirting with any woman within a hundred yards, he added rather sourly, "Besides, what do I know about sex? All I could write would be *The Sensuous Dirty Old Man.*"

Instead of laughing and forgetting about it, Beth Walker took him seriously, and clapping her hands and laughing aloud, she said, "Great! So, you'll do it."

Asimov was cornered. He did not take the idea seriously but could not back out, he simply smiled and waited for the whole idea to fade away. Except it didn't.

---

[1] The *Independent,* April 7, 1992. Obituary by John Clute.

Beth Walker kept phoning and writing to Asimov to get him to accept the contract she had waiting for him for *The Sensuous Dirty Old Man*. He finally agreed, and spent just a single weekend in Janet's apartment, in the middle of his divorce proceedings, writing the sixteen thousand words of the text.

All the time he was writing *The Sensuous Dirty Old Man* he deliberately made sure that Janet could not see what he was doing in case she found the whole thing distasteful. But by the time he had finished it, he rather enjoyed what he had written and found it far funnier than he had thought it would be. It was a humorous little piece, a complete parody of books like *The Sensuous Woman*, and really nothing more than a written version of his flirtatious ways. On completing the first draft he showed it to Janet, who found it not only funny but also totally inoffensive.

Next day, April 26, 1971, immediately before starting the second part of *The Gods Themselves*, Asimov delivered the manuscript to the offices of Walker and Company, and he had a copy of the book in his hands by June 2, little over a month later.

The cover carried a picture of Asimov jokingly disguised with a bra across his eyes, and the author was named "Dr. A" as a parody of the author of *The Sensuous Woman*, "J." The next day Asimov was a guest on the *Dick Cavett Show* and walked onstage with a bra over his eyes.

The book was a success but Asimov decided not to do a sequel; the joke was done. Instead he returned to serious nonfiction and the occasional science fiction short story. But it is clear that the humor bug had bitten him, as by 1974 he was thinking of collecting together a hundred limericks for publication. Walker and Company liked the idea, and in early 1975 Asimov had his hundred limericks. He decided to introduce each one with a little story about how it had been written and how it could be interpreted. Walker and Company loved the manuscript and it was published the same year under the title *Lecherous Limericks*.

In the following years Asimov published several more collections of limericks. He simply loved writing them, and although the books sold in small numbers, Walker and Company assured him that they would keep bringing them out as long as he kept delivering batches of a hundred. And so there appeared *More Lecherous Limericks* (1976) and *Still More Lecherous Limericks* (1977).

One of the last books in the series came about through a collaborative effort with the poet John Ciardi, whom Asimov had known since 1950.

Ciardi was planning to have his own collection of limericks published by Norton. It contained 144 pieces with the planned title of *A Gross of Limericks*. Ciardi wrote to Asimov and suggested that the two of them each contribute 144 limericks and publish a volume twice the size with the title *Limericks: Too Gross*. Asimov loved the idea and the book appeared in 1978.

Three years after publication, *Limericks: Too Gross* ended up at the center of a controversy in Birmingham in the southern U.S. state of Alabama.

A schoolteacher had bought the book to give to her class president as an end-of-year gift. When the eighteen-year-old's parents discovered the book in his room, they went to the school to complain. The teacher was suspended and a court case ensued in which Asimov was asked to give testimony on the suitability of his book for a teenage readership. The teacher eventually won the case, and was reinstated and paid damages.

Asimov found the whole affair bizarre from the start, and if it had not been for such high stakes in the teacher's life and career he would have found the case a joke. The limericks, he believed, were quite inoffensive, and in his opinion, all those involved in bringing up the matter, from the parents to the court, were overreacting in the extreme.

During this period of limerick writing, Asimov was also totally absorbed with straight, serious projects in both fiction and nonfiction. Although he had written a number of quite good science fiction short stories since his general retirement from fiction in the late fifties, none of them had any lasting significance. Then, in August 1974, he began to write one of his best-loved science fiction stories, the critically acclaimed "The Bicentennial Man."

Asimov himself was incredibly pleased with this story and placed it as the second favorite of all the hundreds of short stories he wrote during his career. He also claimed that the ending of the story almost brought him to tears as he wrote it.

"The Bicentennial Man" is definitely one of Asimov's most emotionally charged stories and tugs at the heartstrings in a similar way to his other great favorite, "The Ugly Little Boy." It tells of a robot called

Andrew Martin who, by some positronic fluke, is born with artistic ability. By using his gifts and selling his artwork, the robot makes a great deal of money for his owner.

Being a rather magnanimous chap, Andrew's owner, "Sir," decides that Andrew should be allowed to keep half of his earnings, and so the law concerning robots' rights of ownership are changed (Sir is a lawyer).

Andrew is beloved by his owner's family, the Martins, and when Sir dies, Andrew is kept on by successive generations. Gradually Andrew begins to adopt more and more human characteristics. He saves enough money from his artwork to buy his freedom, he starts to wear clothes, and he is granted civil liberties. At each stage he has to fight a legal battle, which he wins because, firstly, he has the financial resources, and secondly, he uses the legal firm owned by the Martins.

The title of the story comes from Andrew's desire, as he approaches his two hundredth birthday, to actually be made human—by law. Over the two centuries of his existence he has gradually eroded away the distinctions between himself and human beings. He has replaced his body parts with organic material and gained the legal rights of a human being, but now he wants to step over the line into true humanity. Naturally, this final step causes him the greatest difficulty.

The real problem lies in the fact that, unlike a human being, Andrew is practically immortal. The notion of an immortal robot turned human would be offensive to people who live three score years and ten. When Andrew learns of this quite natural prejudice, he decides the only way around it is to undergo an operation to allow his positronic brain to run down and self-destruct so that he will "die" naturally.

When the world learns of this ultimate sacrifice for the sake of gaining humanity, Andrew the robot is granted his wish and "dies," after becoming a real human being . . .

> Andrew's thoughts were slowly fading as he lay in bed.
>   Desperately he seized at them. Man! He was a man! He wanted that to be his last thought. He wanted to dissolve— die—with that."[1]

---

[1] Part 23, *The Bicentennial Man* by Isaac Asimov. First appeared in *Stellar-2,* January 1976.

"The Bicentennial Man" was originally commissioned as the eponymous piece in a collection of stories with the theme of the U.S. Bicentennial of 1976 being put together by Naomi Gordon.

As with "The Gods Themselves," Asimov found that once started, the story ran away with him. He intended to make it seventy-five hundred words in length to suit Naomi Gordon's requirements and found himself passing the fifteen-thousand-word barrier before finishing it. "It wrote itself and turned and twisted in the typewriter,"[1] Asimov later said of the story.

It took Asimov two weeks to write "The Bicentennial Man" while working on other projects. Its completion coincided exactly with the Asimovs' move from Janet's apartment. Dotting the last *i* and crossing the final *t*, he delivered the manuscript to a delighted Naomi Gordon on March 14, 1975.

"The Bicentennial Man" never did appear in Ms. Gordon's anthology. Her project fell through and Asimov returned the advance he had been paid. Instead, the story was published in another anthology, called *Stellar-2*, edited by Judy-Lynn del Rey, in January 1976.

"The Bicentennial Man" was a massive success, and was the only short story to earn both Hugo and Nebula Awards (for best novelette) in 1977.

It was particularly gratifying for Asimov because the double prize complemented the Nebula and Hugo he had won in the novel category four years earlier. Asimov was so pleased that he did not even mind too much when he discovered that the Science Fiction Writers of America who made the award had spelled his name on it "Isaac Asmimov."

Soon after the publication of "The Bicentennial Man" Asimov was asked if he would be interested in the idea of lending his name to a magazine — *Isaac Asimov's Science Fiction Magazine*. The suggestion came from a publisher called Joel Davis, whom Asimov knew from Davis Publications, the publisher of *Ellery Queen's Mystery Magazine*, to which he occasionally contributed straight mystery stories.

Davis was interested in adding to his collection of publications. One of his executives had just returned from taking his children to a *Star Trek*

---

[1] "The Robot Chronicles," introduction to *Robot Visions* by Isaac Asimov. Victor Gollancz Science Fiction, London, 1990 (p. 19).

convention and had suggested that the company try its hand at the science fiction market. Davis's idea was to incorporate a famous science fiction name into the title, and he naturally turned to Asimov.

Asimov took a great deal of persuading over the matter. Initially he did not like the idea of having his name and his photograph splashed all over the cover of a new magazine. The venture might founder and then he would look silly. Also, he would not have the time to become involved on an editorial level, as he was far too busy with his own writing. Davis reassured Asimov that a competent editor would be found for the magazine; all he had to do was to allow his name to be used and a dignified photograph to appear on the front cover.

Eventually Asimov was persuaded, and the first issue, along with the promised dignified image of his face on the front cover, appeared on the newsstands on December 16, 1976. By this time Asimov had grown accustomed to the idea and had been looking forward to the first issue, for which he had written an editorial.

Asimov need not have worried about the fate of the magazine. It did not embarrass him in any way and in fact went from strength to strength. It is still selling well to this day.

By the end of the 1970s, Asimov had begun to slide back into a career as a science fiction writer. Throughout the era dominated by the New Wave, sales of Asimov's books did not drop in the least, and at the end of the decade he could truthfully say that his name as a science fiction writer was even better known than it had been at the beginning. He had regained his footing and self-confidence in the field of writing that had been his first love, and he was never to look back.

From the early eighties on, Asimov was to split his time between writing fiction and nonfiction, but with a greater bias toward science fiction. In the final twelve years of his life he wrote a clutch of novels, each of which commanded large advances from his publishers. These books not only made him one of the wealthiest writers in the world, but, for the first time in his long career, Asimov found himself on the national bestseller list.

13

GENTLEMAN AUTHOR

I saac's heart attack in 1977 still did little to slow him down, but he did agree to take more breaks and, at Janet's insistence, he put away his typewriter when they were on vacation. Perhaps a growing sense of mortality ensured that he started to enjoy activities away from his work.

During the eighties Isaac and Janet continued to travel. They again visited Europe, this time sailing to Paris on board the *QE2*. Other trips revolved around speaking tours. They visited Canada, and spent two weeks in Bermuda each summer, as well as frequently joining Astronomy Island cruises for comet-spotting and stargazing.

Each summer during the 1980s they spent a week in July or August at the Institute of Man and Science, a gathering of American intellectuals, largely scientists and writers, who delivered talks and conducted workshops. It was a satisfying blend of lighthearted chat and intellectual discussion, a little like a highbrow science fiction convention. It was held each year in the tiny town of Rensselaerville, about twenty-five miles south of the Catskills. Each year the organizers chose a different theme upon which the talks and lectures were based, subjects ranging from Space Travel to Society and the Environment.

Despite Janet's insistence on more leisure time away from the typewriter, in the first three years of the 1980s, Isaac's angina grew worse. Late in 1983, his doctor advised him to undergo heart surgery. This involved one of the most complex and risky heart operations—a triple bypass.

Isaac was very nervous about the operation. He had learned from his doctor, Paul Esserman, that during the operation his heart would be stopped and he would be placed on a heart-lung machine. The thought of this sent tingles down his spine. He was particularly concerned because he had recently read that there was a danger of insufficient oxygen reaching the patient's brain during the process. He went to great lengths to explain to the surgeon in charge that his brain was a highly tuned instrument and very sensitive to oxygen, so would he please take extra care.

It was agreed that after the operation Dr. Esserman would test Isaac to make sure that he had been supplied with sufficient oxygen and that his brain was in no way impaired. As soon as the patient came around and was lucid, the doctor asked him to make up a limerick. Isaac began:

> There was an old doctor named Paul,
> whose prick was exceedingly small . . .[1]

At which point Dr. Esserman hurriedly stopped him and declared that his brain was fine.

Isaac had to remain in the hospital for several months, then came a long period of convalescence. For the first time since becoming a professional writer, he was obliged to stop working and allowed to return to it only gradually. Typically, one of the first things he did after leaving the hospital was to write an amusing account of the operation and his time there.

His enforced convalescence did not stop him from socializing. He was released from the hospital on December 31, 1983, and was out celebrating his sixty-fourth birthday on January 2 as he had done for the past six or seven years, with Janet and Judy-Lynn and Lester del Rey. They went to their favorite restaurant, Fleur de Lis, at 69th Street and Broadway.

Isaac enjoyed socializing far more after his return to New York in 1970. He felt relaxed with his close circle of friends and continued to enjoy flirting and playing the rogue until his final hospitalization in 1992.

His closest friends during this period were the same friends he had had since the fifties and sixties—the del Keys, Larry Ashmead, and Martin H. Greenberg. Marty, as Isaac always called him, phoned Isaac

---

[1] *Asimov Laughs Again* by Isaac Asimov.

every evening throughout the 1980s and they would talk on the telephone for at least an hour at a time. They talked about anything and everything, and through this and their lunch meetings Greenberg became Isaac's closest friend.

Another close companion was Larry Ashmead. He and Isaac had worked together throughout the sixties and early seventies, and although they had teamed up on very few books after Ashmead left Doubleday in 1975, they remained pals.

Whenever they were free, the two of them would go out to lunch in style at Peacock Alley at the Waldorf-Astoria. They both loved food and would always order two desserts. As the second dessert arrived at the table, Isaac would always turn to Ashmead and say, "Whatever you do, don't tell Janet."

As well as lunches at the Waldorf, Isaac was a great club man. He had been a member of the Trap Door Spiders since the sixties—a group of successful men from all walks of life who would meet at irregular intervals to eat and drink and exchange humorous stories.

Another organization on which Isaac was particularly keen was the Dutch Treat Club. Isaac and Larry Ashmead were regulars there, and Isaac even became the club president. It was another informal gathering made up of a wide spectrum of men who were all successful in their careers. They regularly booked prestigious speakers to deliver talks at the club, and met once a week to dine and to tell each other ribald stories.

Another important routine in Isaac's life was the role he played in *Isaac Asimov's Science Fiction Magazine.*

In commercial terms the magazine had done well from the first issue, but Asimov's primary interest lay in the fact that it offered opportunities for young, unpublished science fiction writers.

Asimov had always valued the break the pulps had given him during the 1940s and especially the invaluable inspiration offered by John Campbell. In his declining years Asimov saw it as imperative that he give something back to the genre, and the magazine was the ideal opportunity.

Back in 1976, he had agreed to write an editorial for the launch but then decided to contribute to each issue, a routine that he maintained until 1991, when he had to retire from writing altogether.

The present managing editor of the magazine, Sheila Williams, has been an Asimov fan from the age of sixteen. Her father wrote to Asimov asking if she could have a chat with him after a speech he was due to deliver in their hometown. Isaac wrote back to say that if they could hold back the hordes of screaming, fainting fans long enough, then he would be only too happy to talk to them.

The evening of the lecture arrived and Sheila sat in the audience, in awe of her hero up on the dais. At the end of the speech, father and daughter approached Asimov, and sure enough, he remembered them and invited them to sit next to him at the post-talk dinner. Sheila never dreamed that within a decade of that evening she would be in charge of Isaac Asimov's magazine and know the man on a personal basis.

Isaac made a point of turning up at the magazine's offices every Tuesday morning, and although the publication could run perfectly well without him being there, he liked to be involved. He would spend at least two hours each week with Sheila, going through the copy and discussing his editorial, joking around, reciting snatches of Gilbert and Sullivan with improvised lyrics, and making up limericks.

In the early eighties, Isaac was still well enough to entertain friends who visited New York. Both Isaac and Janet hated organizing dinner parties at home, and so they would invariably eat out at one of a collection of favorite restaurants in their area.

Isaac remained in touch with his old friends right up until his death. When Fred Pohl or Harlan Ellison were in town he was always delighted to see them and to catch up with their news. When Ellison called to arrange a luncheon during a forthcoming visit, he would invariably put on a false voice and string Isaac along for a good ten minutes. Isaac never realized who it was.

He attended science fiction conventions less frequently as the decade progressed, unless they happened to be held in New York. Consequently, he had weaker links with the rest of the science fiction community, so visits from old friends within science fiction meant a great deal to him.

After fully recovering from the bypass operation, Isaac was still overweight and decided once and for all to adopt a new regime and to take more care of his health. He adored food, but taking Janet's advice, he tried to cut down on fatty meat, creamy desserts, and sweets. It was difficult for him; he never smoked and rarely drank, but one of his greatest pleasures in life was good food. As a result he did lose weight and felt far healthier for it. In photographs of him taken after 1983, we see a new, unfamiliar Asimov with a slightly gaunt face. The lamb-chop sideburns remained, but as he had lost at least thirty pounds, some of the familiar "cuddliness" had gone, too.

Asimov bought his first word processor in June 1981 and was delighted with it. It was a Radio Shack TRS80. He had always com-plained that electric typewriters moved too slowly for his brain. With this new computer he decided that it was just fast enough to keep up with him. Larry Ashmead's comment to Asimov was: "Isaac, they will never make a machine fast enough to keep up with you."

He never saved on disc anything he wrote, and almost used the PC as a typewriter, printing straight from the screen. Even then he only used it for short pieces and for final copy; he still preferred to use his old electric typewriter for the first draft. This sounds eccentric, but is in fact a prac-tice followed by many writers.

Nor did Asimov ever divide his work into chapters as he wrote; that was always done later, after completion of the first draft. He would then find natural breaks in the text and determine the chapters accordingly. He usually worked for up to ten hours a day, starting early, about six o'clock (he had always been an early riser), and finishing in the late after-noon. He worked in his office across the hall from Janet's office in their apartment. He always worked with the blinds down, distracted only by the occasional phone call or visitor.

In the summer of 1981, a story began circulating in the publishing houses of New York about Asimov's first day with a PC. Having written the rough draft of a new manuscript on his typewriter, he turned to the computer to start the final copy. The computer would not work. After twenty minutes of button pushing and prodding and working himself into a froth, Asimov finally called the manufacturers and complained loudly. An hour later a repairman arrived at the apartment, walked straight up to the machine, and switched it on.

In 1984, Asimov was made Humanist of the Year, an accolade he was par-ticularly proud of. Ever since his first introduction to the movement in the early seventies, he had been keen to popularize humanism and discussed it publicly at every opportunity. By the late seventies, the subject was one of the mainstays of his public-speaking repertoire. He was never antireligious and always respected other people's faith. He believed that arguing against religion was not his domain and was in any case an infringement of others' personal opinions. He conceded that religion lay at the heart of many of the world's problems but also felt that it was so deeply rooted in the emotional makeup of the individual that it was not something he wished to attack.

By the early 1980s, Asimov was back at work on the Foundation books, which, along with his final two robot novels, constituted his most successful literary work of that time. His editor at Doubleday was Kate Medina. In 1984 she had to leave work for a few months, and her editorial assistant took her place, but within days she, too, left Doubleday.

Working as the editorial assistant's assistant was a young woman named Jennifer Brehl, who was fresh out of college and had little editorial experience. She was given the position of editorial assistant and asked to hold the fort until a temporary replacement for Kate Medina was found.

Throughout his career Asimov had placed great importance on maintaining a personal relationship with his publishers, and from the time he moved back to New York in 1970, he visited the Doubleday offices once a week.

One week he turned up at Doubleday and handed Jennifer the completed manuscript of his latest novel, *Robots and Empire*. The two of them chatted for a few minutes and Asimov left.

That evening Jennifer looked through the manuscript Asimov had given her and gave it a light edit. Being fresh to the job and quite inexperienced, she did not want to be too heavy-handed with the book. She knew how illustrious Asimov was and how important he was to Doubleday, and did not want to offend him. Besides, she thoroughly enjoyed the book and found that it only needed a little fine-tuning.

The following week Asimov appeared at the Doubleday offices again and Jennifer handed him back the manuscript with her comments.

For a moment the author was taken aback. He had not realized that Jennifer was going to do anything with the manuscript herself. That evening it was his turn to look over the edited manuscript and read Jennifer's comments.

The following week he returned once more and took Jennifer to one side. He was delighted with her work and much admired her comments, all of which he insisted were improvements. For his part, he had answered all her points and corrected his earlier mistakes.

From that afternoon the two of them became friends, and during the following months Jennifer continued to work with Asimov under the aegis of Kate Medina. Then, shortly after returning to Doubleday, Kate Medina left the company for Random House. At this point, uncertain as to who exactly would be editing his work, Asimov decided to visit Henry Reath, the president of Doubleday, to suggest that with Kate Medina gone, Jennifer Brehl should look after his books.

Jennifer was too inexperienced to be given an editorial position, but Reath decided that she and Asimov should continue working together, while his books technically became part of the editor-in-chief Sam Vaughan's list. Asimov was happy with this arrangement and when, a few months later, Jennifer was promoted to editor and given her own list, Asimov's books were the key element. She then dealt with everything he did at Doubleday from 1984 until after his death, when she was responsible for tidying up the loose ends of his last books.

Jennifer became like a second daughter to Isaac and is also a very close friend of Robyn's. She saw him at least twice a week for the rest of his life and, in terms of organizing his work, grew gradually more and more important to him as he grew older.

One of Isaac's great joys throughout the 1980s was his membership in the Gilbert and Sullivan Society of New York. He had always been a fan of the music and went to almost every production put on by the society throughout the decade. In 1984 he actually performed in a parody created by the society—called *Enraptured Transit; or, Bliss on a Bus,* a Piece in One Act by D. Guarino. Isaac thoroughly enjoyed the experience, and it gave him a further opportunity to show off in front of an audience. He had always claimed that if he had not become a writer, he might well have gone into show business.

Isaac bought Jennifer a membership in the Gilbert and Sullivan Society, and she sometimes joined him and Janet at the society's frequent productions.

During a period in the mid-eighties while working on *Foundation and*

Earth, Asimov was finding the book heavy going. He was also depressed because one of his earlier novels had not made the best-seller list. Jennifer was beginning to worry about him; he could not sleep, was clearly distraught, and concerned that he was letting down Doubleday. He would say things like: "But Jennifer, Doubleday has spent all this money for my latest novel and I'm stuck. What's worse is that the last one didn't even make the list."

Jennifer's protestations that the money did not matter, and that even if one of his books did not become a national best seller they still did very well, seemed to make no difference. She then thought up a way of distracting Asimov from his problems. One evening at home, she wrote on a piece of paper, "Mark Twain" and "Gilbert and Sullivan"—two of Asimov's obsessions. Maybe, she thought, he would like to write a book about one of these.

By the next morning she had decided against Mark Twain because there were already too many books about him in the shops. That afternoon Asimov turned up at the office. He was still downcast, so Jennifer suggested the idea of a book about Gilbert and Sullivan.

It immediately did the trick. Asimov's eyes lit up and he beamed. "I've always wanted to do an annotated Gilbert and Sullivan," he said. "But I never thought for a moment that anyone would want to publish it." He left the office that afternoon his old self and with a new spring in his step.

Six weeks later he turned up at Jennifer's office and placed a huge manuscript on her desk. "What's this?" she asked.

"The Gilbert and Sullivan book," Asimov replied.

Jennifer was panic-stricken. She had not even mentioned the idea to her colleagues, and even an Asimov book had to be approved by the editorial board. She went along to the next meeting and anxiously explained what had happened. Asimov, she said, was really happy and back at work on *Foundation and Earth* and had overcome his disappointment with the previous novel, but he wanted to do a book about Gilbert and Sullivan. To her amazement the other editors loved the idea.

"When can he deliver?" they asked.

"Yesterday?" Jennifer replied.

With the great success of *Foundation's Edge*—his return to the Foundation series in 1982 (discussed in the final chapter)—Asimov had suddenly moved into a different league, and it was his most triumphant period as a writer.

Foundation's Edge was a phenomenal success that was almost impossible to live up to, and indeed, much to his regret, none of his other books were as successful in such a short period of time. Nonetheless, his return to the great series, which he had started forty years earlier, was a source of great pride for him.

January 2, 1985, marked a landmark in Asimov's life and career. It was his sixty-fifth birthday and there was no way he was going to retire. To celebrate the occasion and to declare that he was still in his prime as a writer, he and Janet threw a huge party at their favorite Chinese restaurant, Shun Lee on 66th Street. It was announced as being Isaac's NON-RETIREMENT PARTY. One hundred and fifty guests were invited from all over the world, and it was a rare meeting of all of Isaac's old and new friends. Fred Pohl and Harlan Ellison flew in; friends from Europe crossed the Atlantic; and his friends in New York were also there, the old gang of Larry Ashmead, Martin H. Greenberg, Lester and Judy-Lyn del Rey, as well as his family. The party took over the entire restaurant for the evening and it was remembered as a wonderful event. Isaac and a number of friends gave speeches and the wine flowed. It did not end until the early hours, when the guests dispersed to their various homes and hotels and Isaac and Janet strolled the couple of blocks back to their apartment.

It was the last time this group of friends were to meet; nine months later, on October 16, one of Isaac's closest friends and colleagues, Judy-Lynn, suffered a brain hemorrhage and slipped into a coma. She died shortly afterward. Isaac was devastated by her sudden, early death; she was only forty-three.

In his next editorial for *Isaac Asimov's Science Fiction Magazine,* he composed a letter to Judy-Lynn in which he movingly recounted all the great times they had shared and the many practical jokes she had played on him. He admired her more than anyone else he had met in science fiction and wrote:

> Of all the women I have ever met you were the keenest, the quickest, the most brilliant.[1]

[1] *Isaac Asimov's Science Fiction Magazine.* Editorial 106, "Letter to Judy-Lynn del Rey."

In the letter Isaac recounted the time Judy-Lynn tricked him into believing that she and Larry Ashmead had secretly eloped. Isaac and Janet had celebrated the fifteenth "fake wedding anniversary" with Judy-Lynn, Lester, and Larry in April 1985, a mere six months before Judy-Lynn's death.

He also recalled how Judy-Lynn had worked her way up to become the editor of *Galaxy* magazine in the early seventies. One day he received a letter from someone purporting to be the new editor, a young woman called Fritzi Vogelgesang. Staggered, he called the offices of *Galaxy* and was told that Fritzi was not around. Subsequently they started corresponding. Before two weeks had passed, the letters became intimate and as flirtatious as one would expect from Isaac. It was only then that an angry Judy-Lynn let him off the hook by announcing that she had been Fritzi Vogelgesang all along. She then complained bitterly that it had taken him no time at all to forget her and to start flirting with her successor.

Of course, Isaac never did forget Judy-Lynn when she really did go, and it took him a very long time to overcome the sense of loss her death brought him.

In the autumn of 1990 Isaac heard that Gertrude had died from breast cancer. He had known for some years she was ill. She had been a heavy smoker all her adult life and this obviously contributed to her health problems. Although Isaac had not kept in touch with Gertrude and had seen her only rarely during the twenty years since their separation, he was naturally saddened by her passing.

Of all the family, Robyn was closest to Gertrude and saw her frequently. She was fifteen when her parents separated and it hit her the hardest. By the time Isaac had moved back to New York and left the family home in Newton, David was at college and already drifting away from the family, so it was only natural that Robyn would be caught between her father and mother. Happily, she was able to maintain a close relationship with both parents.

Isaac last saw Gertrude shortly before her death when they both knew that she had little time to live. They were able to talk together calmly, but beneath the outward appearance of civility each still bore great resentment toward the other.

After Gertrude's death he wrote his last humor book, called *Asimov Laughs Again*, which was published a week after his death. It was a collection of jokes and funny stories, but it also contains a number of anecdotes that cast Gertrude in a very poor light. Isaac obviously needed to vent his spleen over his first marriage and felt that he could only do this after Gertrude had died.

During the latter half of the 1980s Isaac once again began to suffer a series of health problems. In his younger days he had had recurring bouts of kidney stones that were agonizing for perhaps a week and would then pass, only to return months or years later. In his late sixties, the on-going kidney-stone problem developed into a sequence of kidney diseases that landed him in the hospital on several occasions. Coupled with his angina, this severely weakened him.

Friends visiting Isaac in the late seventies often found him too sick to leave the apartment, and Janet began to take on a far more protective role. She had always tried to encourage him to look after his own health, to eat better, to exercise more, but her ideas had little influence on him until the triple bypass operation in 1983. When he began to fall prey to a series of illnesses in the late eighties, Janet stepped up her campaign as much as she could. Friends of Isaac's have related how it was almost impossible to get him out of the apartment even if he was feeling well.

According to one of his friends, the biologist Dr. Jack Cohen, he and Isaac's other friends would phone the apartment if they happened to be in New York, and if Isaac answered, he would only be able to meet them somewhere by pretending to Janet that he had to pop out for five minutes on an important business matter. Isaac would then meet Cohen or whoever happened to be in town and they would go to a café or walk through Central Park for a chat.

Janet was probably right in trying to look after Isaac, because he could be quite irresponsible when it came to his own health. On the other hand, toward the end of his life he adhered to the philosophy that as he did not have that long to live, why not enjoy himself a little? He had very few vices, but he did love food, especially the variety he knew was bad for him.

Often, when he was in the hospital and Janet had returned home, he would ask one of his friends visiting him if they could pop out and get him a hot dog or a hamburger because he was sick of the healthy hospital food. They would invariably oblige and make him very happy for ten minutes.

Isaac's health continued to deteriorate throughout the eighties and early nineties. In the summer of 1991 he began to have trouble with his prostate gland, which added another serious complaint to his worsening kidney problems and angina. From the summer of 1991 onward, he was in and out of the hospital with one illness or another. To his great disappointment, he and Janet could not make it to the annual meeting of the Institute of Man and Science in Rensselaerville that summer, an event they had attended every year throughout the 1980s and one of the high points of their social calendar.

One of Isaac's oldest colleagues, Truman (Mac) Talley, who had been involved with some of his earliest science fiction paperbacks, recalls meeting him for lunch in 1991. "He looked very tired and drawn," he remembers. "For much of the meal Isaac was almost silent, which was totally out of character for him. I guess he was taking a great deal of medication."

There were also times when Isaac seemed to temporarily regain his health. Jennifer left Doubleday in 1989 but continued to work as Asimov's freelance editor, collaborating with a managing editor called Janet Hill. The two women became good friends and together often accompanied Isaac on business calls and meetings in New York. He loved the thought of turning up with two young and attractive women, one on each arm, and when Robyn joined them he felt especially pampered.

Jennifer and Janet recalled with fondness Isaac's visit to the 1991 American Book Association meeting in New York. They met him at the apartment and helped him into a cab. It was only as the cab was pulling away that Isaac realized he had left his cane behind. He had been using a cane for most of the year even though he did not like to rely on it.

"I must go back for my cane," Asimov announced.

Whereupon Jennifer and Janet simultaneously answered, "Well, if you haven't noticed until now that you left it behind, it shows you don't really need it."

Isaac laughed and accepted the logic of their argument.

"In the event it was really nice that Isaac had forgotten his stick," Janet Hill recalls. "The whole of the New York literary scene had been buzzing for weeks, claiming that Isaac was on his deathbed, and there he was walking around the stands with us two and no cane. Of course Isaac loved to be the center of attention and the fact that he was attending the ABA with two young women made him feel really good. For that afternoon at least he convinced everyone that there was no substance to the rumors."

However, the sad fact was that the rumors, although greatly exaggerated, bore a grain of truth. It was only a matter of a few months later, in the autumn of 1991, that Isaac stopped writing at his usual intensive level as his illnesses became too much for him.

During this time he relied heavily on both his wife, Janet, and his editor, Jennifer, to help him with his work. Partly as an effect of his medication, by late 1990 his hands had begun to shake quite badly and he was finding it increasingly difficult to use his word processor and typewriters. He took to dictating his latest work to Jennifer, who typed it up for him. They would then go through the typed version together and Isaac would alter the text before it was redrafted.

Throughout the eighties, when Asimov was working on the last Foundation books and the final two robot novels, *Robots of Dawn* and *Robots and Empire,* he still continued to write his monthly column for *Fantasy and Science Fiction,* a magazine to which he had been contributing since 1958. Toward the end of his career and as his health deteriorated, Janet and Isaac had cowritten many of the pieces for the magazine. When he became too ill to write at all, he found that he had delivered three hundred and ninety-nine pieces to *Fantasy and Science Fiction,* and although he and Janet talked about collaborating on a four hundredth piece, to his great sadness it was never written.

Isaac used to always joke that the only way a writer should die was collapsing at the typewriter and being found with his nose stuck between the keys. For him it did not happen this way. Throughout the winter of 1991 and the spring of 1992, he was in and out of the hospital. A sudden attack of flu or a pain in his abdomen would mean that he was taken in for observation. His final attack was precipitated by a seemingly innocent nosebleed.

By this time Isaac had grown accustomed to constant hospital admissions and took it all in his stride. He no longer resisted Janet's insistence that the slightest problem be attended to. He was taken across town to the New York University Tisch Hospital on First Avenue and kept overnight for observation. It was during this visit that he suffered renal failure. His condition weakened and he became semiconscious. According to family friends, even at this stage the doctors thought that he would recover; they did not expect him to die when he did.

The night Isaac died, Jennifer Brehl was at home. She knew that Asimov was slipping away and had left the family at his bedside that evening, fully expecting to hear within twenty-four hours that he had died.

At 2 A.M., she received a phone call from Robyn at the hospital telling her that Isaac had died. She wept for hours until sleep finally overtook her.

Robyn and Janet Asimov had been at Isaac's side until the end. Isaac's brother, Stanley, was immediately informed and a message was sent to California, where David Asimov was living.

Later that morning, April 6, 1992, the world awoke to the news that one of the most famous writers of all time—and certainly the best-loved science fiction author since H. G. Wells—had died.

One of Asimov's last books to be published was *Asimov Laughs Again,* and the concluding item was perhaps the very last thing he ever wrote. It is Larry Ashmead's favorite segment from his friend's long and highly productive writing career. In it Isaac touchingly describes his feelings for Janet and instantly dispels all criticisms that he could not express emotion in his writing:

> Janet and I met on May 1, 1959, and fell in love at once. Unfortunately there was nothing I could do about it. I was married. It was an unhappy marriage, but I was married. And I had two small children.
>
> So we could only correspond and yearn for each other, until my marriage broke up. Since then, we have lived together, gotten married, and the point is that for thirty-two years now we have stayed deeply in love.
>
> I'm afraid that my life has just about run its course and I don't really expect to live much longer. However, our love remains and I have no complaints.
>
> In my life, I have had Janet and I have had my daughter,

Robyn, and my son, David; I have had a large number of good friends; I have had my writing and the fame and fortune it has brought me; and no matter what happens to me now, it's been a good life, and I'm satisfied with it.

So please don't worry about me, or feel bad. Instead I only hope that this book has brought you a few laughs.[1]

[1] *Asimov Laughs Again* (p. 341).

14

FORWARD THE FOUNDATION

F rom the time the Foundation books first appeared in Doubleday editions in the mid-sixties, Asimov had been receiving a constant stream of fan mail begging him to carry on with the series. But despite the obvious public interest, he was never tempted to return to the stories, which had occupied his twenties and with which he had now lost touch. In the end it took a conspiracy between Asimov's publisher and his friends to get him back to work on the Foundation epic.

As early as 1971, Lester del Rey was beginning to badger Asimov over the subject of the Foundation. His argument was that the stories had been left in limbo some four hundred years into the millennium during which the two Foundations would build a new Empire. "Asimov *had* to return to the plot," del Rey complained; he, for one, wanted to know what happened next. It was unfair of Asimov, he said, to leave his hordes of readers in suspense.

Asimov always argued that he had run out of ideas for the series and that he wanted to do other things. Finally, in 1973, after a lunch meeting with Larry Ashmead, del Rey decided that he would push Asimov harder. As Asimov's best friends, they both knew his weakness; together, they cooked up a plan. Del Rey would tell Asimov that he was going to carry on the series for him and prepare a proposal, which he would pass on to Ashmead to back him up.

Naturally, when Asimov heard about this plan he was outraged. He could not allow even one of his best friends to finish his work for him.

Asimov may have grown away from the Foundation saga, but it was his baby. When he told Ashmead about del Rey's plans, the editor simply said, "Oh, sure, he's given me a proposal. It looks good." Asimov was mortified and promised there and then that he would return to Foundation just as soon as he could.

Early in 1973, soon after the publication of *The Gods Themselves*, Asimov did actually start to write a piece of Foundation fiction, his first since "The Psychohistorians," the first chapter of the trilogy compiled in 1951.

Asimov called this new piece *Lightning Rod*. He wrote fourteen pages in one sitting and then put it aside. Somehow he could not recapture the old magic of the original and decided to wait for inspiration while he got on with other things.

Lightning Rod continued to sit under a pile of papers in Asimov's office, and even del Key's threats and schemes could not motivate Asimov. There was always something Asimov had to finish before he could find time to devote to a return to Foundation.

Little changed throughout the rest of the seventies. In 1977, Cathleen Jordan, then Asimov's editor at Doubleday, suggested that he might like to embark on "a large-scale project, an important book—a Foundation book perhaps?" Instead, Asimov decided to write his autobiography and spent the next two years working on the mammoth collection of daily events and family history that appeared in two volumes, *In Memory Yet Green* (1979) and *In Joy Still Felt* (1980).

After allowing Asimov this extravagance, the senior editor at Doubleday, Betty Prashker, came to the conclusion that Asimov had to be leaned on to get him back into the Foundation mood.

In January 1981, the author turned up at the Doubleday offices to see his editor. Cathleen Jordan had left and her successor was Hugh O'Neill. They chatted for about an hour, and after sorting out current business, O'Neill told Asimov that Betty Prashker wanted to see him in her office on the thirty-third floor.

Asimov was fond of relating the story that Doubleday offered him big advances, claimed that a new Foundation book would be a massively successful best seller, and tried every inducement imaginable, but what finally clinched it was the threat that if he did not sign a contract he would be thrown out of the window of Betty Prashker's office.

Short of dropping their favorite author from a great height, Doubleday was very firm with Asimov—if you can call presenting him with a contract and offering him a five-figure advance to get on with a new Foundation novel as soon as possible being firm. Asimov protested that he simply did not have the time and had this and that project to complete, but Doubleday was insistent.

Asimov had always been happy with Doubleday and felt indebted to them as great contributors to his success as a writer. He did not want to upset them and so, finally, on February 5, 1981, he bit the bullet and signed a contract for one new Foundation novel.

Even then Asimov found he could not get straight down to writing the book. He felt incredibly pressured by the size of the advance Doubleday had forced on him. He had always believed that you should be paid for what you do after you have done it, and hated the yoke of a huge check around his neck.

With the pressures of other projects in progress and the writing block created by fears of letting down Doubleday, it took Asimov four months to get started on the new novel.

He decided to reread the first three Foundation books—the first time he had looked at them in nearly thirty years. After he had read the final page of *Second Foundation,* his first thought was: What was all the fuss about? There was no action in the books and the characters did nothing but talk. His favorite section remained "The Mule," but aside from that, he could not see the appeal. Then he read a review by James Gunn, written when the books were first published, and it changed his view. The review read:

> Action and romance have little to do with the success of the trilogy—virtually all the action takes place off-stage and the romance is almost invisible—but the story provides a detective story fascinated with the permutations and reversals of ideas.[1]

---

[1] "The Story Behind the Foundation" by Isaac Asimov. *Isaac Asimov's Science Fiction Magazine,* Edition No. 61.

Asimov dug out the fourteen pages of *Lightning Rod* he had written nearly a decade earlier, reread it, and found it to be as fresh as it had been at the time of writing. He immediately sat down and started on page fifteen.

Before long he was back in the Foundation mood and the words flowed. By the end of the year he had the novel written in draft form and delivered the final copy to Doubleday on January 17, 1982—a year, almost to the day, since Betty Prashker had persuaded Asimov to start the book.

Doubleday was absolutely delighted with Asimov's manuscript. Hugh O'Neill had been receiving the story in batches from Asimov and was very excited by it. The original title had been *Lightning Rod* from the fragment started in the early seventies, but O'Neill wisely insisted that the word "Foundation" should be inserted somewhere in the title. They toyed with *Foundation at Bay* for several months during 1981, but soon after delivery of the final segment, author and editor settled upon the title *Foundation's Edge*.

After reading the last section of the book, O'Neill saw Asimov on his next regular visit to Doubleday and said to him. "Now I'm really mad, Isaac. Why haven't you been writing science fiction all along?"[1]

It is obvious that Asimov himself became very pleased with *Foundation's Edge* and the whole idea of returning to his saga, because he deliberately decided to leave a thread of the story unresolved so that it could lead on to a sequel, a fifth book in the series.

Foundation's Edge is a fine continuation of the trilogy and recaptures the feel and mood of the original series. It deals with the adventures of another classic Asimov hero, Councilman Golan Trevize.

Trevize believes that the Seldon Plan has been irreversibly damaged by the Mule and that the Foundation government is deceiving the people by pretending that the Plan is still a going concern. He also believes that the Second Foundation has not been destroyed but is manipulating the destiny of the First.

Early on in the story, Trevize clashes with the mayor of the Foundation, a woman, Mayor Harla Branno, known as Branno the Bronze. Branno is a tough, elderly woman who has been the mayor for many

---

[1] "The Story Behind the Foundation."

years, during a period of peace and relative calm in the history of the Foundation. She is keen to see some adventure during her time. She, too, secretly believes that the Second Foundation is still a going concern. She manipulates Trevize into a public scandal, arranges for his exile from the Foundation, and sends him in search of the enemy.

The story then transfers to the Second Foundation itself. It is with this device that Asimov makes *Foundation's Edge* into a truly memorable and intriguing addition to the original saga. All readers of the first Foundation stories wanted to know more about the enigmatic Second Foundation. Throughout the first three volumes we learn precious little about it. The only characters who are revealed as Second Foundationers are Bail Channis, Lady Callia of Kalgan, and First Speaker Preem Palver. In *Foundation's Edge* we are taken into the very heart of the Second Foundation, to the inner sanctum, the Speaker's Table.

The Second Foundation has been developing its mental powers since the time of Hari Seldon and can read minds and manipulate the thoughts of others with consummate ease. Although they are few in number, it is the members of the Second Foundation who really control the fate of the Galaxy.

As was revealed at the end of the trilogy, the Second Foundation is based on Trantor—in the old Imperial grounds. The "real" Second Foundationers are a select group of twelve Speakers who run the whole show. There are several thousand other Second Foundationers of lower rank who maintain their society, but it is the Table of Speakers who have the greatest mental powers and most acute mathematical ability. It is they who supervise the Plan and control the Prime Radiant—the guide to the future of the Galaxy.

A young but particularly able Speaker named Stor Gendibal is ambitious and forward-thinking—the equivalent of Councilman Trevize of the First Foundation. In total contrast to the other Speakers, Gendibal, too, believes that the Seldon Plan is failing. He has also come to the conclusion that there is another agency at work in the Galaxy, which is controlling the Second Foundation in the same way that the Second Foundation believes it is controlling the First. In a mirror image of Trevize's fate, it is decided that Gendibal must go off into space to locate and, if necessary, destroy this other agency.

Meanwhile, Trevize has already found this other group—the planet Gaia, a single organism composed of the individual inhabitants who are linked by a psychic net or collective unconscious that creates a super being greater than the sum of its parts. As the tale unfolds we learn that the inhabitants of Gaia are actually robots, and almost in passing, that the Mule was, in fact, a Gaian renegade.

Whereas the Mule wanted isolation from the greater part of Gaia and was a megalomaniac, the rest of the planet believes that it has been guided to override the Seldon Plan to create a better alternative to either the Dark Age produced by the destruction of the old Empire or the alternative—Seldon's two Foundations. Because Gaians can maintain a certain degree of individuality and draw upon the greater power of the united planet, it perceives its way as the best future for humankind—in other words, the creation of a Galactic Gaia.

Gaia is faced with one problem. Because the individual inhabitants are robots, they cannot decide whether their plan is actually for the greater good of humanity, and therefore they are compelled by the Laws of Robots to find a single human with great intuitive power to decide for them. Trevize, it appears, is the chosen one and must decide the future fate of humankind.

The climax of the story is reached when Trevize, Gendibal, and the mayor of the Foundation all arrive in the vicinity of Gaia and engage in a part-mental, part-physical battle of wits and muscle to wrestle for the future of humanity.

Finally, Trevize is forced into making a clear decision. He chooses Gaia, and Gendibal and the mayor are both sent back to their respective people with the belief that they have accomplished their mission, unaware of what had really happened.

The ending of *Foundation's Edge* has Trevize unsure of his decision, but the mechanism for a future Galactic Gaia has been set in motion. Asimov cleverly leaves the conclusion open for a sequel in which Trevize tries to find evidence to support his decision.

In writing *Foundation's Edge*, Asimov was forced to link in the story with the earlier Foundation books, but he also wanted to include new material based on the developments in the real world of the latter half of the twentieth century.

In the original Foundation books, there was no real reference to computers; in *Foundation's Edge,* Asimov exploits computers as fully as possible. He has Trevize piloting a wonderful, ultramodern ship, the *Far Star*—the most advanced machine the First Foundation has yet produced, which is controlled by a computer linked to Trevize's mind.

The most telling influence on Asimov's thinking in this story is the whole concept of Gaia. By the time Asimov was working on *Foundation's Edge,* the British chemist James Lovelock had formulated his Gaia hypothesis. This suggests that the Earth is a single living being that is self-regulating to protect itself against the changes put upon it. Asimov was impressed with this theory, and to a large extent he built the plot of both *Foundation's Edge* and the sequel, *Foundation and Earth,* around it.

Asimov had always been interested in the idea of "super organisms." He had touched upon the idea in his 1956 story "The Last Question," in which, at a certain stage in the tale, human beings have merged to form a super being. The Gaia hypothesis of Lovelock gave Asimov a far more rigid framework in which to build his future vision.

Asimov was also influenced by current affairs. The character of the female mayor of Terminus, Branno the Bronze, is almost without doubt modeled on Margaret Thatcher, who, even by 1981, had become famous as a strong and powerful leader nicknamed the Iron Lady.

Foundation's Edge was constructed in a totally different way from the original Foundation trilogy. Whereas the first three books were written as a collection of short stories composed over a period of almost a decade and only later brought together in book form, *Foundation's Edge* was written as a novel and tells one story set in one time period. It was published in October 1982 and went straight into the *New York Times* best-seller list, where, to Asimov's astonishment, it remained for twenty-five weeks.

Asimov had never written a best seller before. Naturally all of his books had sold well, but they clocked up impressive sales over a long period; his original Foundation books would have been number-one best sellers if they had sold in a short space of time. Now, after a wait of over thirty years, the public was desperate to have the next installment of the saga that had enthralled generations of science fiction readers. By the end of 1984, *Foundation's Edge* had sold over a million copies in the U.S. alone.

Foundation's Edge was not only a best seller but it won the 1983 Hugo for best novel and was warmly received by the critics, who universally acclaimed the book as a worthy continuation of the famous series. Jennifer Brehl believes that *Foundation's Edge* was so good because of the pent-up creativity of thirty years, which all came out in one burst.

Doubleday were naturally delighted with the success of the book and had pushed Asimov into signing another contract long before *Foundation's Edge* was even published. When he protested that he could not afford the time and that he was exhausted from the efforts of writing *Foundation's Edge*, his editor, Hugh O'Neill, simply suggested that Asimov cancel all other commitments and put all his efforts into writing science fiction novels.

When Janet read the final draft of *Foundation's Edge* in the spring of 1982, she said to him, "Isaac, I want you to start the next novel right now."

Even though the thought of accepting another huge advance and commiting himself to another novel sent Asimov into a paroxysm of anxiety, he could do little else but agree.

In many ways it is difficult to sympathize with Asimov's anxiety about accepting large advances from Doubleday. In 1985 Robert Heinlein received a million-dollar advance for the U.S. rights to his latest book, *The Cat Who Walks Through Walls: A Comedy of Manners*, and comparably large advances were not unknown long before that. Coupled with this is the fact that all of Asimov's books had earned their advance and usually made a great deal of money for both publisher and writer. The anxiety lay in Asimov's humble roots; the Brooklyn boy from the candy store found it very difficult to accept a payout before the goods were delivered.

Putting aside his misgivings, Asimov straightaway got to work on a new novel. This time he decided not to return immediately to the Foundation saga, but instead to write a third Elijah Baley and R. Daneel story, a sequel to *The Naked Sun*, which had been published back in 1957.

In the plotting of *Foundation's Edge*, Asimov was already beginning to draw together the various threads of his fiction of the forties and fifties.

Although he has said: "The fact is that for the most part I have been ceaselessly mining the motherlodes I had uncovered by the time I was 22 years old,"[1] Asimov was compelled to go to extraordinary lengths to

---

[1] "The Little Tin God of Characterization" by Isaac Asimov. *Isaac Asimov's Science Fiction Magazine,* May 1985.

amalgamate the workings of the Empire, robots, and even the Eternals of *The End of Eternity* into one vast network of fifteen novels.

With *Foundation's Edge,* he managed to explain the origin of the Mule—a minor mystery brought up in the original Foundation books. His passing reference to the Eternals suggests that it was they who enabled the early colonization of the Galaxy by altering the history of humanity so that space exploration became a possibility. He also managed to introduce the robot factor into *Foundation's Edge,* an element absolutely excluded from the first three Foundation novels.

In *The Robots of Dawn,* his third robot novel and first for twenty-six years, Asimov returned to the theme of the early colonization of the Galaxy featured in his first two robot novels, *The Caves of Steel* and *The Naked Sun.*

He had actually started work on a third robot novel back in 1958, shortly after the publication of *The Naked Sun.* He was planning to call it *The Bounds of Infinity,* but got no further than the first four chapters before discarding it. Asimov claimed the reason for dropping the project was that, with the launch of the Russian satellite Sputnik and the start of the space program, he was captivated by the thought of writing nonfiction. It is also quite likely that he had exhausted himself writing the collection of novels that made his name and had simply run out of ideas.

Thanks to his new impetus to write science fiction in the early eighties, Asimov picked up the threads of his part-finished novel from twenty-five years before and set to work on the new project, which now had the provisional title of *The World of Dawn.* He started work on it in September 1982 and had it finished five months later.

The Robots of Dawn is set on the planet Aurora, one of the Spacer worlds mentioned in the first two robot novels. Most of the characters first appeared in *The Caves of Steel* and *The Naked Sun.* The hero is again Elijah Baley, who, with his robot companion, R. Daneel Olivaw, solves another murder. The genius robot maker Dr. Fastolfe again appears, and a new character, another robot, named Giskard, makes his debut.

Robots and Empire, Asimov's fourth and final robot novel, which appeared in 1985, leads on directly from *The Robots of Dawn* and continues the plot-merging and the hole-filling started in the previous novel. It begins two hundred years after *The Robots of Dawn.* It is therefore the first and only robot novel not to feature Elijah Baley solving a murder. Instead it concentrates on Daneel and Giskard.

By the end of *Robots and Empire,* many of the loose threads of the network of novels are taken care of and Asimov has gone a long way to completely merging his fiction collection.

The most significant development in these novels is the introduction of another Law of Robotics, a Zeroth Law that takes precedence over the other three. It is stated in *Robots and Empire* as:

> "A robot may not injure humanity, or through inaction, allow humanity to come to harm."[1]

Of course, this law comes from a far murkier pool than the clear-cut first three laws, and leads to complications concerning the robots using it and its consequences for humanity. The problem is: who, let alone a robot, knows what is good or bad for humanity? After all, to their cost, the Eternals discovered the complications of this matter in *The End of Eternity.*

In the era described in *The Robots of Dawn* and *Robots and Empire,* the Zeroth Law is known only to the two robots responsible for devising it, Daneel and Giskard. Daneel can cope with it and uses it to good effect in later parts of the network, but poor, confused Giskard is overcome by the unresolvable philosophical ramifications it provides and in the last pages of *Robots and Empire,* he "dies." (Incidentally, Giskard's passing provoked one of the greatest collections of mail from Asimov's legion of fans around the world.)

Toward the end of the novel, Giskard explains his predicament:

> I cannot accept the Zeroth Law, Friend Daneel. You know that I have read widely in human history. In it, I have found great crimes committed by some human beings against each other, and always the excuse has been that the crimes were justified by the needs of the tribe, or of the state, or even of humanity. It is precisely because humanity is an abstraction

---

[1] *Robots and Empire* by Isaac Asimov. First published by Doubleday, 1985. (Quote from Grafton Books edition, p. 384).

that it can be called upon so freely to justify anything at all,
and your Zeroth Law is therefore unsuitable.[1]

This is as philosophical as Asimov had ever been in any of his writing up to
that point, and could have led him into more interesting avenues than the
ones he did actually follow during the rest of his fiction writing career.

Unfortunately, *The Robots of Dawn* and *Robots and Empire* are little
more than fillers for the creation of Asimov's fifteen-novel network. The
stories in themselves are weak and some of the characters tiresome. Elijah
Baley should have been left in relatively dignified mothballs.

Although they showed diminishing returns compared to *Foundation's
Edge*, both *The Robots of Dawn* and *Robots and Empire* did very good
business. The fact that they did not match the heights reached by *Foundation's Edge* perhaps reflected fading public interest in the path Asimov
had chosen to take. Both books remained several weeks on the *New York
Times* best-seller list, and *The Robots of Dawn* sold over a million copies
within eighteen months of its publication, but the critics this time were
divided. California journalist Clinton Lawrence said:

> *The Robots of Dawn* is another fine example of the story-
> telling talents of Asimov. It fits well with its predecessors and
> is full of interesting, thought-provoking themes. It should
> definitely satisfy Asimov's fans.[2]

But science fiction writers and critics Brian Aldiss and David Wingrove
commented:

> In *Robots and Empire* Asimov's message is presented without
> real force or passion. It is as if Asimov himself senses how
> stale the idea is. It is, in the end, only a device to link two very
> different kinds of novel.[3]

---

[1] Ibid. (p. 385).
[2] Clinton Lawrence in *The Californian Aggie,* December 1, 1983.
[3] *Trillion Year Spree: The History of Science Fiction* by Brian Aldiss with David Wingrove.
First published by Victor Gollancz, 1986 (p. 498).

The real problem with these two novels is that they merely fiddle around with issues rather than tackling them head-on. Asimov himself realized that much of his fiction is handled with dialogue, there is little visible action. What makes Asimov's fiction usually so readable is his mastery of pace, his preoccupation with big themes, and his often superb development of intrigue.

In these two robot books, Asimov's pace is tediously slow, the themes are not paramount, and the intrigue is either obvious or centered on irrelevancies.

After completing *Robots and Empire* Asimov returned again to the Foundation novels with the fifth book in the series, *Foundation and Earth*.

Sadly, *Foundation and Earth,* although viewed fondly by Asimov himself, is perhaps the weakest science fiction novel he ever wrote. Leading on from the moment *Foundation's Edge* finished, *Foundation and Earth* returns to the adventures of Asimov's new hero, Foundation councilman Golan Trevize.

With Trevize and the backdrop of the four previous Foundation books, Asimov could have propelled the story on to greater heights and perhaps even topped the success of *Foundation's Edge*; instead he headed off in a direction that made for a disaster of a novel, and in so doing left behind many of the enthusiasts of *Foundation's Edge* and perhaps even a few diehard fans from the old days.

The twin obsessions that spoil *Foundation and Earth* on a plotting level are, firstly, the concept of Gaia and, secondly, Asimov's rather hackneyed devotion to the "planet of origin question," around which a number of his early novels were based.

In *Foundation and Earth,* Trevize is motivated by his desire to find irrefutable proof that his decision to go with Gaia was the correct one. The problem is *that Foundation and Earth* turns into a travelogue. It takes Trevize over five hundred pages to find Earth.

By the end of *Foundation's Edge* the networking of the novels is almost complete and we get a very full account of the past twenty thousand years of history through the device of the robot Daneel Olivaw, who, it appears, is the guardian of the Seldon Plan.

Foundation and Earth did not do as well as *Foundation's Edge,* but by any standards, it still did remarkably good business, chalking up another million sales for Asimov. It was published in October 1986, four years after *Foundation's Edge.* It immediately entered the *New York Times* best-seller list at No. 12 and remained on the chart for fifteen weeks, peaking at No. 7. The *Los Angeles Times* said of the book:

> *Foundation and Earth* is a coherent whole which stands on its own. If it lacks the youthful enthusiasm and inventiveness of the seminal novel *Foundation,* written in 1941 when Asimov was 21 years old, it has the solid workmanship and skill of the mature master.[1]

If nothing else, *Foundation and Earth* is certainly "solid." At 510 pages, it is the longest science fiction novel Asimov ever wrote. Unfortunately the plot drags, and it could have done with being half the published length. The novel is crammed full with exposition, background scientific information, and explanations of trivial side issues.

However, the most distracting aspect of the entire book is the constant bickering between two of the characters, Trevize and the Gaian robot Bliss. Using this device, Asimov tries to resolve the questions troubling Trevize and help the reader to reach conclusions. It fails terribly. By the end of the novel we have been forced along the route to a Galactic Gaia, but Bliss is so irritating and her pro-Gaian arguments so weak that the last thing the reader wants is for the Galaxy to follow the Gaian path.

Ultimately, with *Foundation and Earth* Asimov does not come close to giving us the payoff we deserve after sticking with it for over five hundred pages, and we come away feeling terribly disappointed.

According to his editor, Jennifer Brehl, Asimov was very taken with the concept of Gaia and was particularly proud of *Foundation and Earth.* He saw it as an essential building block in the structure of his grand future history. But is it good fiction, or even entertaining? Asimov may have succeeded in completing his master plan, but it was at the expense of what had made his name—storytelling.

[1] John G. Cramer, *Los Angeles Times*, October 26, 1986.

After completing *Foundation and Earth*, Asimov's original intention was to write a novel following directly on from page 510 and dealing with the threat to humanity from the spooky Solarian, Fallom, whom Trevize picks up during his travels. With Jennifer Brehl's prompting, Asimov eventually decided against this and turned instead to the missing piece remaining in his multinovel saga—the life of the creator of psychohistory, Hari Seldon. It was to this that Asimov devoted the rest of his life as a science fiction novelist, giving us the penultimate Foundation novel, *Prelude to Foundation*, published in 1988, and *Forward the Foundation*, published posthumously in 1993.

Although, with the exception of the very quickly written *The Robots of Dawn*, it usually took Asimov nine months to write a novel—"Just like a baby," as Jennifer Brehl puts it—the author's declining health meant that *Prelude to Foundation* took a little longer. When it did arrive, it proved to be a better book than *Foundation and Earth*, but still not a patch on the original Foundation trilogy.

Asimov always seemed more at home when dealing with Hari Seldon and the mechanisms of his two Foundations. Clearly, the majority of readers also preferred reading these tales. In returning to Trantor in the heyday of the Empire with the character of the young Hari Seldon dominating the story, you get the feeling that Asimov is returning home.

Throughout the original Foundation novels, Hari Seldon is a nebulous figure who only fleetingly appears in person and is long dead before we reach page thirty-five. In *Prelude to Foundation* we learn how psychohistory began.

Unfortunately, *Prelude to Foundation* turns into another travelogue. This time the action is entirely set on Trantor.

After he delivers a talk on the subject of psychohistory at a mathematics convention, Hari Seldon's ideas capture the imagination of various parties who want to use him for their own ends. Poor Hari is then obliged to go on the run to avoid, among others, the agents of the emperor himself. *Prelude to Foundation* is the story of Hari Seldon's flight from those out to get psychohistory for themselves.

Ironically, at this stage, psychohistory is little more than a vague idea and Hari Seldon is quite exasperated that everyone and his brother wants to get their hands on it.

During his travels, Hari Seldon comes through various adventures and in the process manages to answer some of the problems involved with his development of psychohistory. He also meets up with a number of characters who help him in his work and protect him from danger. Chief among these is Dors Venabili, whom Seldon later marries; Yugo Amaryl, a heatsinker who, Seldon discovers, is a great mathematician; and the street urchin Raych, whom Hari and Dors adopt. Naturally, by cleverly weaving the plot, Asimov contrives to bring together more threads from the robot stories and the Foundation saga.

By the end of *Prelude to Foundation*, Seldon has worked out how to proceed with psychohistory. He has also met the guardian of humanity.

The emperor during this era of galactic history is Cleon I, who is advised by his chief of staff, First Minister Eto Demerzel, who, it turns out, is none other than R. Daneel Olivaw. Daneel/Demerzel is at the very center of things and is the real power behind the throne. It is in this role that he is best able to guide events and, most important of all, to nudge Seldon along the correct path toward the development of psychohistory.

Prelude to Foundation is a much better read than any of the three books preceding it. There are none of the tiresome arguments between characters; the weaving of robots and Foundation is far more subtle; and, most importantly of all, the plot is centered upon the aspects of the entire network that the majority of readers find the most interesting—Hari Seldon and the Foundations. Coupled with this is the fact that we learn more about Seldon, which was an obvious gap in the entire collection. Asimov handles this with skill and the portrayal of the creator of psychohistory is convincing.

However, by far the best book in the entire collection of the Foundation/Robot novels of the eighties and nineties is, quite appropriately, the very last, *Forward the Foundation* (1993), written in the final years of Asimov's life.

All the weaknesses that flaw the other novels from *The Robots of Dawn* onward are absent here and, crucially, in *Forward the Foundation* Asimov returns to the original format of his Foundation stories—the collection of novellas.

Forward the Foundation was originally intended to consist of five interlinked novellas. In the event, Asimov's deteriorating health and finally his death curtailed the fifth story in the collection, which was then turned into an epilogue.

With this, his final novel, Asimov picks up the story soon after the conclusion of *Prelude to Foundation*. In the first segment of the book, the story revolves around the relationship between Seldon and Eto Demerzel and their battle to save the throne from an internal rebellion, an event that would have seriously damaged Demerzel's plans for the future of the Galaxy.

By the end of this, Demerzel disappears, presumably to tend to some other problem facing the Galaxy or to return to his hideaway on Earth's moon.

The second story is called "Cleon I." Here Hari is middle-aged, and as a consequence of events that took place in the first story, he is now, quite surprisingly, the first minister. Hari does not want the job, but nonetheless he does it extremely well and is simultaneously able to progress with psychohistory through the goodwill of Cleon, psychohistory's biggest fan.

In the development of his science, Hari is at this time greatly assisted by his right-hand man, Yugo Amaryl, the heatsinker turned mathematical genius. Together they have established a team of mathematicians and psychologists working on the development of psychohistory at Streeling University in the Imperial Sector.

In this second novella, Seldon is again involved in a plot against the throne, which this time ends in bloodshed. The climax of this tale also frees Seldon from his responsibility as first minister and allows him to return to full-time work on psychohistory.

In the third segment, Asimov turns his attention toward Dors Venabili, Seldon's partner. By this time Seldon is aging and he is racing against the clock to develop psychohistory to the point where he can save the crumbling Empire.

To complicate matters, he is faced with an assassination attempt by, so it turns out, one of his team of psychohistorians working with him at the university. He is saved from death by the efforts of his guardian and wife, Dors. With the story's conclusion, Hari's partner of almost thirty years dies, and, for the first time, it is revealed to Seldon that Dors was in fact a robot selected for her role by none other than the ubiquitous Demerzel/Daneel.

The fourth and final novella is set in the twilight of Seldon's life. He is now working flat out on psychohistory, but due to a shift in the political framework of the time, he is perceived as a political undesirable distrusted by those in power as well as the general public. Consequently, he has little backing and is in constant danger of being bumped off or scandalized by his enemies.

The most important character in this segment is Seldon's granddaughter Wanda, who appeared as a small child in the third segment. In the first part of this final novella Wanda is a teenager who gradually takes on a crucial role in the future of psychohistory.

At the point where psychohistory seems to be on the verge of collapse, Seldon's lifework is saved by the discovery that Wanda has mental powers. It is she who, along with a small group of others with similar abilities, forms the core of what becomes the Second Foundation. The fate of Hari Seldon's psychohistory, and with it the future of humanity, is set back on course by these gifted individuals.

By the conclusion of the final novella, the Second Foundation has been established at Trantor University and the Seldon Plan is set in place.

Asimov's fifth segment was originally intended to tell of Seldon's final year of life and the mechanism by which the First Foundation was established on Terminus. Unfortunately, Asimov managed to write little more than two thousand words of the piece, and so his editor, Jennifer Brehl, worked with him in the last weeks of his life to convert it into an epilogue.

This, Asimov's final piece of fiction, is particularly moving because it is a direct reflection of himself—Seldon is dying as he sits alone at his desk.

This short piece features Gaal Dornick, Seldon's right-hand man in the great scientist's last years. Dornick is instrumental in establishing the First Foundation.

So we have come full circle, back to the beginning of *The Foundation Trilogy*, which tells how Gaal Dornick met Seldon and the two Foundations were established "at opposite ends of the Galaxy."

It is clear that toward the end of Asimov's life, Hari Seldon became the author's alter ego, and it is particularly poignant that, as Asimov's own powers declined and it became apparent that he would not die facedown on the typewriter keyboard, Asimov has Seldon dying seated at his desk.

Jennifer Brehl and Asimov often discussed the deeper meaning and the background to the Foundation books and the great network of novels Asimov had created. Once, during his last months, Jennifer asked him why he had not returned to Seldon and given us his story long before. He replied that he had not known Hari Seldon then, that it was only in his own last years that he could understand his most famous creation and know him well enough to write convincingly.

Quite naturally there is much of Asimov's own life in *Forward the Foundation*. Jennifer often discussed the origins of the characters in his final books with him. Wanda, he told her, was, of course, based on his own daughter, Robyn; the elder Dors Venabili was modeled on his real-life guardian, Janet; and the young Dors, featured in *Prelude to Foundation*, was clearly Jennifer herself.

Forward the Foundation is one of the most satisfying pieces of fiction Asimov ever wrote and it is fitting that it turned out to be his swan song. It has the old feel and pace of Asimov at his best and ranks up there with the finest moments from the original trilogy. It caters perfectly to our desire to know more about the man behind the whole saga and delivers a believable and convincing description of the life and times of Hari Seldon. By the time he was writing *Forward the Foundation*, Asimov really did know Seldon. More than that, Seldon was part of Isaac Asimov.

After Asimov's death a number of other pieces of fiction with which he had been involved appeared. Toward the end of his life he had worked in collaboration with his friend Robert Silverberg, and together they had developed old short stories of Asimov's and expanded them into novels. The first of these was *Nightfall*. This was followed by *Child of Time*, which was an expansion of one of Asimov's favorite stories, "The Ugly Little Boy," and the third was *The Positronic Man*, based on "The Bicentennial Man."

These were very successful books, but actually had little to do with Asimov. By the time they were being put together he was too involved in his greatest love, the networking of his novels, to contribute much to these expansions.

During the 1980s, Asimov also worked with Janet on a collection of children's positronic robot books built around a character called Norby. As well as this, he returned to *Fantastic Voyage* with *Fantastic Voyage II: Destination Brain,* which appeared in 1987.

In the late eighties, Asimov wrote a curious little book called *Azazel,* about a tiny imp with magical powers. The book was a collection of shorts that grew out of a simple story that Jennifer particularly liked. The stories were published in magazines, where Azazel became a tiny alien, but Jennifer preferred Azazel as an imp. By the time the book was created, Asimov had decided that he, too, preferred Azazel in his original fantasy form, and so he was converted again.

Coupled with these new works, throughout the eighties, a bewildering number of anthologies of Asimov stories began to appear in the bookshops with titles like *The Complete Robot* (1982), *The Winds of Change and Other Stones* (1983), and *The Edge of Tomorrow* (1985). Many of these were put together by Asimov's close friend, the respected anthologist Martin H. Greenberg.

The last of his books that Asimov actually held in his hands was the collection of humorous stories *Asimov Laughs Again. Forward the Foundation* was in final manuscript form when he died, but he never saw the finished product.

There are some arguments as to exactly how many books Isaac Asimov published. When his author's copy arrived, he always numbered it and placed it in the bookcase in his study. The last one to be numbered by him was book No. 467, but there were at least seven other titles that appeared after this and were in various stages of development when the author died, including *Forward the Foundation.*

And so, at the end of Asimov's life, both his work and the life of his most famous creation had come full circle. Asimov had triumphantly returned to science fiction after two decades as a nonfiction writer, and some of his earliest stories, in the case of "Nightfall," written in his early twenties, had been revisited and made into novels. He had once more adopted the science fiction mantle and done something he had not achieved in the first forty years of his career—written a series of books that appeared on best-seller lists.

During his long career, Asimov had achieved a great and rare thing:

he had crossed the barriers and become successful in two mediums, fiction and nonfiction. He had become a household name as a science expert, and a writer beloved by literally millions of science fiction fans around the world. Most of all, he left the world a legacy that will be cherished for centuries to come: a body of work unparalleled in scope, enlightening, entertaining, inspired, and inspiring.

Asimov's writing and storytelling really peaked with his first wave of science fiction novels. His second wave of fiction did not have the consistent quality of his classic work in the 1950s. *The Gods Themselves*, *Foundation's Edge*, and *Forward the Foundation* are worthy companions to the likes of *The Currents of Space* and *The End of Eternity*; the rest are second-rate in comparison.

He never aspired to imbue his writing with spirituality or even great style. His greatest energy was reserved for producing highly readable novels and crystal-clear nonfiction. Some would call this philistine, an example of a writer sacrificing style for thrills. The many millions who have enjoyed Asimov's stories for over half a century would strongly disagree.

Comparing his writings to a clear glass window, "a stained glass window," Asimov would say, "is very beautiful, but it is usually opaque. When you look at it, you are captivated by the glass itself and full of admiration for the artist who created it. Clear glass is not so striking, but you can see right through it."

Asimov never aspired to a great artist; he was a storyteller, an artisan. And that's all he ever wanted to be.

EPILOGUE

The day after Isaac Asimov died, Robyn Asimov and Jennifer Brehl visited Campbell's Funeral Directors on Madison Avenue to see Isaac one last time and to arrange the funeral details.

Jennifer Brehl describes paying her last respects to Isaac as a very sad and strange experience. A few weeks earlier he had been sitting in his palatial apartment uptown. At Campbell's, Jennifer was shown into a small room, where a plain, rough pine box stood on a pedestal. Within the box lay Isaac, wrapped only in a hospital sheet, his skin gray. On the side of the box, the name ASIMOV had been scrawled in crayon.

Jennifer took a cutting of his hair, which she keeps to this day with a pair of Isaac's glasses and a collection of his bolo ties. Later that day Jennifer and Robyn escorted Janet from her apartment on the West Side to Campbell's for a last sight of Isaac.

Just over two weeks later, on April 22, 1992, Isaac Asimov was honored in a memorial service held at the Ethical Culture Center. With the exception of David Asimov, Isaac's close family were all there, along with his colleagues in the publishing world and his many friends from around the globe.

It was of course a very solemn occasion, but it was also a service full of laughter. Although many of the speakers were overcome by emotion toward the end of their tributes, all the guests shared the feeling that they were there to celebrate a great life, a life full of achievement; to commemorate the passing of a man who had worked as close to his full potential as anyone possibly could.

Asimov did not believe in an afterlife. He believed that when you die, you die. Yet his millions of fans around the world, as well as his close friends and family at the memorial service that day, know that, through his great work, Asimov has attained a form of immortality.

During his lifetime Asimov presented a twofold gift to the world. Firstly, he left behind him a collection of great stories, gripping tales that will entertain readers for centuries to come. Secondly, he imbued all who read his nonfiction with a sense of awe, a feeling of wonderment at just how incredible the universe really is.

During his time on Earth Asimov did not find a cure for cancer, he was not the first man on the moon, he did not snatch a child away from the path of an oncoming truck, but he was a supreme communicator, a man who led others into the great, inspiring labyrinth of human knowledge, and for that he will not be forgotten.

The Order of Service at the Ethical Culture Center included a piece Isaac himself had written. It is perhaps the most touching piece he ever composed.

FAREWELL—FAREWELL

To all my Gentle Readers who have treated me with love for over thirty years, I must say farewell.

I have written three hundred ninety-nine essays for *Fantasy and Science Fiction Magazine*. The essays were written with enormous pleasure, for I have always been allowed to say what I wanted to say. It was with horror that I discovered I could not manage a four-hundredth essay.

It has always been my ambition to die in harness with my head facedown on a keyboard and my nose caught between two of the keys, but that's not the way it worked out.

Fortunately, I believe neither in heaven nor hell, so death holds no terrors for me. It does, however, hold serious terrors for my wife, Janet, my daughter, Robyn—editors such as Jennifer Brehl, Sheila Williams, and Ed Ferman—all of whom will be unhappy if anything happens to me.

I have talked to each one of them separately, urging them to accept my death, when it comes, with a minimum of fuss.

I have had a long and happy life and I have no complaints about the ending thereof, and so farewell my dear wife, Janet, my lovely daughter, Robyn, and all of the editors and publishers who have treated me far better than I deserve.

And farewell also to the Gentle Readers who have been so uniformly kind to me. They have kept me alive to the wonders of science and made it possible for me to write my essays.

So farewell—farewell.

Isaac Asimov[1]

---

[1] From *Isaac Asimov's Science Fiction Magazine* by Isaac Asimov, 1992.

Afterword

A Decade On

I saac Asimov was HIV positive and died from complications associated with AIDS. I was aware of this at the time of the first edition of this book, but chose to honor the wishes of Isaac's family and friends who did not want me to bring this fact into my account.

Isaac contracted the disease after being given infected blood during a surgical procedure, but it was some time before he became aware of his condition and his decline was gradual. However, a few years before his death he learned the nature of his illness and wished to make it known to his public and to bring the matter out into the open. But, according to some sources, he was advised against this because of fears that the news would devalue his apartment in New York. This claim may never be ratified and perhaps it is now quite irrelevant anyway, but what is certain is that from a distance of just over a decade since the death of Isaac Asimov it is possible to put the man's life and work into a clearer perspective, one that was not possible when this book first appeared in Britain in 1994.

As I have said in earlier chapters, soon after Isaac died a number of people began to voice doubts about his importance and his relevance. I heard agents and editors (none of whom knew him) claiming that he was little better than a hack, a man who diversified to the point of absurdity, a man who devalued his capital by writing too many mediocre books. However, I do believe that this attitude has now changed.

Part of the reason for this is that Asimov was a man who was way ahead of his time, and people are only now catching up with the things he said and wrote about. Those who believe he was a hack simply because he was just too darn prolific will never be convinced otherwise, but I think it has at least become clear that Asimov was not just writing for the sake of it, that he was and is still relevant, and that his views were and remain important.

Isaac's fantasy worlds are creations most often set in far-off places and in the distant future, but he also contemplated many issues that were closer to home and closer to our own era. Two books that act as a good marker for his importance as a thinker are *Frontiers* and *Frontiers II*, the first of which was published the year before Asimov died and the second, in 1993, some eighteen months after his death. Between them, these two volumes contain over two hundred Asimov essays, and more than any other books of his oeuvre, they illustrate the astonishing breadth and depth of Isaac's scientific knowledge and experience. They also show that Asimov never lost touch with the world of science that he had done so much to popularize. The topics he covered in these two volumes ranged from archaeology to cosmology, from microbiology to lasers, but whatever they were about they offered insights into the leading edge of research for the time.

Of particular interest to Asimov was the problem of how humankind was mistreating the environment and creating problems for the future. He had of course written on this subject on several occasions (for example, *ABC's of Ecology*, 1972; *Solar Power: New Ways to Add to Our Energy Supply*, 1974; *Earth: Our Crowded Spaceship*, 1974; and *Our Angry Earth* (with Fred Pohl), 1991. His stance was that he was concerned over the clear scientific evidence that humanity was damaging the environment, but his ideas for the best way to deal with these often failed to chime with the standard opinions of many environmentalists during the 1970s and '80s.

Asimov was a great believer in the onward march of technology. He was a humanist and a technophile (although this was purely a theoretical devotion—he was not actually very good with machines!). He supported the development of nuclear energy and saw it as an inevitable step toward the eventual practical establishment of nuclear fusion as a resource. In holding this view, he flew in the face of most Green politics, and his public pronouncements on these issues were often met with suspicion from contemporary environmentalists.

Today, it is evident that much of what Asimov believed was absolutely accurate. Some of the claims made by environmentalist groups during the 1970s and '80s are now viewed with some skepticism. Clearly, there is a danger from man's careless treatment of the environment, and global warming is almost certainly affected by human interference, but there is also no doubt that some of the statements that came out of the 1970s and '80s were sensationalist and ill-informed. At the same time, the use of nuclear power has increased, and although some people are concerned about the dangers and long-term cost of such technology, nuclear reactors are now responsible for providing some 16 percent of the power needs of the industrialized world.

Asimov's dream of creating a nuclear fusion technology is also edging closer to reality. Asimov powered his Foundations with nuclear fusion, and in his fiction it was the power source that took humankind across the galaxy. Asimov also saw it as a possible "real life" salvation in our future and he wrote about this subject at length. In 2004, new breakthroughs have been made in the practical application of a limited form of nuclear fusion (after some fifty years and one hundred billion dollars of research) and it is hoped that the first commercial reactor will be built within twenty years. If this is achieved, we will acquire the technology Asimov hoped for—a clean, almost limitless power source that could one day take us to the stars.

Of course, Asimov was obsessed with space exploration and had been since his childhood. In many ways he would probably have found the last decade or so in this area a great disappointment. However, three high points that would doubtless have excited him have been reached in just the last two years. The first of these is the building of the International Space Station, due for completion toward the end of the decade. The second is the latest scram jet experiments carried out by NASA using a test vehicle called the X-43A, which recently traveled at mach 10 (about 7,000 mph). This achievement indicates that within perhaps a generation we will see intercontinental hyperjet transporters that could make the journey from London to Sydney in ninety minutes.

The third development, and in many ways the most important, is the move toward the commercialization of space that has gained pace since Asimov died. A few hi-tech industries and billionaire philanthropists are growing increasingly interested in the commercial exploitation of space for tourism, mining, and looking further ahead, to colonization of the moon and Mars. Asimov, along with his contemporaries (Clarke, Heinlein, and Van Vogt) all knew this was an essential element in any serious future advancement in space travel, that, along with the design of craft that could somehow circumvent the restrictions of the theory of relativity (still sadly some way off), such entrepreneurial energy would offer the best chance for humans to reach for the stars.

Another area of technological change that Asimov and his contemporary science fiction authors predicted is the huge expansion of the Internet since Isaac's death. In 1992, the Net was embryonic and used primarily by academics to communicate with one another via what they then called "electronic mail." It was only some three years after Isaac died that the Internet really entered the public's imagination.

Since then, of course, the Net has become a part of life, just as computers, cars, and TVs have become integral to our everyday existence. Like most intelligent observers, Asimov would probably have been dismayed by some of the rubbish that clogs up the Net today, but he also understood decades ago that such a system could (and hopefully will) do much to move society into a new era of communication and interrelatedness. Asimov was a liberal and he believed in the theory of world government. He saw as ridiculous the nationalism and the misplaced patriotism of so many people. Within his fictional futures, he described superior worlds and societies to our own; he may well have seen the Internet as a device with at least the potential to change the world for the better.

He would also have been pleased to note the high profile he has on the Internet. Along with *Star Trek*, *Star Wars*, Harry Potter, and *The Lord of the Rings*, Asimov and his work is one of the most popular science fiction/fantasy subjects on the Net and there are close to 500,000 sites that relate to the man and his books in some capacity. I'm sure that if Asimov were alive today we would have seen at least half a dozen books by him dealing with the many facets of the Internet and he probably would be writing a weekly "newsletter" to his fans posted on his official web site.

In purely commercial terms, Asimov's career has not missed a beat since his death. Indeed, if anything, his work has acquired a new standing. The bookshops are still filled with Asimov titles, and well-known science fiction authors have been commissioned to carry on with new series of books set in Asimov's universe, the universe he first created with his Foundation and robot series during the 1940s and '50s. These include Gregory Benford's *Foundation's Fear* (1997), *Foundation and Chaos* by Greg Bear (1998), and David Brin's *Foundation's Triumph* (1999).

However, the most important development of Asimov's work has come from Hollywood. As I mentioned earlier, the Good Doctor had only tangental relationships with the movies and in part this is the reason why it has taken so long for his novels and short stories to become a source of interest to current directors and producers. However, a more significant reason than this is the simple fact that although quite a few of Asimov's stories were optioned by Hollywood during his lifetime, they were for many years caught in "production hell," the wilderness of creativity in which a film option remains stuck and rarely escapes to reach the screen.

Asimov acted as an adviser on many TV and Hollywood productions (most notably in the late 1980s for a series on U.S. television called *Probe*), he was invited to be a science consultant for *Star Trek: The Motion Picture* in 1979, and he wrote and presented some popular science programs and documentaries for TV during the late 1970s and early 1980s. Of course, Isaac wrote copiously about his experiences with the producers in Tinseltown, often in the form of essays that were written in uncharacteristically scathing tones. Most of these were never published, but one, "Hollywood and I" (an amusing portrayal of the film industry meeting science head-on), was published in *Isaac Asimov's Science Fiction Magazine* in May 1979.

Quite a few Asimov stories have been made into video games and TV series, including, in 1964, *The Caves of Steel* for British TV, and a widely disliked adaptation of *Nightfall*, released as a movie in 1988. In 1999, Asimov's *Bicentennial Man* made the screen starring Robin Williams, but it was considered only a modest success.

Although Asimov's influence may be seen in almost all science fiction films and SF TV shows from the 1950s onward (most especially *Star Wars, Battlestar Galactica, Babylon 5*, and *Star Trek*), the first really successful movie adaptation of his work appeared in 2004—the film *I, Robot*, starring Will Smith and directed by Alex Proyas.

The movie has been a great international hit, grossing 52.25 million dollars during its first weekend of release and going straight to No. 1 in the U.S. movie charts. However, anyone going to see the film expecting a faithful adaptation of any of Isaac Asimov's robot stories or novels would have been disappointed.

Critics called the movie a "liberal adaptation" and the makers made no pretense about it, *I, Robot* was a film "inspired" by Asimov's creation. At the core of the movie lies the essence of Asimov's literary work relating to robots—the essential Three Laws, but apart from that there is little relating it to Isaac's fiction. The film's plot, involving a robot suspected of murder, is built upon the Three Laws, and the hero (Will Smith's Del Spooner), with help from Susan Calvin (Bridget Moynahan), uses the laws to solve the mystery, but that's about it.

The success of *I, Robot* has made Asimov's work something of a hot property in Hollywood. His short story "The Ugly Little Boy" has been bought for a seven-figure sum and is to be produced by Denise DiNovi (*Catwoman* and *New York Minute*), and Demi Moore has been lined up to star in it. The rights to the Foundation series (which has now sold in excess of twenty million copies globally) were sold to Fox in 1994, and there are plans to adapt the series as a movie with Shekhar Kapur directing. Meanwhile there are rumors that Ridley Scott is developing a screenplay for *The End of Eternity* with Paramount. With the box-office success of *I, Robot,* all of these projects have been given a tremendous boost.

Indeed, it is becoming clear that although Isaac Asimov wrote some five hundred books and covered every subject under the sun (and many under alien suns), his most lasting legacy will almost certainly be his ideas about robots and the influence his creation continues to exert in that field. Most importantly, Asimov's Three Laws of Robotics (an idea that started out as a framework for a set of fictional stories) are now accepted as the central premises for the construction of real robots. And, although the world is not yet filled with automata and androids as Asimov imagined in his fiction, they may become commonplace within a generation or two.

Early in the twenty-first century robots are beginning to appear in our daily lives in a similar way to that imagined by science fiction writers. Robots in one form or another have been with us for at least a generation— they have been disguised as computers, "intelligent" carpet cleaners, and refrigerators. These machines do some of the jobs assigned to humanoid robots in the fiction of the 1930s, but they do not look the way they were supposed to. However, a number of companies around the world are developing increasingly sophisticated walking, talking robots.

The most famous of these is Honda's robot called ASIMO, which, in spite of looking like a miniature NASA astronaut in full flight gear, is able to "learn" so that it may recognize people and answer questions (albeit using a very limited vocabulary). ASIMO has become quite a star for Honda, and various models tour the world meeting heads of state, actors, and actresses at galas and product launches. A variation on ASIMO is a popular child's toy robot that first appeared in 2004 called Robosapien, which, although still controlled by a remote, is able to "learn" in a very limited sense.

It is a shame Isaac Asimov is no longer with us. Not merely because he was a much-loved father and husband, friend and figurehead for his profession, but because he took such delight in all that is new and innovative. He was always more comfortable contemplating possible futures than musing on the nuts and bolts of the present. That future is here and it is being reinvented each day. He would have been thrilled to be part of it.

BIBLIOGRAPHY OF ISAAC ASIMOV'S FICTION

Pebble in the Sky, Doubleday, 1950

I, Robot, Gnome, 1950

The Stars, Like Dust, Doubleday, 1951

Foundation, Gnome, 1951

David Starr: Space Ranger, Doubleday, 1952*

Foundation and Empire, Gnome, 1952

The Currents of Space, Doubleday, 1952

Second Foundation, Gnome, 1953

Lucky Starr and the Pirates of the Asteroids, Doubleday, 1953*

The Caves of Steel, Doubleday, 1954

Lucky Starr and the Oceans of Venus, Doubleday, 1954*

The Martian Way and Other Stories, Doubleday, 1955

The End of Eternity, Doubleday, 1955

Lucky Starr and the Big Sun of Mercury, Doubleday, 1956*

The Naked Sun, Doubleday, 1957

Lucky Starr and the Moons of Jupiter, Doubleday, 1957*

Earth Is Room Enough, Doubleday, 1957

Lucky Starr and the Rings of Saturn, Doubleday, 1958*

The Death Dealers (A Whiff of Death), Avon, 1958

Nine Tomorrows, Doubleday, 1959

The Rest of the Robots, Doubleday, 1964

Fantastic Voyage, Houghton Mifflin, 1966

Through a Glass, Clearly, New English Library, 1967

Asimov's Mysteries, Doubleday, 1968

Nightfall and Other Stories, Doubleday, 1968

The Best New Thing, World Publishing, 1971*

The Gods Themselves, Doubleday, 1972

The Early Asimov, Doubleday, 1972

The Best of Isaac Asimov, Sphere, 1973

Have You Seen These? NESRAA, 1974

Tales of the Black Widowers, Doubleday, 1974

Buy Jupiter and Other Stones, Doubleday, 1975*

The Heavenly Host, Walker, 1975

Murder at the ABA, Doubleday, 1976

Good Taste, Apocalypse, 1976

The Bicentennial Man and Other Stories, Doubleday, 1976

More Tales of the Black Widowers, Doubleday, 1976

The Key Word and Other Mysteries, Walker, 1977*

The Casebook of the Black Widowers, Doubleday, 1980

The Complete Robot, Doubleday, 1982

Foundation's Edge, Doubleday, 1982

The Winds of Change and Other Stories, Doubleday, 1983

The Union Club Mysteries, Doubleday, 1983

Norby, the Mixed-Up Robot (with Janet Asimov), Ace Books, New York, 1983*

The Robots of Dawn, Doubleday, 1983

Norby's Other Secret (with Janet Asimov), Ace Books, New York, 1983*

Banquets of the Black Widowers, Doubleday, 1984

Norby and the Lost Princess (with Janet Asimov), Ace Books, New York, 1985*

The Edge of Tomorrow, Doubleday, 1985

The Disappearing Man and Other Stories, Doubleday, 1985

Robots and Empire, Doubleday, 1985

It's Such a Beautiful Day, Doubleday, 1985

Norby and the Queen's Necklace (with Janet Asimov), Doubleday, 1985*

Norby and the Invaders (with Janet Asimov), Ace Books, New York, 1986*

The Alternate Asimovs, Doubleday, 1986

Science Fiction by Asimov, Doubleday, 1986

The Best Mysteries of Isaac Asimov, Doubleday, 1986

The Best Science Fiction of Isaac Asimov, Doubleday, 1986

Foundation and Earth, Doubleday, 1986

Robot Dreams, Doubleday, 1986

Fantastic Voyage II: Destination Brain, Doubleday, 1987

Norby Finds a Villain (with Janet Asimov), Ace Books, New York, 1987*

Other Universe of Isaac Asimov, Doubleday, 1987

Prelude to Foundation, Doubleday, 1988

Azazel, Doubleday, 1988

Norby Goes to Earth (with Janet Asimov), Ace Books, New York, 1988[*]

Nemesis, Doubleday, 1989

Puzzles of the Black Widowers, Doubleday, 1990

Nightfall (with Robert Silverberg); first published in the United Kingdom by Victor Gollancz, 1990

Child of Time (with Robert Silverberg); first published in the United Kingdom by Victor Gollancz, 1991

Forward the Foundation, Doubleday, 1993

[*]juvenile fiction

GENERAL BIBLIOGRAPHY

Science Fiction, Robert Scholes and Eric S. Rabkin, Oxford University Press, New York, 1977

Trillion Year Spree, Brian Aldiss with David Wingrove, Paladin, 1988

In Memory Yet Green, Isaac Asimov, Doubleday, New York, 1979

In Joy Still Felt, Isaac Asimov, Doubleday, New York, 1980

Asimov Laughs Again, Isaac Asimov, HarperCollins, New York, 1992

The Science Fiction of Isaac Asimov, Joseph Patrouch Jr., Doubleday, New York, 1974

OPUS 100, Isaac Asimov, Houghton Mifflin, Boston, 1969

Robot Visions, Isaac Asimov, Victor Gollancz Science Fiction, London, 1990

New Maps of Hell, Kingsley Amis, Victor Gollancz, London 1961

Foundations Friends, edited by Martin H. Greenberg, Tom Doherty Associates, Inc., 1989

Bloomsbury Good Reading Guide to Science Fiction and Fantasy, M. H. Zool, Bloomsbury, 1989

The Ultimate Guide to Science Fiction, David Pringle, Grafton, 1990

Odyssey: The Authorised Biography of Arthur C. Clarke, Neil McAleer, Victor Gollancz, London, 1992

The Early Asimov, Vols. 1, 2, and 3, Isaac Asimov, Victor Gollancz, 1973

Appendix:

Chronological List of Isaac Asimov's Books

1950

001 *Pebble in the Sky*
002 *I, Robot*

1951

003 *The Stars, Like Dust*
004 *Foundation*

1952

005 *David Starr: Space Ranger*
006 *Foundation and Empire*
007 *The Currents of Space*
008 *Biochemistry and Human Metabolism*

1953

009 *Second Foundation*
010 *Lucky Starr and the Pirates of the Asteroids*

1954

011 *The Caves of Steel*
012 *Lucky Starr and the Oceans of Venus*
013 *The Chemicals of Life*

1955

014 *The Martian Way and Other Stories*
015 *The End of Eternity*
016 *Races and People*

1956

017 *Lucky Starr and the Big Sun of Mercury*
018 *Chemistry and Human Health*
019 *Inside the Atom*

1957

020 *The Naked Sun*
021 *Lucky Starr and the Moons of Jupiter*
022 *Building Blocks of the Universe*
023 *Earth Is Room Enough*
024 *Only a Trillion*

1958

025 *The World of Carbon*
026 *Lucky Starr and the Rings of Saturn*
027 *The World of Nitrogen*
028 *The Death Dealers (A Whiff of Death)*

1959

029 *Nine Tomorrows*
030 *The Clock We Live On*
031 *Words of Science*
032 *Realm of Numbers*

1968

087 *Asimov's Mysteries*
088 *Science, Numbers, and I*
089 *Stars*
090 *Galaxies*
091 *The Near East*
092 *The Dark Ages*
093 *Asimov's Guide to the Bible: Volume 1*
094 *Words from History*
095 *Photosynthesis*

1969

096 *The Shaping of England*
097 *Twentieth Century Discovery*
098 *Nightfall and Other Stories*
099 *Asimov's Guide to the Bible: Volume 2*
100 *Opus 100*
101 *ABC's of Space*
102 *Great Ideas of Science*

1970

103 *The Solar System and Back*
104 *Asimov's Guide to Shakespeare: Volume 1*
105 *Asimov's Guide to Shakespeare: Volume 2*
106 *Constantinople, the Forgotten Empire*
107 *ABC's of the Ocean*
108 *Light*

1971

109 *The Stars in Their Courses*
110 *Where Do We Go from Here?*
111 *What Makes the Sun Shine?*
112 *The Sensuous Dirty Old Man*
113 *The Best New Thing*
114 *Isaac Asimov's Treasury of Humor*
115 *The Hugo Winners: Volume 2*
116 *The Land of Canaan*
117 *ABC's of the Earth*

1972

118 *Asimov's Biographical Encyclopedia of Science and Technology, 2d ed.*
119 *The Left Hand of the Electron*
120 *Asimov's Guide to Science*
121 *The Gods Themselves*
122 *More Words of Science*
123 *Electricity and Man*
124 *ABC's of Ecology*
125 *The Early Asimov*
126 *The Shaping of France*
127 *The Story of Ruth*
128 *Ginn Science Program—Intermediate A*
129 *Ginn Science Program—Intermediate C*
130 *Asimov's Annotated "Don Juan"*
131 *Worlds within Worlds*
132 *Ginn Science Program—Intermediate B*

1973

133 *How Did We Find Out the Earth Is Round?*
134 *Comets and Meteors*
135 *The Sun*
136 *How Did We Find Out about Electricity?*
137 *The Shaping of North America,*
138 *Today and Tomorrow and —*
139 *Jupiter, the Largest Planet*
140 *Ginn Science Program—Advanced A*
141 *Ginn Science Program—Advanced B*
142 *How Did We Find Out about Numbers?*
143 *Please Explain*
144 *The Tragedy of the Moon*
145 *How Did We Find Out about Dinosaurs?*
146 *The Best of Isaac Asimov*
147 *Nebula Award Stories Eight*

1974

148 *Asimov on Astronomy*
149 *The Birth of the United States*
150 *Have You Seen These?*

1984

1985

333 *Giants*
334 *How Did We Find Out about DNA?*

1986

335 *The Alternate Asimovs*
336 *Isaac Asimov Presents the Great SF
     Stories 14, 1952*
337 *Comets*
338 *Young Star Travelers*
339 *The Hugo Winners: Volume 5*
340 *The Dangers of Intelligence and Other
     Essays*
341 *Mythical Beasties*
342 *How Did We Find Out about the Speed of
     Light?*
343 *Futuredays: A Nineteenth Century Vision
     of the Year 2000*
344 *Science Fiction by Asimov*
345 *Tin Stars*
346 *The Best Science Fiction of Isaac Asimov*
347 *The Best Mysteries of Isaac Asimov*
348 *Foundation and Earth*
349 *Robot Dreams*
350 *Norby and the Queen's Necklace*
351 *Magical Wishes*
352 *Isaac Asimov Presents the Great SF
     Stories 15, 1953*
353 *The Twelve Frights of Christmas*
354 *How Did We Find Out about Blood?*

1987

355 *Far as Human Eye Could See*
356 *Past, Present, and Future*
357 *Isaac Asimov Presents Superquiz 3*
358 *How Did We Find Out about Sunshine?*
359 *Isaac Asimov Presents the Great SF
     Stories 16, 1954*
360 *Young Witches and Warlocks*
361 *How To Enjoy Writing: A Book of Aid
     and Comfort*
362 *Devils*

363 *Norby Finds a Villain*
364 *Fantastic Voyage II: Destination Brain*
365 *Hound Dunnit*
366 *Space Shuttles*
367 *How Did We Find Out about the Brain?*
368 *Did Comets Kill the Dinosaurs?*
369 *Beginnings*
370 *Other Worlds of Isaac Asimov*

1988

371 *Atlantis*
372 *Isaac Asimov Presents the Great SF
     Stories 17, 1955*
373 *Asimov's Annotated Gilbert and
     Sullivan*
374 *Isaac Asimov Presents from Harding to
     Hiroshima*
375 *How Did We Find Out about
     Superconductivity?*
376 *Isaac Asimov's Book of Science and Nature
     Quotations*
377 *The Relativity of Wrong*
378 *Prelude to Foundation*
379 *Encounters*
380 *The Asteroids*
381 *The Earth's Moon*
382 *Mars: Our Mysterious Neighbor*
383 *Our Milky Way and Other Galaxies*
384 *Quasars, Pulsars, and Black Holes*
385 *Rockets, Probes, and Satellites*
386 *Our Solar System*
387 *The Sun*
388 *Uranus: The Sideways Planet*
389 *The History of Biology* (chart)
390 *Isaac Asimov Presents the Best Crime
     Stories of the 19th Century*
391 *Mammoth Book of Classic Science Fiction*
392 *Monsters*
393 *Isaac Asimov Presents the Great SF
     Stories 18, 1956*
394 *Azazel*
395 *Isaac Asimov's Science Fiction and
     Fantasy Story-a-Month 1989 Calendar*

1991

464   *The March of the Millennia: A Key to Looking at History*
465   *The Secret of the Universe*
466   *Isaac Asimov Presents the Great SF Stories 22, 1960*
467   *Atom: Journey Across the Subatomic Cosmos*
468   *Cal*
469   *Isaac Asimov Presents the Great SF Stories 23, 1961*
470   *Christopher Columbus: Navigator to the New World*
471   *What Is a Shooting Star?*
472   *Why Do Stars Twinkle?*
473   *Why Does the Moon Change Shape?*
474   *Why Do We Have Different Seasons?*
475   *What Is an Eclipse?*
476   *Faeries*
477   *The Mammoth Book of New World Science Fiction*
478   *Isaac Asimov's Guide to Earth and Space*
479   *Ferdinand Magellan: Opening the Door to World Exploration*
480   *Our Angry Earth*
481   *Henry Hudson: Arctic Explorer and North American Adventurer*
482   *Why Are Whales Vanishing?*
483   *Is Our Planet Warming Up?*
484   *Why Is the Air Dirty?*
485   *Where Does Garbage Go?*
486   *What Causes Acid Rain?*
487   *Asimov's Chronology of the World*
488   *The History of Chemistry* (chart)

1992

489   *Asimov Laughs Again*
490   *Isaac Asimov Presents the Great SF Stories 24, 1962*
491   *The New Hugo Winners: Volume 2*
492   *The Complete Stories: Volume 2*
493   *Why Are Some Beaches Oily?*
494   *Why Are Animals Endangered?*
495   *Why Are the Rain Forests Vanishing?*

1993

496   *What's Happening to the Ozone Layer?*
497   *Why Does Litter Cause Problems?*
498   *Isaac Asimov Presents the Great SF Stories 25, 1963*
499   *The Mammoth Book of Fantastic Science Fiction*
500   *The Ugly Little Boy*
501   *Forward the Foundation*
502   *The Positronic Man*
503   *Mammoth Book of Modern Science Fiction*
504   *Frontiers II: More Recent Discoveries about Life, Earth, Space, and the Universe*
505   *The Future in Space*

1994

506   *I, Asimov: A Memoir*

1995

507   *Gold*
508   *I, Robot: The Illustrated Screenplay*
509   *Yours, Isaac Asimov*
510   *Magic: The Final Fantasy Collection*

2003

511   *Return of the Black Widowers*

USEFUL WEB SITES

http://www.asimovonline.com

This is the official Asimov site and is packed with excellent information on the Good Doctor.

http://homepage.mac.com/jhjenkins/Asimov/Asimov.html

This is an amazing site created by a man who must be Asimov's No. 1 fan—John Jenkins. It contains lists of all of Isaac Asimov's works and a review of each—an invaluable resource to any obsessive fan.

http://www.asimovs.com

This is the site for *Isaac Asimov's Science Fiction Magazine*. It contains articles, discussion groups, and very useful information for the fan and the casual reader alike.

INDEX

About the Author

During the 1980s Michael White was a member of the internationally famous band the Thompson Twins. He then became a chemistry lecturer at d'Overbroeck's College, Oxford, where he taught for seven years before becoming Director of Studies. Turning to full-time writing in 1991, he is now the author of twenty-five books including the international best-sellers *Stephen Hawking: A Life in Science, Leonardo: The First Scientist, Tolkien: A Biography,* and *The Science of the X-Files.* There are some 140 editions of Michael White books published globally. He was awarded the Bookman Prize in the U.S. for best popular science book of 1998 for his biography of *Isaac Newton, The Last Sorcerer,* an honor he shared that year with the Astronomer Royal, Martin Rees. In 2002, he was short-listed for the prestigious Aventis Award for his book *Rivals* (the prize went to Stephen Hawking that year). Michael White has been a newspaper columnist, science editor for *GQ* magazine and a series consultant for the Discovery Channel's *The Science of the Impossible.* He is a regular on radio and TV around the world. In 2001 he was awarded a Distinguished Talent visa by the Australian government and now lives in Perth, Western Australia, where he is an Honorary Research Fellow at Curtin University. He lives in Perth with his wife and four children.

For more information visit Michael White's web site at: michaelwhite.com.au